THE Great
Departure

Kidnapped Souls:
National Indifference and the Battle for Children
in the Bohemian Lands, 1900–1948

The Lost Children: Reconstructing Europe's Families
after World War II

THE Great Departure

Mass Migration

from Eastern Europe

and the Making

of the Free World

Tara Zahra

W. W. Norton & Company
Independent Publishers Since 1923
NEW YORK | LONDON

to William Irvine

Contents

THE Great
Departure

"Not a Golden Country"

Faustina Wiśniewska was counting the days until she could return home. "I do not understand how the people there look upon this America," she wrote to her parents. "They think that a country like America is made of gold. This is not a golden country, but a new one, . . . and here they exploit people as they did the Jews in Pharaoh's time, 12 hours' work a day." Faustina, a recent Polish immigrant, was not impressed by electric lights or by the Statue of Liberty. Assaulted by the sounds, sights, and foul smells of New York City, she moaned, "Oh, how lonely I am! Here you only hear the noise of thousands of people walking, of the whistling of factories, of the bells of trolleys . . . in place of nightingales and larks. Instead of roses, tulips, and lilacs, barrels of garbage and covered wagons, and stench instead of fresh air." She had abandoned any fantasy of prosperity, yet her parents constantly nagged her to send money home. She and her husband were living hand to mouth. "We cannot live on smelly meat, stale bread, musty cereals. . . . To live in misery or to kill myself in order to save a *grosz*, no, I am not that crazy to work myself to death." She refused, on principle, to sacrifice her few daily pleasures in order to support needy relatives. "I have already suffered a great deal myself and I denied myself the eating of a good breakfast. Now I eat the best meat, the filet. There are those who send money to the old country, but they themselves live like animals."[1]

Faustina took part in one of the greatest migrations in human history. Between 55 and 58 million Europeans moved to North and South America in the period 1846–1940. At the peak of this exodus, in the first decade of the twentieth century, Austria-Hungary was the top supplier of migrants to the United States, sending more than 2 million subjects of the Dual Monarchy through the gauntlet at Ellis Island.[2] The great departure from Eastern Europe was not unique: millions were on the move in other parts of the world as well. Between 48 and 52 million people, mostly from India and Southern China, moved to Southeast Asia and to islands in the Indian Ocean and South Pacific between 1846 and 1940. Another 46–51 million people left northeastern Asia and Russia for Manchuria, Siberia, Central Asia, and Japan.[3] Yet the movement out of Eastern Europe hollowed out villages with particularly dizzying speed. In 1907 alone, more than 300,000 people left the Dual Monarchy for the United States, the most ever to land on American shores from one country in a single year.[4] "Moans are uttered by people here because it seems that all of Europe is depopulating itself and is heading in droves for America," Faustina attested.

When Faustina made her journey, the phenomenon of mass emigration from Eastern Europe was still relatively novel. Before the age of the steamship, the journey across the Atlantic was long (averaging thirty to forty days), expensive, and potentially deadly. But by 1890, when Faustina left home, transatlantic emigration was far less dangerous and somewhat more comfortable, even in steerage. Expanding railway lines and steamship routes reduced the time, cost, and risks of transatlantic travel, and narrowed the psychological distance between Eastern Europe, Western Europe, and America. The insatiable demand for cheap labor in North America's booming industrial cities fueled the growing transcontinental and transatlantic traffic in labor. And the erosion of feudal bonds and labor obligations in Eastern Europe unleashed millions of people from the villages or regions of their birth. By the turn of the twentieth century, it was possible to travel by steamship from Hamburg to New York in only seven days, at cut-rate prices. Fares fluctuated with periodic price wars, but a third-class steamship ticket around 1900 would have cost about thirty dollars for an East European emigrant (approximately eight hundred dollars in today's currency). This was not easy money for the average peasant to come by, but not impossible with the help of family, friends, and credit.[5]

The sudden departure of millions of citizens to foreign lands sent shock waves across Europe and the Atlantic. If the arrival of the "unwashed masses" from Southern and Eastern Europe inflamed xenophobia in Western Europe and the United States in the early twentieth century, those who stayed behind were no less unsettled. Military officials bemoaned the growing number of conscripts who failed to appear for military duty. Landowners worried about where they would find workers to harvest the next year's crop (and about the need to increase wages to compete in a global labor market). Religious authorities warned that peasants would be demoralized and secularized in foreign cities. Family members despaired that they might never see their relatives again. To many, "America fever" (and its cousins "Brazil fever" and "Argentinia fever") threatened to destroy individuals, families, and nations.

Faustina's trajectory was not unique. But in her letters home, Wiśniewska also challenged the story that Americans like to tell themselves about this great departure: that immigrants desired to come and to stay—not that many came reluctantly, pushed by circumstances at home, feeling that they had no other options, and that many wished mightily to return home again. The great story of immigration has generally focused on how many persons the United States (or other receiving countries) would allow in, or keep out, not on the situations those migrants sought to escape, or on the impact of their departure on their homelands, or the role of their own governments in keeping them home. Significantly, it has tended to ignore one of the most consequential political discoveries of nineteenth-century European states: that emigration could be manipulated like the steam valve on a teapot; that encouraging people to stay or go could be used as an instrument of policy, to serve both domestic and international goals. People could be "scientifically" managed, like any other natural resource.

THE STORY OF mass migration has also generally accepted the premise that more mobility meant more freedom. In American political culture, the meaning of the term "freedom" has never been stable, but it has long been defined in relation to movement. Among eighteenth-century political theorists, Thomas Jefferson was one of the most ardent defenders of the right to exit. He insisted that all men possess "a right which nature has given to all men of departing from the country which chance, not choice, has placed him."[6] Freedom has also long been defined in racial terms in America, especially in relationship to slavery and its legacies. Since violent capture, forced transport across the Middle Passage, and the physical bondage of human bodies were essential to slavery, physical mobility became fundamental to abolitionist ideals of freedom in the United States.[7] Within the United States in the first half of the twentieth century, the domestic slave trade forcibly uprooted at least two-thirds of a million people at the whims of their owners. Slaves lived in fear of being arbitrarily sold away from parents, children, spouses, and siblings, a form of (threatened and real) forced migration that emerged as a quintessential symbol of domination and unfreedom for enslaved people.[8] Abolitionists also helped to consolidate a link between free labor and freedom in America, implicitly legitimating capitalism. The notion of "wage slavery," deployed during the Progressive era and beyond, was so powerful precisely because actual slavery was a living memory. In his famous muckraking novel *The Jungle*, the socialist writer Upton Sinclair explicitly compared the East European immigrants in Chicago's meatpacking industry to chattel slaves. "Here was a population, low-class and mostly foreign, hanging always on the verge of starvation, and dependent for its opportunities of life upon the whim of men every bit as brutal and unscrupulous as the old-time slave-drivers," he declared.[9] While particularly powerful in the United States, the ideal of the "free migrant," defined in opposition to the slave or indentured servant, has been a cornerstone of global migration politics since the era of abolition.[10]

In the United States, of course, imagined links between freedom and mobility also reflect the centrality of the frontier to American history and identity. Frederick Jackson Turner's 1893 address entitled "The Significance of the Frontier in American History" is certainly the most famous version of the myth of "frontier individualism." Turner asserted that movement had been the "dominant fact" of American life since Columbus's arrival in the New World. The American conquest of the West transformed Europeans into Americans and bestowed on them a unique attachment to freedom, individualism, and democracy. In Turner's view, physical mobility, social mobility, and political liberty naturally converged in the American West.[11]

Like the movement west, mass immigration tethered the concepts of freedom and mobility in the United States. Mass immigration helped transform freedom into an imagined space or a physical destination, rather than a political or spiritual condition. Migrants were said to travel into or out of "freedom" as they crossed U.S. borders. To East European Jews, "America signifies distance. America signifies freedom," wrote the Austrian-Jewish writer Joseph Roth in 1927.[12] Migrants themselves made, and continue to make, powerful political claims based on the argument that immigration is at the heart of American identity. At the outset of the Second World War, when American nativists cast European immigrants and refugees as a threatening "fifth column," Louis Adamic (himself an immigrant from the Habsburg Empire) maintained that America's immigrants were its greatest strength. "The fact that its population is an extension of most of the Old World, stemming from about sixty different backgrounds, constitutes perhaps one of the greatest advantages which the U.S. enjoys." He even speculated that Europe's descent into fascism was a consequence of mass emigration. "Too many 'Americans,'" whom he defined as "people addicted to liberty," had abandoned Europe for America in the past century, he insisted.[13]

In reality, however, from the very moment that the mass exodus from Eastern Europe began, many Europeans questioned the notion both that emigration should be unrestricted and that moving would lead to freedom or prosperity. Like Faustina and Upton Sinclair, they insisted that emigrants were being delivered to new forms of bondage and misery. Many European and U.S. officials in the nineteenth century believed that producing "free migrants" required regulating the intermediaries—like emigration agents and shipping companies—that facilitated and profited from migration. In Eastern Europe in particular, a conviction grew that emigrants could never be truly free outside their homelands.

These fears were linked to anxieties about the status of East Europeans in global racial and civilizational hierarchies. By the late nineteenth century, when peasants and workers began to move en masse from the East to the West, Europe's continental empires (including the Habsburg, Russian, and Ottoman Empires) self-consciously occupied a precarious position between the imagined "West" and the colonial world.[14] Emigration reformers feared that their citizens would become the slaves, coolies, or indentured servants of the twentieth century—fears stoked by American nativists who questioned the racial "value" of migrants from Southern and Eastern Europe. East European policymakers from the late nineteenth century onward consistently worked to defend and cultivate the status of their citizens as "white" Europeans, and to protect their legal and social equality with white West European and North American workers.[15] To an extent, they were successful. For Jewish migrants arriving in the United States, Roth observed, the image of America as a land of liberty corresponded to a certain reality. "Not because they really are all that serious about liberty in the new country, but because they have people who are more Jewish than the Jews, which is to say the Negroes. Of course Jews are still Jews. But here, significantly, they are first and foremost whites. For the first time a Jew's race is actually to his advantage."[16]

CONCERNS ABOUT THE LOSS of population were hardly new in the late nineteenth century. In the early modern era, vast numbers of Europeans were wiped out in the demographic catastrophes of the fifteenth–seventeenth centuries, in particular the Black Death and the Thirty Years' War. These natural and man-made disasters taught rulers that human beings were a precious resource. Early modern sovereigns generally subscribed to mercantile economic theories, valuing population as a motor of economic development and source of political power. More people, they believed, meant more labor, larger markets, and bigger armies for self-defense. Most early modern states therefore sought to hoard population by restricting emigration. Some, such as Catherine the Great in Russia, even campaigned to attract immigrants to populate and productivize their domains.[17]

By the early to mid-nineteenth century, however, mercantilist theories gave way to Malthusian pessimism throughout much of Europe, as mortality rates declined and population increased. State authorities began to worry less about underpopulation and more about overpopulation and its ugly bedfellows—poverty, disease, famine, and revolution. As a result, authorities eased restrictions on movement. The Frankfurt Parliament of 1848, for example, declared that "freedom of emigration may not be restricted in the interests of the state," while the Austrian constitution of 1867 guaranteed every citizen the right to exit the Habsburg Empire. A growing emphasis on free movement in this period coincided with the general ascendance of political and economic liberalism.[18]

The middle to late nineteenth century has therefore long been remembered as a golden age of unfettered mobility. It was only in the aftermath of the First World War, in this story, that Western xenophobia, the expansion of state power, and economic crisis spelled the end of an era of open borders.[19] This narrative of unlimited migration is incomplete at best, however. Movement could also mean expulsion, even in Western Europe in the nineteenth century. As emigration came to be seen as a potential solution to various social and political problems, several European states developed strategies for encouraging or even forcing the emigration of individuals or groups seen as "undesirable" or "surplus" citizens.

Such practices of human dumping took many forms. In the nineteenth century, the French and British Empires expelled vast numbers of convicts to colonial penal colonies, where many perished from disease, malnutrition, and overwork in brutal conditions. In the British Empire, champions of emigration urged the government to "shovel out paupers" in the 1820s and 1830s. Orphans and "surplus" single women soon joined paupers and convicts in exile. Emigration, in this context, became a strategy for rendering Britain's colonies profitable and ridding the metropole of unwanted elements. And of course, until the abolition of slavery in the Americas, millions of Africans were transported across the Atlantic in chains. Free and unfree forms of migration coexisted throughout most of the nineteenth century and were defined in relationship to one another.[20]

Nor did concerns about emigration ever fully disappear in the Habsburg Empire. In the Bohemian Lands, for example, early Czech nation builders and government authorities responded with alarm to a wave of mass emigration to North America. More than 20,000 Bohemians received passports to emigrate from Austria in the 1850s, part of a broader movement of people from Northern and Central Europe to North America at midcentury. That number does not include individuals who emigrated illegally: the actual number of departures was probably closer to 64,000.[21]

Regional and local officials mobilized to stop this emigration with police measures, including the prohibition of emigration agencies and the prosecution of agents. Liberal Czech "national awakeners" such as playwright Josef Kajetán Tyl, author of the unofficial Czech national anthem "Where Is My Home?" (Kde domov můj?), meanwhile created narratives that explicitly linked emigration to misery and loss. In his 1850 play *The Forest Nymph, or A Journey to America* (Lesní panna, aneb, Cesta do Ameriky), an unscrupulous Jewish emigration agent seduces a party of naïve Czech villagers into emigrating to America; en route they are robbed by gypsies; upon arrival they are attacked by Indians while living in a community of fanatical, hypocritical Quakers. Needless to say, the emigrants come to regret their foolhardy decision to leave home. The play ends with the migrants' return to their Bohemian village, where they joyfully reaffirm their attachment to their homeland. "I now feel as if my heart has burst its strings!" declares one homecoming migrant. "The Bohemian climate—and the beer! America can't measure up to that!"[22]

AS NEWS (AND REMITTANCES) from emigrants trickled home, migrants and their family members and neighbors participated in the heated transatlantic debate about emigration. The questions at stake had no easy answers. Was emigration a solution to a social crisis, a productive outlet for unemployed workers and landless farmers? Or did it siphon off society's most valuable citizens at the height of their youthful potential? Did migrants return home with pockets full of dollars and fresh ideas, or with broken bodies and souls? Was migration a path toward freedom, social mobility, and a better life? Or did it entrap migrants in new forms of slavery?

These debates divided villages and families as well as policymakers in Vienna and Budapest. Growing up in the Austrian village of Blato at the turn of the century (in current-day Slovenia), Louis Adamic recalled that he "experienced a thrill" every time a man returned home from America.

> Five or six years before, as I heard people tell, the man had quietly left the village for the United States, a poor peasant clad in homespun, with a mustache under his nose and a bundle on his back; now, a clean-shaven *Amerikanec,* he sported a blue-serge suit, . . . a black derby, a shiny celluloid collar, and a loud necktie made even louder by a dazzling horseshoe pin. . . . [H]is two suitcases of imitation leather, tied with straps, bulged with gifts from America for his relatives and friends in the village.

Adamic loved to listen to these *Amerikanci* hold court in local cafés, where they treated their audiences to rounds of beer and sausage and dazzled them with tales of their American adventures. In his imagination, America

> was a grand, amazing, somewhat fantastic place—the Golden Country—a sort of Paradise. . . . In America one could make pots of money in a short time, acquire immense holdings, wear a white collar, . . . and eat white bread, soup, and meat on week-days as well as on Sundays, even if one were but an ordinary workman to begin with.[23]

As Adamic plotted his own emigration, however, he realized that his mother did not share his romance with America. She had heard other stories about the fate of emigrants, whispered among neighbors.

> Mother knew of other men in Blato and the vicinity who had gone to America and had sunk, leaving no trace, into the vastness of America. She knew of men in villages not remote from our own who had returned from the United States without an arm or minus a leg, or in bad health. There was an *Amerikanec* in Gatina, the village nearest Blato, who had come home with a strange, sinful, and unmentionable disease, which he later communicated to his wife, who, in turn, gave birth to a blind child. There was a widow in Podgora, another village near by, whose husband had been killed in a mine accident. . . .[24]

Migrants multiplied these harrowing stories in their letters and testimonies. Adam Laboda left Austrian Galicia when he was sixteen years old, joining a party of fourteen boys from his village. He eventually found a job working in a mill in Massachusetts, where he earned $2.77 a week for sixty-four hours of work. When interviewed in 1938, he had no regrets about his decision to come to America. He conceded, however, that not all his traveling companions had been as fortunate. "I will tell you about what happened to those 14 Polish boys who came to America together," he said. "Four of them committed suicide, one shot himself, one hung himself, one took poison, one drowned himself. There is one who is a big contractor in Buffalo, another who has a large store in Boston. The four who killed themselves had left the church and took to drinking and that finished them. The rest are working something like me."[25]

For many migrants, the greatest hope was to return home. At least 30 percent, and perhaps up to 40 percent, of the migrants who came to America from Central Europe at the turn of the twentieth century made a round-trip (or even multiple round-trips). For many, that had always been the plan. "Most of the Bohunks came to America intending to stay two or three years, four at the most, work to the limit of their endurance at whatever they might find, save every cent possible, and then, returning to the Old Country, pay the debt on the old place, buy a few additional fields and heads of cattle, and start anew," recalled Adamic.* Adamic himself remained in the United States, where he became a successful journalist and public intellectual. But others returned disappointed and disillusioned, having found little reward for their hard work, lack of support in times of illness and old age, and questionable moral values in a society where everyone seemed out for him- or herself.[26]

"In America the work is hard—like in the galleys; you sweat

---

* "Bohunk" was a derogatory term for immigrants from the Habsburg Empire (a combination of "Bohemian" and "Hungarian").

more in one day than in a week at home. . . . As long as a man is healthy and can work, then it is good; but if he is not well, he cannot work and then there is only misery,"[27] Joseph Cybulski wrote to his wife, Sophie, discouraging her from joining him. Moses Weinberger, an Orthodox rabbi from Kniesen, Hungary, offered similar advice to his peers in Europe. In an 1887 tract, he counseled, "Stay home. . . . Nothing will be left for you to do save dressing in black, wrapping yourself in shrouds, and rolling from darkness to abyss: from factory to sweatshop to itinerant peddling. For such great success you don't need America!" Weinberger concluded that survival in America required abandoning all scruples. "He who does not know how to deceive, does not live in a world of hypocrisy, does not enjoy leading people astray, and does not consciously bait people by telling them lies—such a one will never see an extra cent in his purse."[28]

Some migrants nursed fantasies of return for decades. In 1912, a letter signed "the unlucky one" reached the editors of *Forverts*, a Yiddish daily newspaper in New York. The writer was contemplating a return to Warsaw after twenty-two miserable years in America. "I am not skilled in a trade, but I am a businessman, and all these years I've struggled because I never made a living. I know English, I am not lazy, I've tried everything and never succeeded." Now that his children were grown and married, he just wanted to go home. "It is very hard to part with the children, but to live in poverty is also bad. It seems strange to me that I must go away from the free America in order to better my condition. But the chances for me are still better there," he reflected.[29] America, these migrants concluded, would never deliver on its promise of bread and freedom, let alone gold, milk, and honey.

These conflicting visions of America and of Western Europe drove and intensified ongoing debates about emigration. When Faustina wrote her letters home, these debates were just beginning.

They would not be resolved in her lifetime. The forces that propelled emigration and shaped migration policies in East Central Europe changed dramatically over the course of the twentieth century, with the rise and fall of multiple empires, states, and political regimes, dictatorships and democracies. This history was defined by extremes: from the extreme mobility of the turn of the century to the virtual paralysis of the Cold War era. From the 1880s onward, however, one constant remained strong: anxieties about emigration were bound up in a broader discussion of the meaning of freedom, free labor, and slavery in a global labor market.

THE MEMORY OF THESE MIGRATIONS has been distorted by the rise of nationalism and ethnic politics in the twentieth century. There are many bilateral histories of migration: Poles in Chicago, Jews in New York, Algerians in France, Turks in Germany. Ethnically defined museums and organizations are often most active in collecting migrants' stories and disseminating them to the public. Ethnic groups play the starring roles in these stories, which often start and end with the question of how migration diluted or strengthened ethnic solidarities. It would be a mistake, however, to assume that migrants always shared these concerns. Louis Adamic recalled that Austrian emigrants in America "thought of themselves as fighters, lovers, poets, dancers, singers, and children of the Almighty before it occurred to them that they were also members of definite national and political groups."[30]

It is impossible, however, to ignore the persistent role that nationalism and nation-states played in the development of emigration policies in the twentieth century, particularly after 1918. In the late nineteenth century, some Austrian nationalists, especially Hungarian and Polish activists, began to see emigration as a potential weapon in a nationalist demographic struggle. They plotted to discourage the emigration of Hungarians and Poles, while encouraging the emigration of other national minorities. Emigration, they hoped, could alter the demographic (ethnolinguistic) balance sheet in their favor. The Russian Empire pursued similar policies of "filtration." As a result, the vast majority of the 2.7 million Russian subjects who left imperial Russia between 1880 and 1910 were Jews, Polish-speakers, or German-speakers.[31]

After the First World War and the collapse of the Habsburg Empire into self-declared nation-states, all of East Central Europe's new governments hoped to "filter" their populations, retaining only the most desirable national citizens. Emigration policy became an explicit tool of new and more violent forms of nation building and population politics. Before World War I, many European states encouraged (or forced) the emigration of "surplus" populations. But they tended to define these "surplus" populations primarily in terms of social class, gender, or occupation. Now, in East Central Europe after World War I, "surplus" populations typically referred to national, religious, or racial minorities.

Ironically, this meant that the most "desirable" citizens from a nationalist perspective tended to enjoy the least freedom of mobility after World War I. Ethnic and religious minorities, by contrast, were free to go, but not typically welcome to return home. The line between encouraging and forcing emigration became increasingly blurry with the onset of the Great Depression and the rise of right-wing fascist regimes in East Central Europe. That line was easily crossed in the context of the Second World War and its aftermath. The violent policies of ethnic cleansing associated with this era, including the deportation and murder of Europe's Jews and the flight or forced expulsion of twelve million ethnic Germans, can be traced to the Wilsonian moment after World War I, when democratic governments began to selectively open and close the migration tap in order to mold nationally homogeneous populations.

Ethnic cleansing and immobility were ultimately flip sides of the same coin in East Central Europe. The more Germans, Jews, and other minorities emigrated or were deported, the tighter the state's iron grip on its "preferred" citizens, who were needed to fill the demographic craters left behind. Immobility was the terrible cost paid by East Europeans for achieving the long-standing dream of homogeneous nation-states after 1945.

Eastern Europe's Jews were the most tragic victims of a growing conviction that emigration could solve the perceived "problem" of national, linguistic, and religious diversity. Well before the Nazi conquest of the East, a broad consensus had developed—among Western diplomats, Zionists, humanitarian organizations, and East European officials, as well as ordinary Jews desperate for a better life—that the "solution" to the so-called "Jewish problem" would entail the mass emigration of Jews from Eastern Europe. The groups and individuals invested in Jewish emigration in the 1930s had very different motivations and vastly unequal degrees of power. While "encouraging" emigration became a soft form of deportation for East European anti-Semites, it was a last hope for many Jews and the humanitarian organizations that tried to save them during the Second World War. But the fantasy that Jews could be relocated en masse to a faraway colonial reservation—like Madagascar, Angola, or Guiana—emerged from a long-standing view of mass emigration as a solution to demographic and social "problems." When the Nazis successfully made Jews disappear, under the pretext that they were being "relocated" to the distant East, it is hardly surprising that so few East Europeans protested: the notion of emigration as a "humanitarian" solution to the "Jewish problem" had been long established, and it helped make the departure of Jews palatable to their neighbors.

The Second World War marked a critical turning point in the history of East European emigration in other ways as well. As some twenty million people were uprooted during the war and its aftermath—the majority from Central and Eastern Europe— governments and international agencies first began to distinguish officially between "economic migrants" and "political refugees." While migrants designated as "political refugees" were favored with new "human rights" to international humanitarian assistance, individuals labeled "economic migrants" were often denied such assistance. These distinctions, formally anchored in international law and humanitarian practice during the early Cold War, have shaped asylum and migration policies ever since. In postwar Europe, the line between "economic" and "political" migrations was from the outset, however, unstable and arbitrary. It reflected the political concerns of the moment and the perceived demands of labor markets as well as the prejudices and whims of border officials. These distinctions served, above all, to privilege certain groups of migrants above others in a brutal competition for visas, recognition, and humanitarian sympathy. Distinguishing between "economic migrants" and "political refugees" also enabled Western governments to square the circle between their ongoing desire to control state borders and a theoretical commitment to a "human right" to emigrate.

Emigration policies in East Central Europe did not simply contribute to the development of border controls and ethnic cleansing, however. The rise of a global labor market raised genuine humanitarian and social concerns about the welfare of migrant workers. From the late nineteenth century onward, reformers typically justified restrictions on emigration in the name of migrants' own well-being. These concerns were often highly paternalistic, presuming that migrants were victims of false consciousness, duplicitous emigration agents, or Western propaganda. But they were also based on a vision of freedom that differed significantly from contemporary liberal visions. Freedom, in this view, was not linked to movement, or to the absence of state intervention in private life. Real freedom required stability, security, and solidarity at home. Workers were to enjoy the freedom to stay home, rather than the illusory "freedom" to cross the ocean in search of bread and employment. Protecting citizens' freedom, in this view, required restricting their movement.

From the vantage point of the post-Communist present, it is easy to dismiss such rhetoric as cynical propaganda. Today the relationship between mobility and freedom seems almost sacrosanct. The Cold War was a critical moment in this development. After the Second World War, the "captivity" of East Europeans behind the Iron Curtain became a quintessential symbol of unfreedom for many in the West. American Cold Warriors depicted the Iron Curtain as an impermeable barrier between a "free world" and a "slave world." In Cold War parlance, "captivity" referred both to the political control of East European governments by Moscow and to the physical captivity of individuals by their own governments.[32] Freedom of movement thus attained the status of a fundamental human right. In 1948, as Cold War divisions hardened, Article 13 of the United Nations Declaration of Human Rights declared, "Everyone has the right to leave any country, including his own, and to return to his country." Over the course of the following four decades, emigrants and anti-Communist dissidents would passionately invoke this right to movement.

By 1989, nothing symbolized the failed promise of socialism so profoundly as the barbed wire and watchtowers that imprisoned citizens in their own states. Communism's collapse remains indelibly associated with images of euphoric Germans dancing, singing, and popping champagne corks atop the Berlin Wall on November 9, 1989. "The sound that you hear and what you're seeing tonight is not hammers and sickles, but hammers and chisels, as young people take down this wall, bit by bit," reported Tom Brokaw from

Berlin on November 10. On that day, commentators insisted, East Berliners were not simply crossing from the East to the West: they were moving from captivity to freedom. As crowds of dazed East Germans wandered the streets of West Berlin for the first time in twenty-eight years, Brokaw declared, "Tonight in Berlin, it is 'Freedom night.' . . . Thousands of East Berliners have been crossing into freedom all day long."[33]

And yet the Iron Curtain did not simply descend from the sky in 1948 or 1961. Nor was it merely a Soviet imposition. It was the culmination of a century-long struggle against emigration in Eastern Europe. The borders erected by Eastern bloc regimes were undeniably murderous. At least 136 people died trying to cross the Berlin Wall between 1961 and 1989. The Iron Curtain was littered with dead bodies, divided families, and constrained lives.[34] But precisely because the campaign against emigration in Eastern Europe was so enduring and so deadly, it is worth taking seriously the rhetoric of "slavery" and "freedom" that helped to radicalize and sustain it.

This campaign was a powerful, but ultimately failed, effort to uphold state sovereignty in the face of globalization. It was simultaneously an effort to establish and protect the status of East European migrants as "white" men and women in the context of global labor markets. Since the 1880s, millions of emigrants from Eastern Europe have successfully settled in places like Chicago, Lille, and London. Thousands of others died trying—whether killed by the guns of East European border guards or the American "paper walls" that trapped Jews in the Nazi empire. Whether these migrants were propelled by hope and ambition or desperation and fear; whether they succeeded or failed in their efforts to go to the West; whether they made permanent homes abroad or ultimately returned home—the great departure from Eastern Europe helped to define the "free world" in the twentieth century.

CHAPTER ONE

Travel Agents on Trial

In the winter of 1889, reporters from across the Austro-Hungarian Empire and beyond flocked to the sleepy Galician town of Wadowice. Wadowice, located about fifty kilometers from Cracow, is today best known as the birthplace of Pope John Paul II. That winter, however, Wadowice played host to a sensational trial that captured the imagination of the Austrian press and public. The defendants were Jewish travel agents from the nearby town of Oświęcim, better known to the world today as Auschwitz.

Oświęcim, conveniently located at the juncture of Prussian, Russian, and Austrian railway lines, had recently developed a booming emigration business. Since 1880, hundreds of thousands of East Europeans had trekked through the town en route to the German ports of Hamburg and Bremen and then to America. The sixty-five defendants in the case were accused of seducing migrants into abandoning their homeland with false promises of an American El Dorado. In reality, prosecutors argued, East European peasants were delivered into hard labor in American factories, mines, and brothels. "What happens to these poor people over there?" the state's attorney demanded. "Each of them left because unscrupulous people convinced them that they would be able to make a good living—and each ends up ruined and in misery." The accused agents stood trial for a host of unsavory crimes: fraud, smuggling, bribery, assault, and generally swindling emigrants out of their last heller as they set out for America.[1]

The Wadowice trial quickly came to implicate much more than a group of corrupt travel agents. As the prosecuting attorney argued in his closing statement, the trial was a referendum on emigration itself, "one of the most important, burning problems of the day." And emigration, he claimed, posed a grave threat to the basic ideal of freedom in the Habsburg Empire. He accused the travel agents of Oświęcim of nothing less than "introducing a slave trade into the free land of Austria."[2]

NEFARIOUS EMIGRATION AGENTS appeared in contemporary literature as well as in law. Henryk Sinkiewiecz, the Polish journalist and Nobel Prize–winning novelist, famously dramatized the tragic plight of Polish emigrants in America in his 1897 novel *After Bread*. The protaganists, the peasant Lorenz Toporek and his daughter, Mary, are seduced to emigrate by the beguiling promises of a duplicitous German agent and his Jewish co-conspirator:

This German expatiated on the wonders and marvels of America. He promised him for nothing more land than the largest farm in Lipintse . . . so that the peasant's eyes beamed with anticipation. . . . [T]he Jew milk-merchant, who accompanied the German, said that the American government gave to everybody as much land as they could use. . . . They tempted the peasant till they secured him. Why should he remain here? . . . He struck hands with the

German, had a mass said to St. Michael, took his daughter—and lo! he was coming to America.

Lorenz and his daughter are robbed of their life savings en route, and of their health and spirits in New York. "The 'inheritance' which they expected was a dream and passed as a dream, and the reality appears in the form of a narrow basement room, deep in the ground, with one window, partly broken; from the walls of the room oozes unhealthy slime and streaks of moisture. . . ." After Lorenz dies of overwork and illness, Mary wanders the docks in New York City each morning begging for passage home. "Should she remain here? Never! She would go to the docks, embrace the feet of the ship captains and beseech them to take her, and, if they would take her across the water, she would walk on foot through Germany and return to Lipintse." But it was not meant to be. "One day she did not appear, and they saw her no more. The next day the papers announced that a policeman had found on the end of a pier the dead body of a girl of unknown name and origin."[3]

Emigration had become such a burning issue for a good reason. Around 3,547,000 emigrants departed Austria-Hungary for overseas destinations between 1876 and 1910, 7–8 percent of the 1910 population. The largest numbers left from the impoverished Austrian provinces of Galicia and Bukovina and from southern and eastern Hungary. Hundreds of thousands of migrants were also moving east to west within Europe. At least 300,000 Austrian workers harvested German fields in Prussia and Saxony; others earned their bread on French farms or in British factories. Seasonal migration within Austria-Hungary or Europe was often a stepping-stone to emigration overseas.[4]

This mass departure was sudden and unexpected; contemporaries described emigration as a contagious "fever" that infected entire villages. Aside from the midcentury wave of Bohemian emigration, relatively few citizens of the Habsburg lands crossed the Atlantic before the 1880s. In 1880, for example, only 17,267 Austro-Hungarians emigrated to the United States. By 1892, that number had more than quadrupled, to 76,937. At the peak of the exodus, several hundred thousand citizens of the Dual Monarchy were emigrating each year.[5] Leopold Caro, a Polish-Jewish lawyer and emigration reformer, described villages that became ghost towns overnight. "Entire regiments left in 1907 in order to earn money in America. Many houses stood empty, and in many others only old women and small children remained behind. In some villages the entire young generation left home. . . . Everyone believed that America was the Promised Land, a true paradise."[6]

In an era in which demographers saw population as a measure of political, economic, and military strength, these numbers induced panic in the halls of government and beyond. Military officials were consistently at the forefront of efforts to curtail emigration in the late nineteenth century, dismayed by the loss of conscripts to America fever. Conservative landowners, social reformers, nationalist activists, religious authorities, and socialists also mobilized against emigration, however. To many, the loss of millions of workers represented a disgraceful symptom of underdevelopment, poverty, and imperial decline.

In the eyes of many reformers, the seductive propaganda of emigration agents was the major cause of the emigration boom. The Wadowice trial of 1889 was one of the most sensational cases in which travel agents were prosecuted, but it was not isolated. In 1905–06, Hungarian authorities arrested or fined two thousand emigration agents and were monitoring more than fifteen hundred individuals who were suspected of encouraging emigration. In 1914, over three thousand agents faced criminal charges in the Austrian half of the monarchy.[7] These arrests and trials were often initiated through anonymous denunciations (sometimes from competing agents and shipping companies, or by local anti-Semites). They were clearly orchestrated as a warning to would-be emigrants about the hazards of leaving home.

In their effort to curb emigration, Austrian officials were not alone in focusing on the middlemen who facilitated migration. Beginning in the nineteenth century, abolitionists and government reformers had begun to crack down on agents as they sought to eliminate various forms of unfree migration. They accused agents of coercing migrants to leave home, swindling them en route, and trapping them in forms of labor that resembled slavery. These concerns stimulated the first attempts to regulate the business of emigration. The English Passenger Vessel Act of 1803, initially intended to monitor shipping firms, were gradually expanded to regulate emigration agents, labor brokers, and rooming houses, in order to protect migrants from unscrupulous brokers. Laws passed in France in 1854 and Belgium in 1876 required emigration agents to obtain licenses. The Swiss government was the first to ban advertising for emigration completely. Closer to home, Bohemian authorities banned emigration agencies in the 1850s. Other laws regulating emigration followed in Japan (1896), Germany (1897), Italy (1901), and Hungary (1903). The Hungarian law was the most restrictive to date, and it became a model for legislation across East Central Europe after World War I.[8]

Beginning in the 1860s, British laws aimed to guarantee that emigrants from China and India were transported by choice, and that they understood the conditions of their contracts. American consuls were required to inspect U.S. ships embarking from Hong Kong and to question migrants to certify that they were departing voluntarily. Officials confronted migrants with a series of ritualized questions (for which many were clearly coached). A British missionary recorded this interrogation in Hong Kong in 1871:

Q: Who induced you to go?

A: No one.

Q: Why do you go?

A: Because I wish to get higher wages and be a free man.

Q: Who sold you the ticket?

A: The elder.

Q: Did you sign any contract to work in America in payment for the ticket?

A: No.

Q: Have you made any arrangement with regard to your labor after arrival in California?

A: No.

Q: Then you declare unqualifiedly that you are under no obligations whatever to any persons, which will bind you to labor for any particular party in the United States?

A: I do.[9]

As of 1885, American immigration laws banned contract labor completely, insisting that all contract labor represented "slavery" in disguise. The ban was also intended to insulate American workers from competition from cheap migrant labor. But the contract labor law created a Catch-22 for migrants, who could be rejected upon arrival in America if they admitted to having a job lined up in advance. In the words of the U.S. Industrial Commission Report of 1901, the migrant "strives to show that he can support himself, and he strives to show that he does not know of any job by which he can support himself."[10]

As Adam McKeown has argued, these laws obscured the fact that the vast majority of nineteenth-century migration conformed to neither extreme of "free," unmediated migration or "slavery." The very ideal of the "free migrant" was based on a mythical prototype: a rational individual who made decisions independent of social pressures, family, or friends. Unsurprisingly, this imagined migrant was also male. Single female migrants, seen as less capable of willfully choosing emigration, were often suspected of being either prostitutes or victims of the "white-slave trade," and their mobility was restricted in the name of their moral protection.[11]

By blaming mass emigration on Jewish agents, prosecutors and social reformers cast migrants as innocent victims of Jewish and capitalist machinations. A 1913 memo from the Austrian Ministry of War to the Justice Ministry expressed the typical view: "It is common knowledge . . . that the majority of emigrants do not actually decide to emigrate of their own initiative, or because of their economic situation, but are rather induced to emigrate by the immoral, speculative activity of emigration agents."[12] Blaming and arresting travel agents was also a far simpler (and less costly) "solution" to the perceived emigration crisis than addressing the deeper social and economic inequalities within Austria and beyond that actually propelled emigration.

There was, however, an obvious contradiction at the heart of the anti-emigration movement. It was painfully self-evident that many Austrians, particularly the peasants and Jews of Galicia, lived in a state of abject poverty. Images of "Galician misery" and backwardness circulated widely in the empire, and justified a range of imperial civilizing and modernizing projects.[13] And yet, a broad constituency of Austrian politicians and social reformers were fully convinced that only the disingenuous promises of travel agents induced Austrians to emigrate. These reformers were intent on hanging on to Austria's population even though there was not enough land, food, or work to go around.

In part, the preoccupation with maintaining population in imperial Austria was linked to the explosive growth of popular nationalist movements at the end of the nineteenth century. In the nationalist battle for supremacy, numbers mattered. Beginning in 1880, when citizens were first asked about their "language of daily use," the imperial census escalated into a high-stakes campaign for citizens' allegiances, as the number of Czech-speakers, German-speakers, Polish-speakers, or Ruthene-speakers counted came to be seen as a measure of national strength. Increasingly, numbers determined how state resources were allocated, where schools were built, and in which languages children could be educated.[14]

It follows logically that nationalists would mobilize to prevent the emigration of members of their own national community and encourage the exodus of national rivals. The Hungarian government, which operated somewhat like a nation-state within the Dual Monarchy (sharing only a common foreign policy and military with Austria), did just that. As of 1904, two-thirds of the emigrants leaving the Hungarian half of the monarchy were not native Hungarian-speakers. A secret memorandum from the Hungarian undersecretary of state to the Hungarian prime minister explained, "For the institution of national statehood it is absolutely necessary that the ruling race . . . become the majority of the population. . . . Providence . . . has granted another population factor which has significantly raised the proportion of the Hungarian element at the expense of the nationalities. . . . This important new factor is the mass emigration of the non-Hungarian population."[15]

In Russia as well, imperial authorities began to encourage Jewish emigration in the 1890s, while restricting the emigration of nationally "desirable" citizens. The Russian government allowed the Jewish Colonization Association (JCA) to set up branches across the empire beginning in 1892, effectively legalizing Jewish emigration, even though emigration remained illegal for non-Jewish Russians. The JCA had established four hundred offices throughout Russia by 1910, providing migrants with information about opportunities to emigrate and assisting with the burdensome paperwork.[16]

In Vienna, by contrast, imperial authorities officially mourned the loss of all the kaiser's subjects equally. In 1905, out of 111,990 emigrants from Austria to the United States, 50,785 (45 percent) were Polish-speakers, 14,473 (14 percent) spoke Ruthene (a language later known as Ukrainian), and 11,757 (10 percent) were Czech-speakers. In contrast to their proportion in the emigration from imperial Russia, where anti-Semitic persecution was much more severe, Jews were not heavily overrepresented among emigrants from the Dual Monarchy. Out of a total of 275,693 emigrants from Austria-Hungary in 1905, for example, 17,352 emigrants (6 percent) were Jewish, only slightly more than the percentage of Jews in the total population in 1900 (4.7 percent in Austria, 5 percent in Hungary).[17]

At the provincial and local level, however, Polish nationalist activists began to worry that Polish emigration would play to the advantage of Ruthene-speakers. Representatives of growing populist and anti-Semitic parties, meanwhile, began to suggest that the emigration of Jews to Palestine or North America represented a potential solution to the "Jewish problem." In 1901, after being informed that sixteen thousand Jewish Galicians had emigrated that year, the anti-Semitic priest and peasant organizer Stanislaw Stojalowski quipped, "A pity there were not three times as many."[18]

At the Wadowice trial, the prosecutor Heinrich Ogniewski condemned the loss of "Polish souls" to emigration. "Over a million Polish souls have been swept away by America fever," he lamented. In America, these migrants "are dispersed in all of the businesses, mines, and factories, and crushed by foreign elements, and in time they cease to be Poles. This denationalization takes place in the course of only a few years. Are we really so numerous that we can be indifferent to the loss of over a million Polish brothers?"[19] In spite of such nationalist concerns, however, it was not until after 1918 that Austria's successor states began to follow the Hungarian example, deliberately manipulating emigration to engineer homogeneous populations.

If emigration agents and nationalist agitation were not behind the emigration craze, what was its source? The motivations of individual migrants were predictably diverse and complex. In the short term, letters and money sent home from relatives and friends were often the most persuasive form of "propaganda."[20] "I want to write to you the truth about the freedom and goodness of America. There is happiness here," wrote M. Celmer in Detroit to his family back home in 1891.[21] Not all such letters can be taken at face value, however, since some migrants surely felt compelled to obscure their struggles and failures. Joseph Roth observed,

> Most Jewish emigrants are too proud to write when things are going badly for them, and most are eager to play up the new home at the expense of the old. . . . In a small town in the East, a letter from an émigré creates a huge stir. All the young people in the place—and not a few of the old— are overcome by itchy feet. They want to leave the country where a war might break out from one year to the next, and from one week to the next, a pogrom. And so they leave, by foot, by train, on board ship, for Western countries where a different, somewhat reformed, though no less dismal ghetto offers its own brand of darkness to the newcomers who have barely managed to escape the clutches of the concentration camp.[22]

In Hungary, a poem mocked the tendency of emigrants to exaggerate their success:

If he writes home
What does he tell his wife?
Boastful and self-satisfied
He tells of his good life.

If he picks turnips for a farmer
He'll write he's bought a farm.
Hundred and sixty acres' yield
Will soon fill his barn.

Or if he is a laborer
He's sure to be in foreman's rank.
He gives his orders in the bar
But neither at work nor at the bank.[23]

On the other hand, many migrants openly described the hardships they endured to friends and family at home. These letters fueled the anti-emigration lobby, as they seemed to expose the illusory nature of both "freedom" and prosperity in the New World. Simon Sosieński discouraged his brother from joining him in America.

In the old country, you can work the way you like and every Sunday and holiday you can rest. But here in America . . . you have to work day and night and holidays and non-holidays and every Sunday. Because even if you want to have a day of rest, they will not give it to you; but rather you have to work straight through just like the horses or oxen do back home. Yet not even like that because horses and oxen are idle every Sunday and holiday there.[24]

If family members and friends proved most persuasive (or discouraging) to individual migrants in the short term, deeper social and economic inequalities clearly stimulated emigration over the long term. Landholding and inheritance patterns in Galicia, in particular, left peasants with tiny plots of land that could not possibly sustain a family. Emigrants themselves consistently cited poverty, lack of employment, or the desire to save money to buy land or a home as their primary motivations. Anna Kupinsky emigrated from Bukovina to New Jersey at the age of eight, in 1914. The family left Austria, she recalled, because "life was hard in Europe. . . . We were poor. We didn't have any luxuries. We hardly had enough for food."[25]

In a context in which the decision to emigrate was seen (at least by government officials) as morally suspect and possibly illegal, however, migrants may have been inclined to justify their decision to emigrate in terms of economic hardships. They were likely to downplay more individualist motivations: a yearning to escape the confining routines of village life; personal ambition; an oppressive family situation or unwanted pregnancy; the desire to escape military service.

Two equally mythical views of America—and of the global labor market itself—thus propelled emigration and the emigration debate in fin-de-siècle East Central Europe. To some, America was a golden land of social mobility and adventure; emigration agents were purveyors of freedom and the good life. But to the adherents of a growing Austrian anti-emigration movement—and to many disillusioned migrants themselves—emigration represented a nefarious form of "human trafficking," as agents sold their victims into a life of hardship and exploitation.

EMIGRATION was in fact a big business by the end of the nineteenth century. The route from east to west was littered with opportunities for exploitation and profit. The most practical path to America from northeastern Europe was through Germany. Between 1871 and 1914, 38 percent of emigrants embarking at the ports of Hamburg and Bremen were Russian citizens, and 51 percent were Austrians.[26] Transmigration alone brought droves of migrants through Austrian cities and railway stations. More than 2,771,900 Russian citizens emigrated to North and South America between 1880 and 1910, and many traveled through imperial Austria, arousing anti-Semites and stirring accusations of espionage and smuggling along the way. A journey by train from Brody, on the Austro-Russian frontier, to Bremen took only a day by the turn of the twentieth century (today it would still take almost fourteen hours). The trip required serious endurance, however. Emigrating legally from Russia posed particular challenges. A passport enabling travel abroad cost 17.25 rubles in 1910, equal to around one month's wages for an agricultural worker. It was possible to acquire an "emigrant" passport for free, but this was a one-way ticket, since return was forbidden. That meant virtually cutting off family ties, and brought the risk of statelessness if a migrant was rejected or deported by American immigration authorities.[27] For many it was simply less expensive and troublesome to cross Russia's western frontiers illegally, with the help of a smuggler or agent. That also entailed considerable risk, however. Philip Cowen, a Jewish-American journalist and immigration inspector at Ellis Island, made an undercover journey to the Russian Pale of Settlement in 1906 to investigate Jewish emigration. He reported that upon crossing the Russian border—with a smuggler's or agent's assistance—"the emigrant is often despoiled of all that he possesses."[28]

The path from east to west was obstructed, in part, by racist and anti-Semitic fears of East European (i.e., "Jewish") dirt, disease, and backwardness.[29] In 1892, German authorities had blamed Russian Jews en route to America for a severe cholera outbreak in

Hamburg.[30] In response, the American government suspended emigration for several weeks. German authorities quickly erected new delousing and disinfection stations along Germany's borders with Russia and Austria-Hungary, turning back migrants who were sick as well as those without sufficient funds for the journey. The idea was to stop immigration at its source.[31]

These efforts to police hygiene were good business for HAPAG (Hamburg Amerikanische Paketfahrt Aktien-Gesellschaft) and the NDL (Norddeutscher Lloyd), the two major German shipping firms. HAPAG and the NDL controlled the new sanitary stations, acquiring a virtual monopoly on emigration traffic from Eastern Europe. Before the sanitary stations were created, approximately 40 percent of Russian emigrants left the continent through British ports. After 1895, when the checkpoints went into operation, that number dropped to 4 percent. Many emigrants were forced to buy new tickets on HAPAG or the NDL if they reached the border with a ticket for a non-German shipping line.[32]

After 1892, Russians who crossed directly into Germany were typically expedited to Ruhleben, near Berlin, sometimes in cattle cars ("For 8 Horses or 32 Men").[33] In 1894, thirteen-year-old Mary Antin traveled from Polotzk in Russia to Boston. She recorded her experiences in her journal shortly afterwards. The newly established sanitary station at Ruhleben was particularly terrifying, as were procedures for "disinfecting" migrants:

> This was another scene of bewildering confusion, parents losing their children, and little ones crying. . . . [O]ur things were taken away, our friends separated from us, a man came to inspect us, as if to ascertain our full value; strange looking people driving us about like dumb animals, helpless and unresisting; children we could not see, crying in a way that suggested terrible things; . . . our clothes taken off;

our bodies rubbed with a slippery substance that might be any bad thing; a shower of warm water let down us without warning. . . . We are forced to pick out our clothes from among all the others, with the steam blinding us; we choke, cough, entreat the women to give us time; they persist, "Quick, quick, or you'll miss the train!" Oh, so we really won't be murdered! They are only making us ready for the continuing of our journey, cleaning us of all suspicions of dangerous germs. Thank God![34]

While emigration was a particularly harrowing experience for Russians, Austrians also encountered serious obstacles on the route overseas. Before 1867, very few Austrians enjoyed the right to emigrate. Craftsmen and journeymen, elites, and refugees were among the few who could legally traverse Austrian frontiers.[35] In 1867, Austrians theoretically acquired a new, constitutional right to move freely within the empire's borders, as well as the right to venture beyond them. Article 4 of the Austrian constitution of 1867 specified, "Freedom to emigrate is limited only by the obligation to military service."[36]

There remained, however, a big difference between the letter of the law and the reality on the ground. While the government couldn't forbid emigration outright, it could and did throw plenty of roadblocks on the route overseas. Almost every district adopted its own policies to limit mobility, an arbitrary and frightening situation for migrants. Gendarmes patrolled train platforms, and in some districts detained all men of military age. In other localities, they apprehended all single women, who were suspected of being prostitutes or victims of sex traffickers.[37]

The Austrian government also tried to limit emigration by regulating shipping companies. By the early twentieth century, shipping firms were forbidden to employ traveling sales agents to sell tickets. Printed advertisements for emigration were banned, except for basic information about ship schedules, dates of departure, and ports of call. It was also illegal for shipping companies to accept passengers with "prepaid" tickets sent by family members or friends abroad, or to sell tickets to men under the age of fifty who had not completed their military service.[38]

Additional obstacles came in the form of administrative decrees from the Galician governor's office, the Trade Ministry, and the imperial parliament. On March 27, 1877, for example, the governor's office in Galicia ordered all local prefects "to impede the emigration of the peasantry, to advise farmers against emigration, and if this is unsuccessful, to require the possession of 160 florins and a passport."[39] And when the effort to stop emigration didn't succeed, Austrian authorities attempted to entice migrants to return home. In 1907, Emperor Francis Joseph issued an amnesty for draft dodgers—intended in part to encourage the return of Austrian emigrants. That same year the Hungarian government formulated an explicitly nationalist repatriation campaign, aimed at luring Magyar-speaking emigrants (but not German- or Slovak-speakers) back to Hungary (the plan was never implemented).[40]

Then, in 1903, the Hungarian government passed one of the most restrictive emigration laws to date in Europe. Baron Louis de Levay, the Hungarian royal commissioner of emigration, explained that the legislation was a direct response to the "abominable artifice of the secret agents and their accomplices." While many in the press and in parliament "demanded that the emigration evil should be ended by formal prohibition," he elaborated, "the principle of personal liberty, maintained by us," rendered direct prohibition impossible. The law therefore instead simply aimed to "prevent emigration and to protect people from the fever of emigration."[41]

Henceforth, Hungarian men were not legally permitted to emigrate after their seventeenth birthday without written permission from the Defense and Interior Ministries. Parents were required to provide proof that they had made arrangements to support their offspring. In addition, the Hungarian law empowered the government to "forbid emigration to any state or region where the life, health, morality, or property of emigrants is endangered." It was illegal either to speak publicly in favor of emigration or to advertise opportunities for emigration; violators of the law were subject to imprisonment for up to two months as well as to serious fines. The law became the model for restrictive legislation in all of Austria-Hungary's successor states after 1914.[42]

Enforcement of these regulations was haphazard (and often arbitrary), but the constitutional guarantee of free movement clearly had little purchase locally. Simon Herz and Julius Löwenberg, the principal defendants in the Wadowice case, cited the many barriers to emigration in their defense. "After many difficulties, obstacles, and detours, in constant fear and danger of being arrested and returned home, a traveler finally succeeds in arriving in our agency in Oświęcim. . . . He knows that this is an officially sanctioned agency. Is it necessary to force such a traveler to purchase a steamship ticket, to threaten him with violence?" More often, Herz and Löwenberg maintained, emigrants "kissed the ground in joy" at having finally reached the office.[43]

Upon arrival in Oświęcim, emigrants typically spent a night or two at a local hotel or boardinghouse and then caught a train to their port of call. Hamburg and Bremen were the most common outlets for East European emigrants, but it was also possible to depart from Rotterdam, Antwerp, or Liverpool. First, though, the migrant had to get into and across Germany, no simple feat.

If and when migrants finally made it to a port of call, they had to find lodging and food until their departure, typically in hotels and boardinghouses. These facilities were potential sites of further exploitation, and also became objects of reform and regulation. In 1901, HAPAG constructed an enormous depot for emigrants in Hamburg well outside the city. The idea was to completely isolate East European migrants from the German population.[44]

When the American immigration inspector Terence Powderly visited the depot in 1906, 1,184 emigrants were in residence, mostly Russians, Austrians, and Hungarians. The entire facility was divided into "clean" and "unclean" sections. Emigrants were subjected to daily medical examinations. Powderly praised the institution as evidence of America's civilizing effect on the world. "Our laws . . . are educating foreign people in the use of soap and water," he boasted. "If cleanliness is akin to godliness these people are becoming more godly every time an immigrant is sent back from an American port for having some disease that a due regard for sanitation and clean habits would have averted." Many migrants begged to differ, condemning the depot as a prison. Whereas Austrians could choose whether or not to stay in the Emigrant Hall, Russians were forcibly quarantined there.[45]

Even with the new health screenings in Europe, migrants feared rejection upon arrival. In 1892, the Ellis Island reception center was opened in order to facilitate more rigorous inspection of immigrants. Beginning in 1891, the American government barred migrants who were sick, suspicious, "likely to become a public charge," or involved in "criminal" or "immoral" activities. The category "likely to become a public charge" was particularly elastic. It extended to almost all single women, unless they intended to work as domestic servants. Any unmarried or pregnant woman was considered "likely to become a public charge" (or likely to become a prostitute) by definition, and turned back to Europe. After 1907, a "poor physique" became grounds for rejection, even if a migrant had no actual medical condition. Simply being frail or underweight could get a migrant sent home. In practice, this clause was applied most rigorously to Jews.[46]

The number of immigrants rejected at Ellis Island was still small—only 1.7 percent in 1907—but the inspections were often terrifying. Louise Nagy arrived on Ellis Island from Warsaw in 1913, at the age of ten. She recalled "noise, the talk, everybody was speaking their language." In a huge room with acoustics "like Grand Central Station," there were lines, more crowds, and the dreaded medical exam. She was petrified of being sent home. "Whatever they would have found wrong with me at the time, they could have sent me back without my parent's permission, whether my parents cared, or wanted me to go. . . . I was just lucky that we came through and nobody was held back." Not everyone was so fortunate, however. "Consumption was a horror word, and I remember one man in particular, he must have been found consumptive and I remember him crying, that meant he had to go back."[47]

Joseph Roth described the experience of being detained upon arrival in America:

The medical examination in the European port was bad enough. Now there is a still-more-rigorous one. And something turns out to be not quite right with your papers. . . . And so the Jew winds up in a kind of prison that goes by the name of "quarantine" or somesuch. A high fence protects America from him. Through the bars of his prison, he sees the Statue of Liberty, and he doesn't know whether it's himself or Liberty that has been incarcerated.[48]

By the turn of the century, emigrants from Eastern Europe were obliged to navigate a gauntlet of confusing and often frightening situations en route to the West. Russian and Austrian gendarmes, German doctors, and American immigration officials all had the power to send them home with little explanation. Anti-emigration activists consistently blamed emigration agents for "artificially" inflating emigration. Given the obstacles faced by emigrants, however, it is difficult to imagine making the challenging journey without professional assistance. In the end, it was clearly not emigration agents who stimulated emigration, but the many barriers to mobility that swelled the demand for the services of agents.

THOSE WERE THE CONDITIONS that brought migrants to the offices of Simon Herz and Julius Löwenberg, the chief defendants in the Wadowice trial. On November 19, 1889, reporters from across the empire and as far away as England, France, and America crowded the few hotels and guesthouses in the Galician town, located about fifty kilometers from Cracow.[49] Sixty-five defendants faced charges in the case, including a number of mid-level Austrian civil servants, railway employees, and police officers accused of accepting bribes from the agents. The proceedings did not end until March 12, 1890, after fifty-five days of testimony.[50] The number of spectators (and defendants) was so large that the trial had to be held in a local gymnasium.[51]

The complete trial records of the Wadowice trial appear to be missing.[52] Local, regional, and imperial newspapers all sent reporters to Galicia, however, and published daily updates, commentary, and transcripts of the proceedings.[53] It is unclear what precipitated the arrests in Oświęcim, but the Austrian War Ministry clearly had a hand in the affair. Beginning in 1888, military authorities had become increasingly alarmed about the number of Galician men who failed to appear for (mandatory) military service. Emigration, they claimed, was draining the supply of new recruits. In

May 1888, the Interior Ministry ordered Galician authorities to mobilize against illegal emigration, and on June 17 the Galician governor ordered the prefect of Biała to scrutinize the activities of the emigration agencies in Oświęcim in particular. A month later, police raided the agents' offices and made the arrests.[54]

The primary defendants in the case were all Jewish emigration agents. In the early 1880s, Simon Herz and Julius Löwenberg founded a travel agency in Oświęcim, located in the first floor of the Hotel Zator, across from the train station in nearby Brzezinka (also known as Birkenau). In 1887, the Herz-Löwenberg firm merged with Jakob Klausner's agency, affiliated with the HAPAG shipping line. Five agents—Herz, Löwenberg, Klausner, Arthur Landau, and Abraham Landerer—formed a partnership. Their primary competitor was another local agency affiliated with the NDL, established in 1888. Fierce competition for customers soon developed between the Herz agency, the NDL agency, and a plethora of itinerant agents who sold steamship tickets and services to emigrants on the sly.

The trial at Wadowice reflected and promoted the conviction that agents were to blame for mass emigration. The anti-Semitic *Deutsche Volksblatt* declared, "There is no doubt that this massive emigration . . . was not the consequence of overpopulation or economic conditions in the province, but that it was artificially nourished by the propaganda of agents."[55] Austrian and American officials also found a convenient scapegoat in travel agents. In an 1899 speech, the Austrian foreign minister denounced "the artifices of unprincipled agents who carry on a lucrative business in this new kind of traffic in human beings."[56] An American consul in Budapest concurred that Slovak peasants emigrated mostly because of agents "who are managing the business a good deal in the manner of the 'Coolie trade.'"[57] In reality, concluded an Austrian investigation in 1905, agents defrauded fewer than a thousand emigrants each year (out of hundreds of thousands of migrants).[58] These facts did not stop reformers from blaming agents for the exodus of millions. "The propaganda conducted by steamship ticket agents is undoubtedly the most important immediate cause of emigration from Europe to the United States," insisted the U.S. Immigration Commission in its 1911 Dillingham report.[59]

These discussions reflected a widespread assumption among elites that migrants themselves were ignorant, gullible, and deluded about their own interests. Leopold Caro lamented, "The uneducated are most easily induced to emigrate by agents and village pub owners; these people are the easiest targets and the most docile material. Illiterates will believe almost anything." According to Caro, agents had recently convinced Ruthenian peasants that Brazil was an Austrian territory, that the emperor himself recommended emigration, and that monkeys did all the household chores in Brazil. Subsequent economists challenged Caro's assumptions. They found that emigration actually increased among peasants with a basic primary education. The poorest and least educated, those on the brink of starvation, tended to remain home, since they lacked the necessary funds to travel. Migrants themselves were highly aware of their own economic interests, and sensitive to very small shifts in the labor market abroad (which fueled the high rate of return migration).[60]

The specific accusations against Herz and his colleagues in Oświęcim went well beyond merely inducing emigration, however. Prosecutors depicted a mafia-like organization in the town, masterminded by Herz and his colleagues. Train conductors, police officers, cab drivers, and government officials were all allegedly on Herz's payroll.[61] The most sensational accusations concerned the treatment of migrants as they passed through the town. When trains full of migrants arrived in Oświęcim en route to Germany, thick-muscled "drivers" employed by the competing travel agencies allegedly surrounded them on the platform. These "drivers" did not shy from violence in their competition for customers. According to the *Deutsche Volksblatt*, "It often came to bloody fights between the drivers. They beat each other with fists and sticks, and after fighting it out, these henchmen drove the captured emigrants to the agencies like cattle."[62] Several of the agents had once been livestock traders (a common occupation for Galician Jews), and prosecutors and the anti-Semitic press accused them of treating their human cargo no better than animals.

The fraud allegedly continued once the "herd of slaves" arrived in Herz's office. Löwenberg, costumed in the uniform of an Austrian civil servant, reportedly met incoming emigrants at the office. His colleagues addressed him as "Mr. Prefect." Photos of Emperor Francis Joseph and imperial insignia supposedly adorned the office walls, in order to give the impression of a government office. The agents first ordered migrants to turn over their passports and money, strip-searching them to extract bills sewn into their clothing or hidden in their socks and undergarments. They determined the price of steamship tickets on the basis of how much cash migrants had on hand. Agents then informed unsuspecting peasants that it was illegal to purchase a ticket from any other firm, and threatened them with arrest and violence if they refused. Gendarmes paid by Herz stood by to carry out the threat if necessary.

Even once the beleaguered emigrant agreed to purchase a ticket, the abuse didn't end. The agents now reportedly insisted that it was necessary to make a "phone call" to Hamburg, in order to reserve a place on the ship. A second fake call went out to the "Emperor of America," in order to reserve space in the golden land. Emigrants were charged for both calls, which were made by means of an alarm clock. Finally, Herz informed emigrants that they would not be permitted to enter America wearing traditional peasants' clothing. Fortunately, they could purchase brand-new "American" suits (at outrageous prices) in Löwenberg's store next door. Prosecutors claimed that agents held emigrants captive while they waited for the train to Germany, sometimes for days, locking them into "pig stalls" and dark basements, where they were charged exorbitant prices for bad bread and weak beer.[63]

The prosecution's case was a shocking litany of violence, exploitation, and corruption. But what did emigrants themselves have to say about their experiences? From December 17 to December 20, 1889, migrants and their relatives took the stand in Wadowice. Many had traveled long distances on foot or by train to testify. Some witnesses were family members whose relatives had emigrated; others had crossed the Atlantic and returned home again. Many were themselves Jewish. Some accused the agents of swindling them, whereas others insisted that they had been treated fairly. All were adamant, however, that they had decided to emigrate of their own volition. Anna Fujarkos, an eighteen-year-old Slovak, wanted to join her husband in America. Janos Hrzesko, aged sixteen, testified that he decided to emigrate because he was poor and hungry. Maryanna Gnapp insisted that poverty and lack of employment alone had caused her to seek a livelihood in America.[64] On December 17, the *Bukowinaer Rundschau* reported, "A series of witnesses, farmers and citizens from the area, testified under oath that it is untrue that emigrants were deprived of their personal freedom in the agency, and that the rumors to this effect were spread by the local anti-Semitic club."[65]

The defendants' lawyers frequently complained that public opinion had been poisoned against their clients by the barrage of anti-Semitic cartoons, caricatures, and editorials circulating around the trial. In one image, dark-skinned agents with hooked noses and malicious facial expressions trick gullible-looking peasants with an alarm clock.[66]

The travel agents of Oświęcim, depicted swindling
emigrants by the anti-Semitic press.
Proces Wadowicki z illustracyami z natury wziętemi (Cracow, 1890).

The Wadowice trial clearly reflected the growth of an increasingly vocal Austrian anti-Semitic movement. The activities of Jewish emigration agents in Austria had become a favorite theme of
the anti-Semitic press, which played a pivotal role in sensational-
izing the trial. The *Deutsche Volksblatt*, founded in Vienna in 1888,
printed extensive coverage of the trial, pressuring the government
to take action against agents.[67] Many of the most dramatic charges
against the agents originated in local denunciations by anti-Semites. Shortly before the arrests, a group of Poles in Oświęcim
addressed a petition denouncing the agents to Georg von Schönerer, the anti-Semitic leader of the Austrian pan-German movement. In 1887, Schönerer had even sponsored a bill to restrict the
immigration of Russians and Romanians to Austria-Hungary—

a movement facilitated by smugglers and emigration agents in border towns such as Brody.[68]

Vincenz Gawronski, a craftsman in town, was a leader of the local anti-Semitic club. On December 12, he reportedly testified in Wadowice that they had written the petition "because we saw with our own eyes how the Jews sent young men who had not completed their military service to America, whereby our army lost many valuable soldiers."[69] Josef Stancyk, a local real estate agent, had also signed the petition and concurred, "All of Oświęcim was outraged by the Jewish agency, since we could see how the Jewish drivers abused the emigrants, and the poor peasants often cried and complained that they had been robbed and plundered in the Jewish agency."[70]

It is impossible to know precisely what percentage of emigration agents were actually Jewish. Emigration and travel agencies were relatively new businesses in the late nineteenth century, but facilitating emigration was a classic middleman trade. It required familiarity with multiple languages and contexts. The emigration business also extended logically from other occupations—in retail sales, trade, and hospitality (hotels, pubs, and restaurants)—traditionally occupied by Jews in Eastern Europe. It is clear that Jews were heavily represented in the ranks of agents prosecuted by the Austrian government, however. A 1910 list of agents suspected of criminal activity in Galicia included 64 agents, 53 of whom had Jewish names.[71] Out of a sample of 284 criminal cases against agents under way in November 1913, 156 of the defendants had Jewish names.[72]

The period from 1880 to 1900 saw the rapid rise of populist anti-Semitic movements across Europe, accompanied by a rash of anti-Semitic trials. Within a period of twenty years, blood libel trials took place in Tiszaeszlár, Hungary (1882); in Xanten (1892) and Konitz (1900–01), Prussia; and in Polná, Bohemia (1899). A spectacular, anti-Semitic trial of accused "white slavers" was held in L'viv/Lwow/Lemberg in 1892.[73] Fleecing migrants was a less scandalous charge than blood libel or sex trafficking, but the Wadowice trial borrowed heavily from the scripts of these courtrooms. The language used to denounce the agents—as "human traffickers," "parasites sucking on our blood," and "vampires"—echoed the standard vocabulary of anti-Semitic trials. "This trial is taking place because it is impossible to tolerate the existence of a human trafficking at the end of the nineteenth century, a trade in the blood of ten thousand impoverished people," insisted the prosecuting attorney Heinrich Ogniewski in his closing statement.[74]

The link between sex trafficking and emigration was particularly significant. Anti-Semites in Eastern Europe frequently depicted Jews as sexual predators. Now the anti-Semitic press deliberately linked emigration and sex trafficking in an effort to criminalize Jewish emigration agents. Both the "white slavery" panic and the emigration panic targeted Jews for their alleged role in moving people across borders and commodifying human beings.[75] And just as sultry accounts of "white slavery" played on racial anxieties, stoking alarm that white women would be reduced to the status of black slaves, emigration reformers stirred fears that East European men and women would be treated like nonwhite colonial labor, Chinese "coolies," or enslaved Africans.

Even Jewish activists involved in the campaign against sex trafficking associated the trade in women with the broader emigration crisis. The Austrian-Jewish feminist Bertha Pappenheim (also known as Freud's Anna O.) traveled to Austrian Galicia in 1903 to gather information about sex trafficking there. "The cardinal point of any campaign against the traffic in women is that emigration should receive the greatest attention," she insisted. Pappenheim, who founded the middle-class Jewish Women's Association in Germany, shared the paternalistic attitudes of middle-class social reformers at the time, blaming emigration on the ignorance of migrants and dishonesty of agents.

> The eagerness of the population to emigrate is abetted by . . . the absolute ignorance of the people, which enables the business of unscrupulous agents. Since they don't know that America is not a city near London . . . since they can neither read nor write, and therefore do not expect letters or direct news and cannot verify their authenticity, every girl who emigrates and leaves her hometown . . . is vulnerable to all forms of danger and vice.[76]

As Pappenheim's words suggest, both anti-trafficking and anti-emigration reformers tended to deny the underlying economic conditions that propelled emigration, as well as the agency of individual migrants. Yet female migrants were not shy about expressing their own interests. In the 1890s, for example, Habsburg authorities attempted to crack down on the trafficking of Austrian women to the Ottoman Empire. The effort failed miserably, because the women involved resisted all such efforts to "save" them. In one embarrassing incident, the Dual Monarchy's consul in Constantinople detained a group of Austrian prostitutes on an Austrian Lloyd steamer. The consul attempted to persuade the women to return home and offered them financial support. They adamantly refused his assistance, insisting that they were better off in the brothels of Constantinople than back home in Austria-Hungary. They declared, moreover, that if repatriated by force, they would return at the first opportunity. The consul was forced to conclude, "The tales of slavery and the dark cellar belong to the realm of legends."[77]

The travel agents of Oswięcim, meanwhile, also defended the autonomy of migrants, contesting the charges lodged against them. In an appeal written (and published in pamphlet form) after the trial, Herz and Löwenberg denied that they had ever induced emigration. The exodus out of Eastern Europe had begun twenty years earlier and only escalated after the agents were arrested. Besides, Austrians had a constitutional right to leave their country, the defendants insisted: "The freedom of every individual to travel for the sake of earning a livelihood is legally guaranteed, and if our concessioned agency facilitated the travel of workers to America . . . we did no differently than any railway office or travel agency that sells train tickets to go abroad."[78]

Above all, the defense contested the notion that a single travel agency could persuade thousands to leave their homes and seek work abroad. In his closing statement, the defense attorney declared, "You cannot solve social problems with prison sentences. You'd have to forbid emigrants returning from America from bringing home the money they'd saved . . . or you'd have to put an end to the ruthless exploitation of agricultural workers in Galicia. If you did all that, emigration would stop immediately."[79]

WHILE THE WADOWICE TRIAL reflected a growing movement against emigration, there was clearly no consensus about emigration in late imperial Austria. The participants in the trial took part in a raging debate among Austrian experts about the economic causes and consequences of emigration, as well as its costs and benefits. Some of the most vocal opponents of emigration were in fact Polish and Hungarian nobles who feared losing cheap agricultural labor to American factories and mines. Ignacy Daszyński, a Social Democratic delegate to the Galician diet, reflected in his memoirs, "Frightened with the loss of the world's cheapest workers, the *szlachta* thrust upon the clergy especially the duty of restraining emigration by frightening the village folk from the pulpit with the greatest tales of horror which awaited the emigrants."[80] It would nonetheless be a mistake to dismiss the campaign against emigration in Eastern Europe as a feudal hangover. Rather, emigration reformers drew on mercantilist and populationist principles that were well entrenched in European political and economic thought by the late nineteenth century—particularly the conviction that population was a precious state resource and that more people translated into more economic, military, and political power.[81] In a 1912 treatise against emigration, for example, the Austrian economist Friedrich Hey warned that proponents of emigration had "forgotten the basic principles and theories of political economy, which teach that the human is an essential link in the chain of the economy; that his labor is a valuable asset, and that the use of this labor, this asset, is above all the right of the state that has made the effort to raise and educate this human material."[82]

These concerns about population escalated alongside a more general European and transatlantic battle for economic power and imperial prestige. Meanwhile, toward the end of the nineteenth century, the goal of increasing population was refined by eugenic theories that focused on the biological quality of the state's "human material." Anti-emigration activists warned that the harsh physical labor and long hours endured by workers in America posed a deadly threat to the physical and moral health of Austrian citizens. Hey contended that 33,000 Austro-Hungarian citizens were killed on the job in American industrial accidents each year, and that another 10,000 were murdered annually, thanks to America's lax approach to law and order (no source was provided for these numbers, which were certainly exaggerated). An even greater number of emigrants allegedly returned home physically decimated, becoming public charges "as a consequence of forced, enervating labor that is detrimental to physical health."[83]

This rhetoric was typical of what one American consul described as a systematic Austrian campaign to deter emigration:

> In the public press of Austria, one will look in vain for important news from the United States. . . . But if there has been an atrocious murder committed anywhere within the republic, or if a great conflagration has destroyed a large amount of property, or a cyclone attack has struck a village in the far west, or the Apaches have attacked a settlement on the frontier . . . the Austrian press will publish the news with all its horrifying details and the frightened reader is supposed to abandon at once and for ever all intention of emigrating to the United States for the purpose of bettering his fortunes.[84]

Whether these horror stories had any effect is another question. Louis Adamic recalled that Slovene nationalist newspapers frequently published sensational tales of American violence and exploitation before the First World War. In these stories, "America broke and mangled the emigrants' bodies, defiled their souls, deprived them of their simple spiritual and aesthetic sensibilities, corrupted their charming native dialects and manners, and generally alienated them from the homeland." But rather than deterring young people from leaving home, such tales only "stimulated our passion for America," he confessed. "It would be, we thought, exciting to live in such a country."[85]

As political economists in Austria debated the impact of emigration, they attempted to meticulously calculate the costs and benefits of such adventures. According to Hey, the Austrian state lost more than 870 million crowns a year because of emigration (whereby each Austrian worker killed in American mines and factories was valued at 5,000 crowns, and the labor of one worker was valued at 2,000 crowns annually). The estimated 300 million crowns in remittances flowing back to Austria hardly made a dent in this loss.[86]

Other economists and politicians held more positive views, however. Representatives of the Galician peasantry in the regional diet praised the tremendous flow of remittances into the province, where American dollars expanded peasant landholdings, renovated churches, and provided relief in cases of natural disaster. By the eve of World War I, economists estimated that 160 million crowns in remittances were flowing into Galicia each year. Emigration also improved the fortunes of workers who remained home. Wages in Western Europe and the United States were two to three times higher than wages in Galicia. In those regions most heavily afflicted by emigration, domestic wages for agricultural workers rose as employers were forced to compete in a global market. According to Daszyński, "The labor of the peasant in foreign lands has saved the country from abject poverty." Economists have since demonstrated that transatlantic emigration did actually increase wages in the regions most affected by emigration in the nineteenth century.[87] Another Austrian socialist, Wilhelm Ellenbogen, insisted on the futility of efforts to insulate the Austrian empire from global economic forces. "One might want to stamp out emigration with police measures, but political measures cannot override the laws of the global economy, however finely crafted they are. . . . The decisive cause of emigration is not so much the activities of agents as the fact that in Galicia and Dalmatia nothing is being done to further economic development."[88]

These views did not, however, win out in Wadowice in 1889 or in Austrian society more generally. In his closing statement, Ogniewski contested the imagined links between social mobility, physical mobility, and freedom that were so central to the American dream. Protecting Austrians' freedom and well-being, he insisted, required measures to curtail emigration. "With respect to the accusation that the prosecution does not respect the personal freedom of emigrants, I have to say that this allegation must appear to be a truly bitter irony, in that it is made by people who have introduced a slave trade to the free land of Austria, and who have erected an entire system of human trafficking."[89] He appealed to the jury to convict "the parasites that have lived from the blood of our peasants" in the name of "the land of our fathers, for the good of the state, and for the defense of them both."[90] The jury obliged. On March 12, Herz, Löwenberg, and Landerer were each sentenced to four years imprisonment, Landau and Klausner to three.[91]

Ogniewski's words and the outcome of the trial reflected the greater significance of the movement to curtail emigration. The growing barriers to international mobility of the early twentieth century were never simply a one-sided consequence of Western restriction and xenophobia. They were the product of collusion between East and West, as East European officials sought to protect the "freedom" of citizens by keeping them at home.

UNSURPRISINGLY, the imprisonment of Oświęcim's travel agents did nothing to slow the steady flow of humans out of East Central Europe. The number of Austrians who left for North America instead ballooned in the 1890s and the first decade of the twentieth century, when mass emigration reached its peak.[92] Government concerns about emigration also escalated throughout the same period. The number of conscripts who failed to report for duty provoked particular alarm among Austrian and Hungarian military officials. Charles Selmsley reported in 1907 that in the Hungarian town of Bartfa, 700 recruits were called up for medical inspection, but only 200 showed up, since "the rest had emigrated to America."[93] When war broke out in the Balkans in 1912–13, officials took more direct action, anticipating that Austria-Hungary would soon be drawn into the conflict. In early 1913, the minister of the interior reported that about 120,000 recruits had been missing from the last call-up, 80,000 from Galicia alone. Panic ensued in the War Ministry.[94]

Once again, officials blamed emigration agents, rather than Austria's more deep-rooted economic inequalities, for shrinking military ranks. And once again, the campaign against agents was fueled by a concerted press onslaught led by anti-Semitic newspapers such as the *Deutsche Volksblatt* and the Viennese *Reichspost*.[95] Anonymous denunciations also led to a growing wave of arrests. One such denunciation to the Ministry of War claimed that in Muszyna, Galicia, "entire regiments of Hungarian conscripts have simply been stolen away by the local Jews, with the intention of weakening Hungary."[96] A letter to the Justice Ministry from a group of self-designated "loyal Austrians" accused emigration agents of "selling slaves" and "sapping the blood from the humanity of the Monarchy like nibbling worms."[97]

The government responded with escalating police measures intended to seal Austria-Hungary's borders. The Galician governor's office ordered prefects and police departments in Cracow and Lwow to closely monitor local emigration agents. Police also alerted officials about common tactics used by emigrants to cross borders illegally. Many Austrian men reportedly sneaked across the German border with forged Russian passports.[98] German officials seized at least eight hundred fake passports per year, according to the Viennese police department. The vast majority of illegal emigrants simply crossed the border on foot, pretending to be seasonal workers. Police even warned local officials to be on the lookout for illegal emigrants posing as religious pilgrims.[99] In November 1913, a special branch of the Viennese police department was established to patrol emigration. The Cracow police arrested an average of ten illegal emigrants per day at the Cracow train station in October 1913. By early 1914, control stations had been erected all along Austria's western borders, and both customs officials and railway employees were deputized to apprehend suspicious travelers.[100]

In reality, some Austrian men did attempt to evade military service by emigrating. Josef Krochmal from Lemberg, arrested for illegal emigration in 1913, was a typical offender. He was a wage laborer with no previous criminal convictions. A friend persuaded him to go to America. He decided to take his chances overseas "since my parents are poor, and there is a shortage of work here," he later testified. An agent told him that he did not need a passport for the trip and that he could simply delay his military service for two years. Krochmal was arrested in Cracow and sent home, so he returned to the agency and demanded his money back. The agent encouraged him to make a second attempt, but he was caught again. The third time, the agent decided to "make a Russian out of him." He furnished Krochmal with a forged Russian passport and instructed him to pretend he was a Pole from imperial Russia. This time, he successfully made his way to Germany and then on to Canada. Unfortunately for him, upon arrival in Quebec, Canadian authorities rejected him on medical grounds and sent him home, at which point he was arrested for a third time.[101]

In what quickly became an international incident, on October 6, 1913, Austrian police arrested Samuel Altman, general representative of the Canadian Pacific Railway Company (CPR, also a shipping company) in Austria and nineteen of his associates. Austrian police shut down and searched the CPR's offices, seized its books, and confiscated its property. Altman himself was a naturalized American citizen who had left Hungary years earlier.[102] He was charged with facilitating the illegal emigration of tens of thousands of Austrian and Hungarian citizens liable for military service.[103] On the day of the arrests, the Viennese *Reichspost* claimed that the CPR had "unleashed a band of agents on the population of Galicia and Bukovina, who hunted for humans as though they were wild game."[104]

Competing shipping lines were almost certainly behind the attack on the CPR. In the previous year, there had been a shake-up in the cartel arrangement that governed the shipping industry. Until the end of 1912, the CPR was party to the so-called Continental Pool, a cartel established in 1892, which included the Hamburg-America Line, the North German Lloyd, the Red Star Line, the Holland America Line, the Cunard Line, and the Austro-Americana shipping firm. On January 1, 1913, the CPR withdrew from the pool and opened a new route from Trieste to Canada, in direct competition with the British Cunard Line (from Fiume) and the Austro-Americana (from Trieste), both members of the pool. In retaliation, the pool immediately launched a vicious press campaign against the CPR. [105]

Arthur Grünhut was the chief instigator in the case. He personally sent multiple denunciations to government ministries and the press. A Viennese police investigation determined that Grünhut was an unreliable informant. He had married a wealthy woman from Philadelphia in 1909, and then returned to Vienna, where he lived off her dowry and a monthly allowance. "He does not enjoy the best reputation in social or business circles," the report conceded. At least thirty-five cases had been filed against him in Austrian civil courts, and he had been thrown out of the Viennese jockey club because of unpaid debts. He had no stable profession, but variously claimed to be an architect, a civil servant, and a real estate developer. Although Grünhut swore that he had no connection to the Continental Pool, he admitted to receiving large payments for his "research" on the CPR.[106]

In reality, the CPR was responsible for only a tiny percentage of the total emigrant traffic out of Austria. Members of the pool had transported the rest.[107] Altman was released on a bail of 150,000 crowns (about $30,000) in May of 1914. He was eventually allowed to leave for America on the condition that he return to Austria for his trial. Thanks to the outbreak of the First World War, however, the trial never took place.[108]

By the eve of the First World War, Austria's borders were virtually sealed. A few Austrian politicians and intellectuals denounced the new restrictions on travel as an ominous "turn in the direction of a police state."[109] Ignacy Wróbel, a Galician socialist delegate to the Austrian parliament, protested in early 1914, "The entire empire has been surrounded by a police barrier, so that even a bird might not be able to fly across our borders." He insisted that the new barriers to emigration violated Austrians' constitutional right to free movement, and demanded that the Interior Ministry guarantee that workers were "actually able to make use of their constitutionally protected right to free movement, particularly in the search for a livelihood."[110] The Austrian law professor Alexander Loffler compared the new restrictions on mobility to feudal bonds. "The tendency is developing to view our laborers as a type of serf, not bound to a specific estate, but certainly to the territory of the state," he warned. But in the context of the rush to war, these protests were isolated. Amid growing fears of mass desertion (and under the pretext of protecting Austrian citizens from travel agents), Austrian policymakers casually sacrificed the right to exit on the eve of World War I.

The war temporarily "solved" the emigration problem. Transatlantic passenger travel virtually ceased during the war. The emigration debate did not disappear, however, as Austrian officials began to plot for the postwar era. Many anticipated a massive return of Habsburg subjects from America and Western

Europe after the war. In 1917, the Austrian diplomat Baron Hugo Sommaruga estimated that one million people would rush home to Austria-Hungary following the armistice. Most returnees, he speculated, would be motivated by curiosity, as well as the assumption that the monarchy would be in need of labor. Xenophobia in America, as well as the prohibition on alcohol, "for which our co-nationals have little understanding," would also encourage a mass homecoming, he predicted.[111]

Meanwhile, in St. Paul, Minnesota, the Austrian vice-consul Edgar Prochnik proposed that the Austrian government ban all emigration to the United States after the war. This would enable Austria to retain its valuable "human material" for its own use and bring the U.S. steel and mining industries to their knees. "I need only mention the large quantity of valuable human material that is thrown into the great sieve at Ellis Island each year," he explained. "It is precisely the most physically and intellectually productive elements who are lost to their homeland, and the qualitatively less valuable human material, the crude rubble . . . that remains at our disposal."[112]

The proposal was taken seriously, and circulated among government ministries in both Austria and Hungary. While most officials disagreed with Prochnik, they did not take issue with the principle behind the plan. They simply recognized that it was impractical. The Hungarian interior minister (presciently) understood that far more radical measures would be required to truly seal the empire's borders. Emigration could be successfully curtailed altogether, he argued, "only if all our neighboring states take the same position with respect to emigration, which we can hardly count on."[113]

Other ministers responded to the memo with more constructive ideas, predicting trends that would develop between the wars. The Austrian interior minister conceded, "Efforts to stop emigration with prohibitions, border control, and other police measures have been unsuccessful." Emigration, he insisted, had deeper roots. "Austrian emigration, as a mass movement, cannot be seen only as an artificially created phenomenon, sustained by large transportation firms. . . . It must rather be traced back to very serious economic, social, and political sources at home."[114]

Even the War Ministry was seeking new approaches by the end of the war. In August 1917, it released a memo advocating a shift toward more progressive policies to retain population. These included measures to promote economic development, including land reform, investment in new technologies, the expansion of industry, and the creation of state-run employment agencies and public works jobs for unemployed citizens.[115] These proposals were too little, too late for the Austro-Hungarian Empire, but they foreshadowed the ways in which the fear and reality of emigration would inspire the expansion of welfare states and efforts to facilitate economic development in East Central Europe after 1918.

FROM THE WADOWICE TRIAL of 1889 to the end of World War I, Austro-Hungarian citizens were engulfed in a heated debate about the consequences of mass emigration. They were simultaneously arguing about the relationship between mobility and freedom in a globalizing labor market. The defense attorneys at Wadowice repeatedly insisted that government measures to restrict and police emigration infringed on the constitutional rights of Austrian citizens to emigrate. "In a modern state citizens should no longer be treated as living inventory which is bound to the land!" one defense attorney proclaimed.[116] The state's attorney disagreed, however, countering that the right to emigrate was an illusory "freedom" that delivered Austrian citizens to wage slavery. In an era in which many could still recall American slavery and European serfdom, these charges of "human trafficking" represented more than hyperbole. The mass movement of East Europeans from rural farms to American factories, mines, and plantations raised pressing questions about the meaning of free labor in the industrial age.[117]

This debate hinged on competing views of both America and Eastern Europe. American authorities, not surprisingly, typically upheld a vision of America as a beacon of freedom and opportunity, linking physical mobility directly to liberty and democratic values. In 1911, the report of the Dillingham Commission emphasized the "civilizing" impact of a sojourn in America on East Europeans:

> He leaves his village, a simple peasant in his peasant dress, usually not only unable to read and write, but not even desiring to. Ingrained in him are the traditions of his obligations to the church and to his superiors. . . . [W]hen he goes back to his old home he is a different man. He is more aggressive and self-assertive. His unaccustomed money gives him confidence and he is no longer willing to pay deference to his former superiors. Frequently, too, the church has lost the influence it had had with him. Moreover, if he has not learned to read and write himself, he has at least seen the value of that ability and is more anxious than before to send his children to school.[118]

Emigration and return migration, in this self-congratulatory tale, would "modernize" and "democratize" East Central Europe. In the context of growing anti-immigration sentiment, however, many U.S. authorities began to question whether particular groups of migrants (defined in racial terms) were capable of "handling" the responsibilities of freedom. The American consul Henry Stern reported from Budapest in 1886, "Crude as these Slovacks [sic] leave their country crude they also return, for their exclusiveness and love for herding prevents that while in America any 'real' American ideas reach them and instead of ideas of real 'liberty' there is only the danger that they bring with them ideas of 'license.'"[119] U.S. Consul Edmund Jussen (himself a German emigrant) was equally pessimistic about migrants' capacity for freedom and self-governance. Emigrants from Eastern Europe, he warned, "have perverted ideas of liberty, and think of the United States as a country where no police interferes with freedom of action. . . . Many of them think they have been governed too much at home and hope to find a country where they will not be governed at all."[120]

After World War I, nativists would impose dramatic limits on immigration in the name of protecting American freedom. Yet they did not necessarily have the final word. In their sheer determination to emigrate, and in their own testimonies, many migrants continued to link emigration to both freedom and social mobility. Over time, their views have tended to shape America's self-image, if not actual immigration policies. In the words of John Szabó of Chicago, writing in 1909, "Although in the beginning I had to do without, and even now I am not bathing in milk and honey, I feel that now I am that man who at home I only had a presentiment that I had a right to be, that is: an independent, free man."[121]

CHAPTER TWO

"The Man Farthest Down"

In 1910, Booker T. Washington and the University of Chicago sociologist Robert Park set out for Europe. Their goal was to determine what was propelling millions of Europeans to American shores. "I was curious . . . to learn why it was that so many of these European people were leaving the countries in which they were born and reared, in order to seek their fortunes in a new country and among strangers in a distant part of the world," Washington explained.[1] Eschewing "palaces, museums, art galleries, ancient ruins, monuments, churches, and graveyards," he embarked on an inverted grand tour, determined to immerse himself in the "grime and dirt of everyday life."[2]

Washington's self-proclaimed mission was to hunt for "the man farthest down" on the European continent. In this quest to explore "the worst" that Europe had to offer, he found rich terrain in Austria-Hungary.[3] During their two-month scavenger hunt for misery, Washington and Park toured Cracow's Jewish ghetto, Prague's YMCA, Bohemian mines, Hungarian farms, Viennese slums, Adriatic ports, Galician border towns, and tiny Carpathian villages.

Booker T. Washington hoped that by locating the man farthest down in Europe, he would not only diagnose the root causes of emigration but also find new salves with which to heal American social and racial inequalities. "I believed . . . that if I went far enough and deep enough I should find even in Europe great numbers of people who, in their homes, in their labour, and in their manner of living, were little, if any, in advance of the Negroes in the Southern States," he reflected. "I wanted to study first hand . . . the methods which European nations were using to uplift the masses of the people who were at the bottom in the scale of civilization."[4] As he projected the racial politics of the American South onto the terrain of the Austrian empire (which he identified as part of "Southern Europe"), he found many parallels. By the time he returned home, he had concluded that the situation of the Slavs of Austria-Hungary was "more like that of the Negroes in the Southern States than is true of any other class or race in Europe." Not only were Slavs, like African Americans, "an agricultural people." They were also distinct from and discriminated by what Washington called "the dominant classes" of Austria-Hungary. "Although they were not distinguished from the dominant classes, as the Negro was, by the colour of their skin, they were distinguished by the language they spoke, and this difference in language seems to have been, as far as mutual understanding and sympathy are concerned, a greater bar than the fact of colour has been in the case of the white man and the black man in the South."[5] Indeed, Washington concluded that the peasants, workers, and Jews of Eastern Europe actually lived in more debased conditions than African Americans in the South. "There are few plantations in our Southern States where . . . one would not find the coloured people living in more real comfort and more cleanliness than was the case here," he observed, after touring a desolate Bohemian farm. "Even in the poorest Negro cabins in the South I have found evidences that the floor was sometimes scrubbed, and usually there was a white counterpane on the bed, or some evidence of an effort to be tidy."[6]

By the time he returned to America, Washington was so disturbed by the poverty he encountered in Austria-Hungary that he began to sympathize with the American movement to restrict immigration. The arrival of millions of destitute East Europeans threatened to create a new kind of "racial problem" in America, he warned. "Whatever else one may say of the Negro, he is, in everything except his colour, more like the Southern white man, more willing and able to absorb the ideas and the culture of the white man and adapt himself to existing conditions, than is true of any race which is now coming into this country."[7] These conclusions aligned conveniently with Washington's message to African Americans, which encouraged cooperation with whites (rather than confrontation over segregation) along with gradual social "uplift" through agricultural and technical education. In any event, American nativists shared Washington's fears about the threat posed by European migrants: within a decade, a new quota system suppressed mass immigration from Eastern and Southern Europe, on the grounds that these migrants diluted America's racial stock.

AUSTRIAN OFFICIALS meanwhile mapped out a very different geography of misery, nourished by their own fears of racial contamination. Washington's musings about the fate of Austrian workers on southern plantations were never purely philosophical. The trip had been partly inspired by efforts to recruit East European peasants to the American South "to take the place of the Negro on the sugar plantations and in the cotton fields."[8] In 1907, the Austro-Americana shipping line even launched direct service between Trieste and Louisiana. As recruiters from Louisiana and

Georgia began to prowl the East European countryside in search of cotton pickers, Austrian officials responded with alarm. Polemical denunciations of the emigration business as a form of "human trafficking" reached a high pitch as rumors spread that Austrian peasants were literally replacing former slaves. Far from seeing immigration to America as a route to freedom or social mobility, Austrian officials began to worry that emigration threatened the very status of the empire's citizens as "white" Europeans and free laborers.

In 1908, the Austrian general consul Baron Hoening of Atlanta toured Florida, Georgia, Alabama, and South Carolina to investigate working and living conditions in the South. He reported grim prospects for Austrian immigrants. "All examples have proven that racial mixing brings forth very unfortunate results. . . . [T]he states with a large mixed population are culturally, economically, and morally backward." Since Austrian migrants would inevitably "live and work with the blacks" on southern plantations, he insisted, "the only possible consequence is that our people will be brought down to the level of the blacks, and that they will hardly be better treated."[9] That same year, the Austrian Interior Ministry alerted Galician district and provincial officials, "Complaints about the entrapment of immigrants in unfree, slave-like conditions—peonage—have not been hushed and have, in some cases . . . proven to be well-founded."[10]

It is unclear whether Austrian emigrants heeded government warnings or simply preferred to settle in the Northeast and the Midwest, where many already had friends and family (and earned better wages), but that same year the Austro-Americana canceled its service to New Orleans.[11] In truth, East European migration to the American South never amounted to more than a trickle. But the ink spilled around the issue on both sides of the Atlantic reflected the high stakes of emigration and immigration politics.

At the turn of the twentieth century, Americans and Europeans looked into the eyes of emigrants and saw their own societies reflected back at them. Through mass migration, they debated and defined the differences between the Old World and the New—where could one live better, eat better, work, pray, and marry better? They often saw severely distorted reflections in the transatlantic mirror. The emigration panic nonetheless inspired more than imagined distinctions between the Old and the New Worlds, and more than repressive forms of border control. The movement of millions across the ocean genuinely transformed the individuals and families who left home, as well as those left behind. As husbands, wives, parents, and children were separated, emigration unsettled traditional gender and family relations, in particular. In some cases, migration became a path to greater independence and authority for women and children. In others, the departure of breadwinners left wives and children abandoned and impoverished.

These developments alarmed emigration reformers and inspired new social theories and reforms. As policymakers recognized that they could not completely seal their states' borders, they increasingly sought to control and redirect emigration for the good of both migrants and the state. Two strategies served these goals: transforming mass emigration into purposeful forms of "colonization," and expanding social protections for citizens abroad, creating what amounted to new transnational welfare states. Both strategies reflected anxieties about the place of East Europeans in global civilizational and racial hierarchies. As anti-immigration movements in the United States increasingly questioned the racial "value" of migrants from Southern and Eastern Europe, East European officials struggled to guarantee that their citizens would be recognized and treated as "white" Europeans overseas.[12]

———

THE HABSBURG EMPIRE and its successor states are rarely
remembered for their colonial exploits. This seems like a forgiv-
able oversight. Aside from Austria-Hungary's 1876 occupation and
1908 annexation of Bosnia, the Dual Monarchy had few colonial
conquests of which to boast. More commonly, East Europeans are
remembered (and remember themselves) as objects of imperial
ambition and victims of conquest by more powerful and milita-
rized neighbors.[13]

And yet, in the late nineteenth and early twentieth centuries,
Austria-Hungary and its successor states did nourish their own
fantasies of expansion. The Austro-Hungarian Colonial Society
was founded in 1894, followed by a naval league in 1907. The colonial aspirations that developed in East Central Europe in the
first half of the twentieth century differed in many ways from
the colonial practices of the British and French Empires in the
same period. Most significantly, they were not initially oriented
toward formal territorial annexation or conquest. East European
colonial advocates generally acknowledged that they had arrived
too late to the starting line in the race for colonies. There were few
territories in the world where they could stake a flag and claim
formal sovereignty. Instead, their goal was to create autonomous
"colonies" of settlers within existing empires or states (in places
like Brazil, Argentina, Madagascar, and Palestine).

Austrian colonial ambitions were inspired by the policies of
Italy and Germany, both also latecomers to the scramble for colonies, and both lands of mass emigration. Italian and German
policymakers began to see emigration as a potential substitute for
colonial conquest in the 1890s, as a way of "peacefully" expanding
export markets and projecting influence around the world. Both
countries simultaneously stepped up efforts to retain strong political and cultural ties to migrants. Other countries that experienced
mass emigration in the late nineteenth and early twentieth centu-

ries, such as Mexico and China, also aimed to protect and support emigrants overseas rather than prohibit emigration.[14]

In imperial Germany, nationalist and imperialist reformers hoped to direct emigrants toward rural colonies in Africa and South America, where they would supposedly retain their language and culture (and become healthy farmers rather than degenerate industrial workers). Germany's 1913 citizenship law extended citizenship to children born to Germans abroad, consolidating the ideal of a German diasporic community defined by descent.[15] The Italian government was meanwhile determined to generate and sustain Italianness abroad. By 1908, there were 1,403 Italian associations with more than 200,000 members in America, all partially supported by the Italian government. A 1912 law made it easier for emigrants and their children to retain Italian citizenship. In Buenos Aires, as of 1910, there were 74 Italian mutual aid societies with 52,000 members, several Italian schools, an influential Italian newspaper, and several Italian-Argentinian banks. Austrian reformers like Leopold Caro urged officials in Vienna to follow Italy's lead. "The Italians do great things for their people in America," he explained in 1912.[16] Many Italian officials explicitly viewed emigration as a substitute for colonial conquest. These policies continued until 1927, when Mussolini began to restrict emigration in favor of formal colonial expansion and internal resettlement.[17]

In East Central Europe, emigration reformers and colonial pressure groups hatched similar schemes. Leopold Caro promoted emigration to South America as "an instrument of national expansion, a means of peaceful extension of national frontiers."[18] This was admittedly a consolation prize in the scramble for colonies, but it would have to do. The colonial advocate Friedrich Hey reasoned, "Since all of the appropriate parcels of African land have long been in secure hands, we have no choice but to content ourselves with the surrogate of peaceful colonization."[19]

These reformers dreamt of isolated colonies in South America where migrants would remain politically and culturally bound to their homeland. Instead of sweating and suffering in American factories and mines, Austrian peasants were to settle in Brazil, Argentina, and Uruguay, where they would manage small family farms and maintain ties to home. Hey explained, "These enclosed colonies would remain in lasting contact and economic relationship with their homeland to the benefit of our industry, our shipping firms, our commerce and trade."[20]

For the most part, such ambitions never developed beyond treatises and adventure novels. The vast majority of migrants were indifferent to the imperial or nationalist ambitions of their governments. They continued to follow the lead of family and friends who had migrated before them, heading toward North America or Western Europe rather than South America or Africa.

One East European scheme to direct mass emigration toward colonial settlement did, however, take root in the twentieth century. To be sure, Zionism differed in important ways from other Austrian and East European colonial projects. Zionist and other Jewish nationalist movements responded to a variety of specific concerns about the future of Jews in Europe. These included existential fears about the physical and political security of Jewish communities, as new forms of violent, racial anti-Semitism swept the Continent from the 1880s onward. The Russian pogroms of 1881–82; the Dreyfus Affair (1894–1906), witnessed by Theodor Herzl as a Viennese reporter for the *Neue Freie Presse*; the rise of Karl Lueger's anti-Semitic Christian Social Party in Vienna in the 1890s; a wave of blood libel trials in Central and Eastern Europe— all suggested to many Jews that their future in Europe was precarious. Many Zionists coupled concerns about anti-Semitism with positive visions of Jewish social, psychic, and political regeneration in Palestine.[21]

Perhaps most significantly, the fundamental goals of Zionists differed from those of other East European advocates of emigration or colonial settlement. Their aim was to create a new state or homeland outside of Europe rather than to expand an existing state. Zionism was often justified by an ideology of "return" to an ancient homeland, while the settlements imagined by Austrian, Czech, and Polish reformers were all organized by and intended to serve a metropole in Europe.[22]

Yet Zionism also shared several features with other East European movements to channel emigration toward nationalist or imperial goals. In all of these visions, emigrants were to settle in less-developed regions of the world, where they would become self-sufficient landowners, farmers, or managers. Rather than assimilating to their surroundings, settlers were to live in enclosed communities and maintain or regenerate their cultural and national loyalties. Zionists, like other European proponents of colonial settlement, were also convinced that European settlers would play the role of "civilizers" vis-à-vis natives. Early Zionists commonly held that Arabs would applaud Jews for bringing European civilization to Palestine. "We will endeavor to do in Asia Minor what the English did in India—I am referring to cultural work and not to rule by force. We intend to come to Palestine as the emissaries of culture and to expand the moral boundaries of Europe to the Euphrates," proclaimed Max Nordau at the Eighth Zionist Congress, in 1907.[23]

Both Jewish and non-Jewish settlement schemes outside of Europe and North America also seemed fraught with peril, however. What if instead of becoming self-sufficient pioneers and landowners, or bringing "civilization" to native inhabitants, East European workers sank to the status of (nonwhite) slave labor? An outbreak of "Brazil fever" in the 1890s brought both the perceived dangers and the allure of settlement in South America to the forefront of public debate among Jews and non-Jews. The Brazilian government, seeking white settlers to populate its vast domain, offered free transportation to migrants from Eastern Europe. The response was overwhelming. Beginning in 1890, over 100,000 citizens of imperial Russia and Austria set out for Brazil, dreaming of rich farmland, warm weather, and relief from poverty. Many settlers were Polish- or Ruthenian-speaking peasants, and the exodus generated intense debate among Austrian social reformers. Large landowners were particularly distressed by the potential loss of their abundant supply of cheap farm labor. Conservative newspapers dispatched reporters to Brazil. Their sensational exposés warned of terrifying attacks by natives, locusts, and ants, and declared that settlers were working in slavery-like conditions on the brink of starvation. The Hungarian government eventually banned emigration to Brazil completely.[24]

Other reformers held more positive views of emigration to South America, however. Some Polish nationalists even envisioned the creation of a prosperous "New Poland" in Brazil. An informational guidebook published in 1896 cautioned peasants against "ill-considered departure from the land of your fathers," and tried to direct migrants away from the coffee and sugar plantations of São Paulo and Espírito Santo, where conditions were considered unsuitable for "white" Europeans. The authors saw brighter prospects in Paraná, where Poles could acquire land and form isolated colonies. "Without doubt there are not, in the whole territorial expanse of the state of Brazil, more favorable conditions for European immigrants than in the state of Paraná," they enthused. "Build, then, fellow countrymen, Polish churches and schools, establish societies and libraries, venture into commerce and industry . . . maintain close spiritual and economic ties with Poland—and God will bless your work."[25]

Jewish settlement projects were animated by similar hopes and

fears. In the 1890s, Baron Maurice von Hirsch's Jewish Colonization Association (JCA) began to fund Jewish agricultural colonies in both Argentina and Brazil. By 1896, the year of the baron's
death, the JCA had settled 6,757 Russian Jews in Argentina.[26] The
Zionist press in Austria attacked the JCA colonies throughout the
1890s. Like other Austrian emigration reformers, Zionists feared
that Jewish migrants would be reduced to the status of colonial
or slave laborers in South America. In March 1898, for example,
Die Welt published a letter from a Jewish emigrant in Ecuador.
Many countries in Central and South America were recruiting
Russian Jews as emigrants, the correspondent reported. Some
even offered free land. He warned prospective migrants not to be
seduced by these offers, since "the goal is to attract colonists and
use them to cultivate deserted or worthless state lands. And this
cultivation is almost impossible for a European." In addition to
poor land, settlers in Argentina were forced to contend with yellow fever, mosquitoes, flies, rats, scorpions, and Indians, as well
as a native population that was allegedly "lazy, idle, cowardly,
sneaky, and bigoted." Jews could supposedly not compete with
these native workers. While agricultural work in South America
was not suitable for Europeans, "the Indian, mestizo, and black
man can survive, because he does the hardest work in this barbaric
climate with ease, and needs no more than some oranges, bananas,
a little rice, . . . a straw house with a roof of leaves and a hammock
inside."[27]

A few months later, reports surfaced that many migrants
who had settled in Argentina under JCA auspices were returning
home "as beggars."[28] S. Werner, writing for *Die Welt*, depicted the
Argentinian colonies as cesspools of misery and hardship. "The
grasshoppers which destroy the entire harvest; the storms that
kill the cows; the wild natives whose sole occupation is robbery
and murder, and finally the [JCA] administration, which sees tor-

menting the colonists as their calling—those are the conditions under which the settlers must live." According to Werner, a group of colonists had complained to officials in Buenos Aires about their plight. The officials replied that there was nothing they could do, since it was illegal to interfere in conflicts between "masters" and their "peons." Outraged, Werner exclaimed, "What does 'peon' mean? Peons are men in bondage, slaves! That's how we learned that we are officially seen as slaves of Baron Hirsch."[29] The message was clear: emigration to South America was a shortcut to slavery and ruin, not to freedom.

What were the alternatives, however? Early Zionists, including Theodor Herzl, had famously considered options ranging from Argentina to Africa before finally settling on Palestine as their goal. Even once Zionists officially had set their sights on Palestine, organized movements to channel Jewish emigration toward other parts of the world persisted. When delegates at the Seventh Zionist Congress, in 1905, voted against a plan to establish a Jewish colony on British territory in what is today eastern Kenya (the "Uganda plan"), a group led by Israel Zangwill seceded and established the Jewish Territorial Organization. This "territorial" movement continued to promote the settlement of Jews in colonies other than Palestine as late as midcentury.[30]

Especially in the late nineteenth century, Palestine competed with Western Europe and North and South America for the same prospective Jewish settlers. In spite of Zionists' insistence that *aliyah* to Palestine was fundamentally different from emigration, Jewish migrants to North America and Palestine shared similar (typically nonpolitical) motivations, fears, and hopes.[31] Zionists therefore tended to promote their own project by publicizing the hardships faced by Jewish settlers outside the Promised Land.

In 1897, for example, O. Fadeuhecht from Kolomea, in Austrian Galicia, wrote a letter to the Austrian Zionist newspaper *Die Welt*, in which he sought to expose the "miserable situation of Russian Jews in London and their bleak future." Tens of thousands of Jews from the Russian Empire were living in East London, he reported, where they worked long hours for pitiful wages, producing cheap clothing for export to the Levant, Egypt, and Central Africa. They were forced to work on the Sabbath, and were unable to raise their children "in a Jewish spirit." The export trade was largely "in Christian hands," and workers had little hope of profiting from their own labor. Instead, their arrival depressed wages for all textile workers, provoking anti-Semitism. In Whitechapel, "where all the Russian Jews live in abominable apartments that mock the most primitive notion of hygiene," a local anti-Semitic newspaper had recently appeared. In the British Parliament, a campaign to restrict Jewish immigration from Eastern Europe was gaining traction. Fadeuhecht saw in Zionism a solution to the plight of London's Jewish immigrants. "Why should the Russian Jews flock to London, where they struggle against a difficult and hopeless future, and not immediately to southern Palestine?" In Palestine, they could raise their own sheep, spin and weave their own wool, and create a new clothing export industry that would profit Jews. They would also retain their Jewish faith and culture. It was a solution that "must succeed, because it links material interests with the highest interests of humanity."[32]

In addition to shared concerns about the racial and social status of emigrants, Zionists and East European reformers both promoted colonial settlement as a weapon against denationalization. For Habsburg and East European reformers, the goal was to prevent emigrants from being "lost" to the empire or nation in North American cities. Proponents of colonial settlement believed that emigrants could avoid this fate by settling outside of Europe and North America in isolated rural colonies, where they would supposedly retain their language and ties to home. Sigismund Gargas, an economist from the University of Cracow, recalled that Brazil was chosen for Polish settlement because the "relatively lower culture of Brazil in comparison to the Anglo-Saxon culture of North America . . . poses less of a national threat than immigration to the United States."[33]

Many Zionists likewise insisted that Palestine was the one place where Jews would remain tied to the Jewish community, however defined. For Zionists and other diaspora nationalists, however, assimilation appeared to threaten Jewish communities in Europe as well as in North America. It is perhaps no coincidence that conversion rates in Vienna, the birthplace of Zionism, were the highest in Europe at the turn of the twentieth century. The German Zionist Arthur Ruppin was particularly concerned about the danger of Jewish "degeneration" through conversion, intermarriage, and assimilation in Western Europe. He also advocated the separation of the Jewish and the Arab populations in Palestine, warning that Jews would otherwise assimilate to Arabs.[34]

Jewish identity appeared to be equally threatened by emigration to rural areas of North America. In 1903, the German Zionist David Trietsch denounced the Jewish Agricultural and Industrial Aid Society (an organization that emerged from a merger of the Baron de Hirsch fund and the Jewish Colonization Association) for its efforts to disperse Jewish immigrants across rural America. These Jews immediately lost their "national unity" and abandoned their religious faith, he insisted, since they were isolated from one another and could not establish synagogues. "The principle of dispersal," he declared, represented nothing less than the "downfall of Judaism and a continuation of the thousand-year-old war of annihilation against the Jews." The only solution, in his view, was the establishment of compact Jewish settlements. "It is clear that if we want to replace the thinnest dispersal of Jews around the world with the most compact settlement possible in one country, then that country can be no other than our land of Palestine, because the unification of all Jews in any other country is unthinkable."[35]

While both Jewish and non-Jewish visions of resettlement were intended to consolidate national loyalties, there were important differences between them. For most non-Jewish proponents of colonial settlement, the ideal of isolated agricultural colonies was profoundly anti-urban, as was the entire anti-emigration movement. Settling peasants on the land was supposed to prevent their moral and physical degeneration in urban factories and mines. East European emigration reformers tended to represent colonial settlement as a project of social and national preservation. They hoped to freeze what they represented as the "traditional" values and social structure of the rural peasantry.

Zionists, by contrast, explicitly envisioned emigration to Palestine as a vehicle for social, psychological, and even physical transformation. The Zionist ideal of "productivization," in particular, called for the transformation of petty traders and merchants into hearty and masculine "muscle Jews."[36] These goals shaped Zionist attitudes toward and relations with Arabs in Palestine. Zionists generally held a positive view of physical and agricultural labor in Palestine, seeing it as a form of work that benefited the national collective. Labor Zionists, who dominated Jewish politics in Palestine from the turn of the century until the 1930s, extolled the virtues of manual labor, insisting that Jews had to render the land fertile by their own hands. "Our settlers do not come here as do the colonists from the Occident to have natives do their work for them," insisted Martin Buber. "They themselves set their blood to make the land fruitful."[37] While other European settler colonies tended to force indigenous populations into the labor market through coercive measures, Labor Zionists drew fire for displacing Arab workers and landowners in their effort to employ "Hebrew labor."[38]

Poster advertising transatlantic passenger service from Trieste to North and South America on the Austro-Americana shipping line.

The East European dream of channeling emigration toward colonization was linked not only to imperial ambitions but also to a general rise in concern for the health, welfare, and social protection of workers in the late nineteenth century. In addition to intensifying border control and planning colonial settlements, reformers in the Habsburg Empire and its successor states responded to mass emigration by creating new forms of social protection that extended beyond the frontiers of the state. Like colonial aspirations, these reforms were propelled by anxieties about the civilizational status of East European workers in a global labor market.

At the very moment that mass emigration from Eastern Europe to America reached its peak, intensive social reform efforts were under way on both sides of the Atlantic. Growing trade union movements and socialist parties campaigned for the rights of industrial workers in Europe and America. In American cities, progressive muckrakers and social workers built settlement houses and preached social reform. Upton Sinclair's novel *The Jungle* is best remembered for its stomach-churning exposé of the meat-packing industry, but it can also be read as an anti-emigration parable. Although Sinclair was American, *The Jungle* confirmed all the worst fears of East European emigration reformers; Jack London called it the "*Uncle Tom's Cabin* of wage slavery." The novel's protagonist Jurgis Rudkus, a Lithuanian immigrant, is swindled and exploited at every turn in Chicago's Packingtown; he loses his health, his savings, his home, his family, and his innocence in the American jungle. His wife is raped by her boss and dies in childbirth because she can't afford a doctor. His son drowns in the street, his father dies of a lung infection, and a cousin becomes a prostitute. A nephew is devoured by rats on the frozen floor of a meat processing plant. Rudkus and his family would certainly have been better off had they never left Europe.[39]

The tragic fate of the Rudkus family reflected broader concerns about migration in Europe and America. In the eyes of many emigration reformers, particularly religious officials, emigration posed a mortal threat to the traditional family structure. Emigration separated parents and children and husbands and wives, and isolated couples from extended kin. It catapulted peasants from tight-knit rural villages to anonymous cities, exposing them to new forms of temptation and vice. Social reformers and theorists constantly bemoaned the allegedly destructive effects of migration on family life and gender roles, and sought ways to keep transnational families and "traditional" values intact.

Growing cadres of professionalized experts (including social workers, psychiatrists, and doctors) were central to the social reform movements that targeted migrant families at the turn of the century, as they were to progressive movements in general. Emigration from Eastern Europe also profoundly shaped new forms of expert knowledge, including the discipline of sociology itself. Robert Park, who accompanied Booker T. Washington on his journey through Europe, was not the only University of Chicago sociologist to study East European migrants. Most famously, in 1918–20 his colleagues William I. Thomas and Florian Znaniecki published *The Polish Peasant in Europe and America*, a five-volume work that shaped the study of migration in the United States for several generations.[40] Like Upton Sinclair, Thomas and Znaniecki were interested in the fate of the tens of thousands of migrants laboring in Chicago's steelmaking and meatpacking industries.

The Polish Peasant was not the work of disinterested observers of mass migration. Like *The Jungle*, it can be read as an anti-emigration polemic. Znaniecki was a recent transplant from Poland, having arrived in Chicago in 1914. He had been barred from holding any academic appointment in Warsaw before World War I because of his Polish nationalist sympathies. Instead, he presided over the Polish Emigration Society (*Polskie Towarzystwo Emigracyjne*), the major Polish association for the protection of emigrants. Upon meeting Znaniecki for the first time in 1913, Thomas concluded that the purpose of the Emigration Society was to "facilitate the emigration of undesirable citizens and to hinder the emigration of the desirable."[41]

Znaniecki and Thomas completed the research for *The Polish Peasant* during the First World War, when Chicago was a hotbed of East European exile nationalism. American authorities fostered this nationalism, hoping to incite Austria-Hungary's Slavic minorities to rebel against their rulers. Tomáš Masaryk, the future president of the first Czechoslovak Republic, lectured at the University of Chicago in 1902 and 1907 and returned to the city in May 1918 to rally its Czech and Slovak community in support of an independent Czechoslovak state. Znaniecki was part of this milieu. By 1918, exiled nationalists were lobbying for the Austrian empire's dismemberment under the banner of the Wilsonian principle of "national self-determination." Znaniecki himself triumphantly returned in 1920 to the new Polish nation-state, where he occupied the first Polish chair in sociology at the University of Poznań.[42]

The Polish Peasant was a product of this revolutionary nationalist context. Not surprisingly, it depicts the Polish immigrant community as both unified and homogeneous. Yet there was no Polish state when it was researched and written. The Republic of Poland was founded in 1918, the same year that the first volume of *The Polish Peasant* appeared in print. The borders of the new Polish nation-state were violently contested until 1921. The migrants described in the study would all have been citizens of Austria, Russia, or Germany, hailing from regions with distinctive political and economic systems, as well as diverse local cultures. Many came from multilingual and multinational communities. Thomas and Znaniecki downplay these and other divisions (including differences of social class, gender, politics, and religion), since the invention of the "Polish peasant" as a sociological type was part of a larger nationalist project: inventing the "Polish nation" as a unified community and state.

Znaniecki and Thomas describe the Polish nation as a "society without a state, divided among three states and constantly hampered in all its efforts to preserve and develop a distinct and unique cultural life."[43] They depict this "society" as an organic community encircled by hostile "races" and "nations." "Surrounded by peoples of various degrees of cultural development—Germans, Austrians, Bohemians, Ruthenians, Russians, Lithuanians—having on her own territory the highest percentage of the most unassimilable of races, the Jews, Poland is fighting at every moment for the preservation of her racial and cultural status," they contend. "The fight of races and cultures is the predominant fact of modern historical life, and it must assume the form of war when it uses the present form of state-organization as its means."[44]

This assertion of a Polish "race" war with surrounding nations was no empty metaphor in the years 1918–21. At that very moment, the Polish army was engulfed in a bloody war against Ukrainian and Soviet forces to determine the new state's eastern borders. For Znaniecki and Thomas, however, the "clash of civilizations" extended across the Atlantic. In *The Polish Peasant*, Polish immigrants in America also appear to be at war, as they struggle to defend a homogeneous, traditional Polish culture against the "American" values that encircle them. The authors transpose an interpretative lens generated by a specific, ultranationalist historical moment in Eastern Europe onto the American cities of the early twentieth century.

Throughout the study's five volumes, Znaniecki and Thomas depict the Old World of the Polish countryside and the New World of the American city as mutually exclusive ideal types. Poles are characterized as traditional, hierarchical, and bound by their collectivist family values. Americans are modern, individualistic, and amoral. According to Znaniecki and Thomas, upon arrival in America, Polish families collapse, social hierarchies crumble, and migrants develop egotistical worldviews. In the worst-case scenario, they descend into criminality. Fears of gender disorder and family breakdown pervade their analysis. In fact, *The Polish Peasant* directly shaped decades of sociological theories and social policies that pathologized urban minority communities (including African American ones) in terms of alleged family breakdown and "cultures" of poverty (including, notably, the 1965 Moynihan report).[45]

Znaniecki and Thomas define both Polish and American communities in terms of family systems. The Polish peasant family is solidaristic and harmonious. Everyone willingly accepts his or her place in an established hierarchy. All willingly sacrifice for the good of the whole.[46] By contrast, Znaniecki and Thomas describe the "modern" American family as atomized and fragmented. Upon arrival in America, Polish peasants abandon their collectivist values as they adapt to American mores. Slowly but surely, the migrant begins to resent family obligations:

> When the boy leaves his family in Poland and comes to America, he at first raises no questions about the nature of his duties to his parents and family at home. He plans to send home all the money possible. . . . He writes: "Dear Parents: I send you 300 roubles, and I will always send you as much as I can earn." . . . But if in the course of time he has established new and individualistic attitudes and desires, he writes: "Dear Parents: I will send money; only you ask too much."[47]

Znaniecki and Thomas condemn this newfound independence as a sign of "demoralization." In many cases, they argue, the bonds of family solidarity are already ruptured back in Europe, through the emigration of husbands without their families. Total breakdown ensues as wives become more independent and strong willed.[48] Znaniecki and Thomas do not see the emigration of entire family units as a more desirable alternative, however. "The most complete break between parents and children—one presenting itself every day in our juvenile courts—comes with the emigration of the family as a whole to America," they contend. When an entire family emigrates, a culture war erupts within the family itself, between "traditional" parents and "Americanized" children, such that "the mutual hate, the hardness, unreasonableness, and brutality of the parents, the contempt and ridicule of the child—

ridicule of the speech and old-country habits and views of the parent—become almost incredible."[49]

In letters to family members back home, Polish immigrants in America frequently complained about the disobedience of their children, which they blamed on unsalutary "American" influences. In June 1908, Helena Dabrowski, a Polish immigrant in Union City, Connecticut, wrote to her sister Teofila, expressing her frustration with her sons. "They will not listen to their mother," she lamented. "They were good in the beginning but now they know how to speak English, and their goodness is lost. I have no comfort at all."[50] Teofila advised her sister to beat her sons, but Helena replied, "In America you are not allowed to beat; they can put you into a prison. Give them [food?] to eat, and don't beat—such is the law in America. . . . Nothing can be done." She deeply regretted her decision to bring her sons to America and worried that they had been spoiled by the ease of life there. "In our country perhaps they would have had some misery, and in America they have none, and because of this many become dissolute."[51]

The children of immigrants often saw things differently, of course. One anonymous Polish woman interviewed through a 1938 oral history project developed a deeply antagonistic relationship with her father after joining him in America. She arrived from Congress Poland at the age of twelve. Her father had abandoned her mother in Europe and remarried in Connecticut. She traveled to America with her mother, who was hoping to track her husband down. Her mother died tragically in childbirth on the ship en route (it was unclear who had fathered the child). As soon as she arrived in Connecticut with her infant brother, her father put her to work in a factory, although she couldn't read or write in Polish or English. She recalled decrepit living conditions. "Mother of God, it must have been the worst in the Polish colony of Waterside: ramshackle, tumbledown, with no running water or electric light and no bath or indoor toilet." A local priest reported her to the authorities for being truant, and her father was eventually forced to send her to school. Years later she was still bitter about her father's "old world" attitudes:

> The little runt couldn't get it through his thick skull that girls rate the same treatment as boys in the U.S.A. To him a girl was good for just two things—work and producing boys who'd grow up and help the family out financially.... But education—hell! A girl was born with all she needed.... [H]e's still a damned foreigner who doesn't know what it's all about.[52]

Znaniecki and Thomas had little faith in the ability of social workers or other authorities to mediate such family conflicts. To the contrary, any kind of outside "supervision and interference" in family life only hastened the family's ultimate disintegration.[53] When Znaniecki and Thomas speak of preserving family "solidarity," however, they are primarily concerned with preserving male authority. The very possibility of divorce in America, along with the ability to call on the assistance of social workers and police officers, results in an "exaggerated feeling of coercive power on the part of the woman," they argue. "Under the old system she had in fact a part in the management of common affairs almost equal to that of the man, yet in cases of explicit disagreement the man had the formal right of coercing her." In America, it was not only possible for a woman to refuse coercion, "but she can actually coerce the man into doing what she wants by using any act of violence, drunkenness, or economic negligence of his as a pretext for a warrant." Intoxicated by this newfound power, immigrant women were purportedly unable to resist the urge to enlist the law against their husbands in petty domestic quarrels. "The action once taken is irreparable, for the husband will never forget or entirely forgive an act which introduced foreign official interference into the privacy of his conjugal relations, humiliated his feeling of masculine dignity, and put him for the time on the same basis as a criminal," Znaniecki and Thomas lament. "Naturally, unless much attached to his children or indolent by temperament, he tends to run away at the first opportunity."[54]

UNEASE ABOUT EMIGRATION's impact on family life resonated well beyond the University of Chicago. Austrian officials, Catholic and Jewish religious authorities, and American and European social workers alike also worried about the breakdown of emigrant families.[55] Like the Chicago sociologists, they were particularly alarmed by the threat emigration seemed to pose to paternal authority. In 1912, Budka Nykita, editor of the Polish magazine *Emigrant*, blamed Jewish emigration agents for both emigration and family dissolution:

> Entire villages have been ruined to such an extent that fathers can no longer say a sharp word to their sons, or else he immediately gets the response: "Give me my inheritance and I will emigrate to Canada." The local agent is typically the Jew in the village pub. The young man goes to the Jew, drinks the entire week away, and then secretly (because he is liable for military service) steals away to Myslowitz. . . . The parents are powerless. The priest is also powerless, because no one listens to him, and the agent has the final word.[56]

Austrian religious authorities were among the most concerned about emigration's disruptive impact. In 1914, three Austrian bishops painted a catastrophic portrait of family breakdown among emigrant families:

> The husband goes to America, for two or three years—or so he says—to quickly earn some money and then return home. . . . Or the young wife leaves her family to work as a domestic servant. . . . It is only natural that family life is disturbed and, if this situation continues, is totally destroyed. Without the supervision of their father the children become dissolute. . . . It's a far greater evil when a wife leaves her husband and children to find work abroad. . . . The man begins to neglect himself . . . and finally to visit the pub. This becomes his second home, he ruins his health and life, marital fidelity is endangered, and both, husband and wife, begin to live only for themselves.[57]

Worries about the breakdown of patriarchal authority may not have been entirely unfounded. In one Hungarian town, so many men took off to America that women reportedly took up most of the positions in the local government. More often change was more subtle and gradual. When their husbands left for America, many women took on new responsibilities within their families and communities, as well as new economic roles. In August 1912, Józefa Pawlak in Budziwój wrote to her husband in America that she had harvested the rye and barley crops, and sold the pig. Her husband sent her his earnings, which she diligently saved. A year later, she purchased a new house for the family, and even put the house in her own name.[58] Piotr Olszak's wife in Poland also managed the family farm in his absence and engaged in important financial transactions, borrowing seed from a neighbor for interest. "Don't worry, I shall manage everything," she assured him.[59]

Thanks partly to emigration, women and children at home also worked longer hours for higher salaries, as they replaced men who had gone overseas, much as they would replace the men who went to fight in the Great War. A 1914 study of Hungarian emigration found that between 1900 and 1910 the average daily wage for a woman in Hungary increased from 90 hellers to 143. Women worked an average of 164 days in 1906 and 188 days in 1910—an increase the authors attributed entirely to male emigration overseas.[60]

In other cases, emigration enabled young women to make decisions for themselves that normally might have been made for them, including the choosing of a spouse. Konstancya Walerych emigrated from Congress Poland to Greensboro, Pennsylvania, to work as a domestic servant in 1913. Within a year, she had gotten married to another immigrant—a man not even from her own province—without alerting her parents beforehand. She wrote to them,

> Dear Parents . . . I inform you that I married a man from Galicia. Our marriage occurred on the twelfth of January; my husband is named Jan Czarnecki. Now, dear parents, I beg you heartily, don't be angry with me for marrying so hastily and a man from so far a country and for not even writing to you about it. . . . [A]s you know, the girls who married with us and took husbands from the same village, were most unhappy afterward.[61]

Helen Słoński, who emigrated from Congress Poland to the United States, also married without asking her parents' permission. "Dearest Mommy, do not be cross that I was married without your knowledge," she appealed. "I did it so you would not forbid me to get married in America. . . . [T]he man who is now my husband pleased me; he loves me and will never stop loving me."[62]

In Habsburg Austria, Louis Adamic claimed, it was common

for young men and women to attempt to avoid unwanted arranged marriages by fleeing to America, an escape route that disappeared once America closed its gates. A young man "sometimes broke with his father over a girl, told him to keep his old homestead or give it to the next oldest son, and went to America," he recalled. "Today, with America's 'Welcome!' sign down, that is almost out of the question. The young man usually suppresses his romantic feelings and marries sensibly."[63]

Other women emigrated in order to circumvent the financial transactions that accompanied marriage. Pauline Reimer left Galicia for the United States at the age of seventeen. "At home they give you money when you get married. If you got more money, you get a better husband. You got less money, you know what it is," she recalled. She said to her parents, "Send me to America. I don't want to be here. You can't marry me off, and I don't want to get married either." Her mother cried and objected, but eventually let her go. She joined her aunt in Wilkes-Barre, Pennsylvania, and never looked back.[64]

Mary Kustron also left Galicia for Chicago in 1912, at the age of twenty. Although her parents were opposed, they had no choice but to accept her emigration, given the lack of options at home. "Well they didn't like it, but you know . . . everybody gotta go their own way," she reflected. Kustron first worked as a hotel maid and then, during World War II, took the night shift in a rubber factory. She was proud of her ability to support relatives back home. During both world wars, she boasted, "nobody help as much as I help and I don't see a hole in my pocket yet."[65]

Not all women experienced emigration as a form of liberation, however. Some came to America with their husbands and felt isolated and homesick for their extended families and friends at home. In America, they found themselves lonelier than ever. Nor were female migrants automatically liberated from the authority of male relatives. One young woman arrived at the home of her cousin in Waynesboro, Pennsylvania, from Galicia in 1907. That evening, a young man appeared, and her cousin yelled out to him, "Mieczek, your wife has arrived! Come see her!" The woman recalled, "I was dumbstruck with fear. I didn't want to get married except in my village."[66] She eventually consented to the marriage anyway, knowing it would be an unhappy one. Going home did not seem like an option.

The emigration of a husband could also mean emotional and financial abandonment. Spouses separated by the Atlantic were dependent on unreliable postal services (in Russia, for example, mail was often intercepted by censors and never delivered). They often feared that they had been completely forgotten. Unanswered letters provoked anxiety, anger, and depression. Walter Borkowski of Pittsburgh wrote to his wife, "I have written two letters to you, and I have not received an answer to any. I do not know if my letters are reaching you, or is it that you have completely forgotten that you still have a husband here on this earth. . . . I am terribly lonesome without my children and also without you."[67]

These fears of abandonment were sometimes well-founded. A series of letters between Adam Struciński, in Glassport, Pennsylvania, and his wife, Broncia, in Poland, document the couple's gradual estrangement. In November 1910, shortly after Adam emigrated, his letters were full of affection. "My success is pretty good, only . . . I am lonesome without you, for what is the use of this work and money if I do not have and do not see you. So, I ask you, beloved angel, to send me your little face, that is a photograph, just as I send to you. Although we are on inanimate paper, nevertheless we shall see and in our souls we shall have our tender kisses." Only a year later, however, the relationship was strained. There was no further mention of "tender kisses" in Adam's letters. On November 26, 1911, he wrote to Broncia, "Although you write to me that I love the money better than you, nevertheless you see that I love you and the money." By 1912, Broncia was fed up and begging Adam to come home. Adam replied that he couldn't return, because he would be drafted into the army. A year later, in February of 1913, he was still making excuses. "It is true that I promised you too much about my coming, but what could I do if it did not come out as I thought. But I hope in May I shall be in my home, if not sooner. I beg your pardon, dear Broncia. Do not be angry with me, forgive me, and when I come then we will reconcile." May came and went, and Adam still did not return. His final letters—before he stopped writing altogether—were filled with more vague excuses.[68]

Teofila Borkowska endured more than seventeen years of separation from her husband, Władek, ending in total abandonment. Her letters to Władek grew increasingly desperate, his replies increasingly sporadic. "I don't know why you do not want to write to me. Evidently you don't want to, for I have sent you four letters and begged and implored you to write at least a few words, but you don't write at all," she appealed in January 1910. "Evidently you don't wish to care for me any more." She had reached the end of her rope. "What can I do now . . . since I cannot earn enough for my living. Nothing more is left for me except to stretch out my hand and beg on the street, or to take my life away."[69] Deserted wives had little chance of obtaining alimony or child support from delinquent husbands, given the logistical, linguistic, and legal complexities involved in a transnational separation.

Whether they experienced emigration positively or negatively, it is striking that women and men alike often described the differences between Europe and America in terms of gender roles and family relations. Terence Powderly, an American immigration inspector, was scandalized by the female workers of Eastern Europe. In Hungary, he observed "barelegged" women who "did the work of men who had gone to America or were in the army," including "working on the streets carrying stone, mortar, and other material used in the construction of buildings," cleaning streets and public parks.[70] For Booker T. Washington, the hard labor performed by East European women provided clear evidence of American superiority and modernity. He estimated that "three fourths of the work on the farms, and a considerable part of the heavy work in the cities of Europe, is performed by women." These scenes led him to a surprising conclusion: "The man farthest down in Europe is woman. Women have the narrowest outlook, do the hardest work, stand in greatest need of education, and are farthest removed from influences which are everywhere raising the level of life among the masses of European people."[71]

Not everyone agreed that women were better off in America, however. Louis Adamic insisted that America, rather than Europe, was the site of greater hardship. "Back in Slovenia, Croatia, or Dalmatia women stayed young longer. There they worked outdoors most of the time. They were spiritually alive and stimulating even at the age of seventy or eighty." In American cities, by contrast, "Bohunk women were indoors most of the time. They were part of the industrial system. They ran boarding-houses for unmarried immigrants in grimy coal or steel towns, or worked in silk or hosiery mills. . . . The strain of life in the industrial, chaotic, unsettled America . . . aged them and robbed them of their best human qualities."[72] Adamic's lament is tinged by nostalgia for the old country. Like *The Polish Peasant*, his book reflects unease about the unsettling of traditional gender roles and family life. But it is striking that whether they construed emigration as a route toward emancipation or toward demoralization for women, gender relations were central to how contemporaries imagined the divide between America and the old country.

THIS DISCUSSION was not only theoretical. It led to concrete transformations in the realm of social protection and family policy on both sides of the Atlantic. Anti-emigration activists in Europe often contrasted the exploitative practices of American capitalists to the supposedly more humane treatment afforded to workers at home, in the form of workers' compensation, health insurance, and social insurance. They also linked harsh working conditions in America to moral as well as physical degeneration. The Austrian War Ministry, for example, claimed that "hard labor and an unfamiliar climate, along with the absence of any kind of social protection" resulted in the "complete physical and moral breakdown" of Austrian workers in America. "In most countries outside of Europe, the emigrant enjoys no legal protection and is delivered to the arbitrary will of his employer."[73]

These accusations were not entirely unfounded. Austria-Hungary was actually far ahead of the United States in terms of providing basic health and accident insurance for workers in the late nineteenth and early twentieth centuries. In the 1880s, a coalition of Austrian provincial nobles, social Catholics, and Czech and Polish politicians introduced protective legislation targeting industrial workers, particularly women and children. Following Bismarck's example in Germany, Austria in 1888 created a comprehensive health and accident insurance program for all industrial workers.[74] In the United States, by contrast, workers would have to wait until the early twentieth century for workers' compensation, which was then introduced only on a state-by-state basis (forty-four states had adopted such laws by 1920); health insurance would remain an elusive "benefit" for many throughout the twentieth century.[75]

The absence of effective legal protection and social insurance for migrant workers in America meant that left-wing socialists (like

Upton Sinclair), as well as right-wing conservatives, nationalists, and Christian Socialists demanded immigration reform. While prominent Austrian socialists such as Otto Bauer generally defended the right of workers to leave their country in order to earn a living, many simultaneously demanded better conditions for Austrian citizens abroad. Ignacy Daszyński, a Social Democratic delegate to the Austrian parliament from Galicia, testified in a 1912 Trade Ministry investigation, "In all of Pennsylvania, in the coal mines of Pittsburgh and in other factories and mines, there are swarms of crippled Austrian subjects who have received no compensation at all for their misfortune." He blamed these tragedies on a lack of American or Austrian government oversight. "Capital is the true ruler in North America, and our people go there without basic information, without help in their first days, without protection in the months and years that follow."[76]

Anti-emigration propagandists also frequently insisted that familial, religious, and charitable bonds were tighter in Europe than in America. In Henryk Sienkiewicz's 1897 anti-emigration novel *After Bread*, the Polish emigrant Lorenz Toporek ends up impoverished and ill in America. Before his untimely death, Lorenz reflects,

> In his country, among his own, if he had lost his all, if sickness had ruined him, or his children had put him out of the house, he would have taken a staff in his hand and would have stood under a cross by the wayside or at the entrance of some church and sung for alms. The gentleman passing that way would have given him a dime . . . ; a peasant would give him a loaf of bread and a woman a slice of bacon, and he could live. . . .

In America, by contrast, "he was lost among all, like a stray dog in a strange yard—timid, trembling, bent, and hungry."[77]

Migrants themselves were often shocked by the ragged appearance of their conationals in the United States. Morris Kavitsky, who emigrated from Russian Poland in 1914, was appalled by the physical condition of fellow Jews on the Lower East Side of New York City. "I had never seen so many people with false teeth and eyeglasses. Was it part of the process of becoming Americanized?" He attributed their poor health to American factory conditions. "People worked harder here; they worked twice as hard as they did back home. This surprised me. Where was the great prosperity which was so widely advertised?" And yet, speaking to a WPA interviewer in 1939, Kavitsky had no second thoughts about his own decision to leave Eastern Europe. "I did not even stop to think whether or not I was satisfied in coming here. Neither did I have a desire to go back home. I came here for the purpose of settling and bringing my family over, and I meant to stick to my purpose."[78]

Alarming reports about the physical deterioration of emigrants inspired plans for new forms of social protection for Austrian workers abroad and at home. Ignacy Daszyński urged the Austrian government to create institutions to protect emigrants in major transit cities, including emigration offices, waiting halls, and boardinghouses. He also proposed the creation of government-run employment agencies, which would place Galician workers in jobs in other parts of the monarchy (such as Bohemian factories) rather than in American mines. Finally, he promoted seasonal migration within Europe as a desirable alternative to emigration to America. Not only did seasonal migrants enjoy better social protection than workers in America, but they were more likely to return home from Germany or France than from across the Atlantic.[79]

In 1913, Austrian legislators answered calls for reform with a new emigration law, modeled on existing Hungarian legislation. The legislation included ambitious measures to guarantee workers' rights abroad, as well as new restrictions on mobility. Even though the draft was never ratified (thanks to World War I), it set important precedents for the bilateral immigration treaties that were signed between East European governments (such as Czecho- slovakia and Poland) and France after World War I, and became the model for new emigration laws in all of the postwar successor states.[80]

The law stipulated that Austrian citizens would henceforth be permitted to emigrate only if "precautions are taken with respect to the economic and hygienic protection of the emigrant, and the government [of the receiving country] guarantees the emigrant's legal security, the preservation of his nationality and confession, and the undeniable right of the Austrian citizen to return home." Contracts for migrant workers had to be written in their own native language and to include precise information about work- ing conditions, hours, and pay. Employers were threatened with heavy fines for breaking these contracts. Shipping companies would be required to transport destitute Austrian citizens abroad back home for half price. The law also included harsh penalties for crimes such as sex trafficking and fraud.[81]

Another important social institution that emerged from emi- gration reform efforts was the emigrant boardinghouse. By erect- ing state-sponsored homes for emigrants in major cities, Austrian officials hoped that they could directly supervise and safeguard their citizens. The Austro-Hungarian Society of New York founded the first Austrian immigrants home, on Greenwich Street, in 1897. Each year, the home became the initial stop in America for sev- eral thousand newly arrived emigrants. In 1911, the home housed 2,164 people, 1,847 men and 317 girls. It served 16,342 free meals and located employment for nearly all its residents. The represen- tative of the home also intervened in 440 deportation cases on Ellis Island.[82]

In spite of noble intentions, however, the Austrian boarding- house also became a notorious site of corruption, conflict, and

scandal. It was ultimately an embarrassing emblem of the Austrian state's failure to protect its citizens. Between 1904 and 1914,
the Austrian home of New York and American immigration
authorities were locked in a particularly bitter struggle, as the
immigration commissioner William Williams repeatedly cen-
sored the Austrian home and society for poor sanitation. While
this battle was fought in terms of dirty toilets and rotten meat, a
deeper question was at stake—the same question posed by Booker
T. Washington: On which side of the Atlantic was "the man farthest down"? Who had the migrant's best interests at heart, and
who was entitled to defend his or her social welfare and moral virtue? The boardinghouse became not only a site for making claims
on immigrants' political and national loyalties but also a venue
for defining and imposing "American" standards of hygiene and
morality on newcomers.

Private boardinghouses for emigrants were commonplace long
before governments got into the business. These homes, typically
managed by immigrant women, became centers of immigrant
sociability. There, Louis Adamic recalled,

> one could not only drown one's sorrows, overcome one's
> weariness from hard and long toil, and meet one's fellows;
> one could also buy steamship tickets and money-orders for
> folks in the Old Country, play poker, eat, dance, have one's
> letters written, enjoy a girl, subscribe to newspapers, pay
> one's lodge and club dues, and—if the saloon-keeper was
> on friendly terms with the priest, which was not unusual—
> even one's church dues![83]

Emigrant families operated informal boardinghouses as well,
putting up newly arrived migrants in whatever space they could
spare. Murray Koch recalled that in Newark, New Jersey, in the

1890s, "almost every Polish family in town had two to five boarders. There would be two or three boarders in one sleeping room. . . .
Hallways were dark and dirty, and the rooms had no heat."[84] The
U.S. Immigration Commission found that 53.4 percent of Mag-
yar families, 42.7 percent of Polish families, 36 percent of Slovene
families, and 34.6 percent of Slovak families earned extra income
by housing lodgers. "Boarding mistresses" who ran larger homes
became powerful figures within immigrant communities, as they
mediated between immigrants and employers, peddlers, politicians, and associations.[85] Immigration and emigration reformers
generally perceived these private boardinghouses as unsanitary
hotbeds of corruption and vice. One Austrian consular official
reported from New York in July 1911,

> Previously when the European emigrant landed on Amer-
> ican soil . . . he was immediately surrounded by a crowd of
> so-called "runners," who determined his nationality with
> a single glance, greeted him in his native language . . . and
> immediately seized his luggage. The newcomer, generally
> unable to speak English, would go along with this so-called
> friend, who would immediately lead him to a boarding-
> house of the lowest quality. Together with the hotel owner,
> who would charge him exorbitant prices for lodging and
> food, he would then proceed to swindle, cheat, and rob him
> in the most shameless manner. When the emigrant ran out
> of money, he was unceremoniously thrown out onto the
> street.[86]

Austrian and American authorities wanted to put these "emigrant catchers" out of business. Officials at Ellis Island therefore
granted philanthropic organizations and governments the right
to establish their own immigrant homes and send representatives

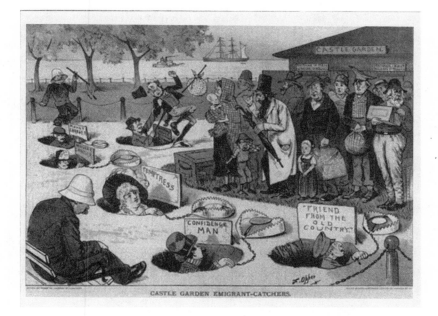

Frederick Opper, "Castle Garden Emigrant
Catchers," *Puck*, June 14, 1882.

directly to Ellis Island. On Ellis Island, delegates of the approved
boardinghouses had first access to migrants fresh off the boat and
were empowered to perform social and legal services on their
behalf. They helped with appeals when emigrants were rejected or
deported, located the addresses of friends and relatives, provided
affidavits for migrants without contacts or adequate funds, offered
housing to newly arrived emigrants, and frequently placed them in
their first jobs. Particularly for foreign governments interested in
the welfare (and supervision) of citizens abroad, the right to have
a boardinghouse and a delegate on Ellis Island was extremely
valuable.

In order be represented on Ellis Island, however, a boardinghouse also had to meet requirements set by American immi-

gration authorities. These included the maintenance of "good sanitary conditions," the employment of a matron to supervise female immigrants, and a pledge not to run illegal businesses on the side (like selling steamship tickets or procuring prostitutes). The American immigration commissioner was empowered to banish a house's delegates from Ellis Island if these conditions were not met.

In 1904, Commissioner William Williams barred the Austrian boardinghouse's delegates from Ellis Island for the first time.[87] American records suggest that the Austrian home was in deplorable sanitary condition and managed by corrupt profiteers, although it received a yearly subvention of 10,000 crowns from the Austrian government, about $4,000. A New York City Health Department report from 1903 described "old and dilapidated" buildings, with a leaky roof and damp walls and ceilings. The bathrooms were filthy, the floors and toilet covered "with excrement and urinary deposits." Women slept in an unventilated attic with thirteen beds.[88]

Soon afterward, the Austro-Hungarian Society divided into separate Austrian and Hungarian associations. In 1907, a new Austrian home was established under the same name, now with an annual subvention of 20,000 crowns from the Austrian government. But in 1908, the home was again cited for violations. This time, two female immigration inspectors conducted an undercover sting operation. One of them went to the home and requested "a girl to serve in a manicuring parlor with 'business on the side.'" Without blinking an eye, the manager offered her a girl; the inspector, in turn, gave the manager a one-dollar "donation."[89] When the Austrian home was readmitted to Ellis Island, it was not for long: by January 1911, it had been barred twice more. In one incident, a representative of the Austrian Trade Ministry secretly visited the home's new premises on 84 Broad Street. He reported that it was "in one of the dirtiest and most dilapidated buildings on the street, with peeling paint and dirty windows, but is nonetheless proudly marked by a sign that reads, 'Austrian Home.'"[90]

The failure of the Austrian home of New York City marked a small defeat in the larger struggle to control emigration, but it was emblematic of the broader failures of Austrian emigration policies. Other European lands of mass emigration, such as Italy and Germany, successfully created lasting ties to emigrants abroad, by providing valuable social services in the form of boardinghouses, mutual aid societies, and cultural organizations, as well as through the establishment of compact colonial settlements. The Austrian government actively imitated these efforts. Why did it fail where Germany and Italy succeeded?

Austrian officials tended to blame politics. According to the Austrian consul in New York, boardinghouses sponsored by foreign governments ran in direct opposition to American immigration policy, which favored quick assimilation and naturalization in the United States. As a result, U.S. authorities tended to treat their home with excessive scrutiny.[91] Perhaps the real answer has to do with Austria-Hungary's multinational and multilingual character, however, and the challenges it created for the government's quest to make loyal "Austrians" abroad. Many emigrants from Italy famously recognized themselves and each other as "Italians" (as opposed to Sicilians, Calabrians, Lombardians, and so on) only once they were overseas.[92] Austro-Hungarian efforts to retain emigrant loyalties faced competition not only with private boardinghouses and charitable homes run by religious organizations but also with growing nationalist movements in the United States. Self-identified Polish, Slovak, Czech, or Hungarian associations, homes, and cooperative societies increasingly offered assistance and community to migrants. They encouraged migrants to think of themselves as Polish Americans, Czech Americans, or

Hungarian Americans, rather than as loyal subjects of the Austrian kaiser.[93] "The Polish home, like the Slavic home, is of the newest type: homes that are devoted to a specific nationality or race without consideration of citizenship. They appear to enjoy the good grace of the Americans, who are happy to allow immigrants to use and cultivate their native language and customs, so long as they acquire American citizenship," reported one Austrian consul. "I am convinced that both the Slavic home and the Polish home are mainly serving the cause of Americanization." These national homes were "founded precisely on the rejection of Austrian patriotism," another consul lamented.[94] The services and solidarity provided by ethnically defined associations were, however, increasingly popular with emigrants themselves. By the eve of the First World War, the Austrian home had clearly been defeated in its struggle for legitimacy in the eyes of the U.S. government and in the eyes of migrants themselves. In August 1915, the Austrian home closed its doors, because it had no more emigrants to house. Three years later, at the end of the First World War, the Austrian empire itself dissolved into self-declared nation-states.[95]

CHAPTER THREE

Happy and Unhappy Returns

arel Čapek's 1933 novel *Hordubal* offered a sober lesson about the perils of emigration. Juraj Hordubal, the novel's protagonist, has been living and working in America for eight years when the Great Depression strikes hard. Unemployed, he returns to his native village of Kriva in the Subcarpathian Rus of Czechoslovakia. With seven hundred dollars in his pocket, he expects a hero's welcome and looks forward to a happy reunion with his wife, Polana, and his daughter, Hafia. His first night home, Hordubal visits the village pub, eager to show off his success. "When a man returns from America he must show himself in the pub, meet the neighbors, stand them drinks. Let them all see that he has not come back empty-handed, and in disgrace," he thinks. Unfortunately, the bartender of his youth is long dead, and his old friends barely recognize him. Hafia does not remember him at all and is unimpressed by his gifts from America. Worst of all, when Hordubal attempts to reclaim his place in the marital bed, Polana rejects him. She prefers to sleep with the farmhand hired to care for the homestead in Hordubal's absence. "I've been as far as America; and what have I got for it?" he wonders a few days later.

"I can't even understand my wife." Polana turns out to be pregnant by the farmhand, who eventually murders Hordubal in cold blood in order to marry his wife and steal his farm. Hordubal loses his friends, daughter, wife, and ultimately his life thanks to his stay in America.[1]

Čapek was an ardent Czech patriot, and Hordubal's fate reflected the preoccupations of East Central Europe's new self-declared nation-states. One of the first priorities of these fledgling democracies was to prevent people from leaving them. Only then could they achieve their other goals: reconstructing war-devastated industries and farms, stabilizing families and communities unsettled by war, and creating nationally homogeneous populations.

While claiming to represent the nation in a liberatory revolution in 1918, many national leaders worried that citizens would not stick around for the hard work of reconstruction. More than just a matter of national security or labor supply, emigration was now considered a threat to the very existence of Eastern Europe's new states. "The government is fully cognizant of the extent to which the emigration of the healthy Slovak population . . . threatens the Republic, and will stop at nothing to ensure that this emigration is reduced to the smallest level possible," proclaimed the Czechoslovak Council of Ministers in 1921.[2] In Hungary, the head of the State Statistical Office agreed in 1918, "Now, after the war, it is even more necessary to avoid . . . and counterbalance the harmful economic and demographic effects of emigration."[3] East European officials did not simply ban emigration outright, however. They took a realist approach, building on the efforts of Habsburg emigration reformers before them. If they couldn't stop emigration completely, they would minimize the damage, by channeling emigration toward desirable destinations and extending the state's protection abroad.

The new institutions created to regulate migration after World War I were intended to signify the expansion and consolidation of national sovereignty and national "self-determination." In reality, however, they often underscored sovereignty's limits.[4] East Central European governments often found themselves at odds with their own citizens with respect to migration policies. Most migrants were simply unconcerned about principles of political economy or population politics. It ultimately took the threat of physical force after 1945 to bring migration fully in line with the state's priorities.

The leaders of East Central Europe's new nation-states cast pre–World War I emigration as a symptom of backwardness and the indifference of Habsburg rulers. In the new promised land of the nation-state, no one would be forced to travel across the ocean in search of a livelihood. In 1923, Leopold Caro declared, "We should not permit emigration, especially permanent emigration, from our country. When, before the Great War, masses of our peasants were forced to emigrate to other parts of the world and place their labor at the disposal of foreign countries—this was the shame of our people."[5]

Concerns about the racial and civilizational status of East European migrants also multiplied after World War I, when American quota laws officially restricted immigration from Eastern and Southern Europe in order to protect America's "racial fitness." Thanks to the American Immigration Act of 1924 (the Johnson-Reed Act), the number of people leaving East Central Europe did decline dramatically after the First World War. The new quota system allowed only 3,078 Czechoslovak citizens to immigrate legally to the United States in 1924. This was less than one-tenth the number of Czechs and Slovaks who applied for emigration passports to the United States that year. The Polish quota in 1924 was only 25,800, although more than 100,000 Poles per year requested emigration visas to the United States in the early 1920s.[6]

Even the wives and children of American citizens faced serious obstacles to emigration. In 1927, for example, Esther Reisfeld appeared at the U.S. consulate in Warsaw to request visas for herself and her two daughters, aged fourteen and fifteen. Her husband was already in the United States and was an American citizen. She was nonetheless informed that she would have to pass an IQ test to get a visa. After failing to answer questions such as "What is more necessary, the fly or the butterfly?" Esther was denied a visa on the grounds that she was "mentally defective." Within a few months, thirty-three other women, all Jewish women married to American citizens, endured similar exams. In a letter of protest to the U.S. surgeon general, an attorney representing Jewish emigrants in Poland compiled a list of questions the women had failed to answer. "How many feathers does a goose have?" "How long is a rope?" "How many stars are there in heaven?" "Which is heavier, one pound of corn or one pound of feathers?" "How many legs does an American cat have?" The surgeon general's reply defended the intelligence tests. "All aliens are not subjected to such intensive examination; only those are so subjected who are suspected of being mentally defective," it explained. "These questions are manifestly ridiculous and readily recognized as such by people of normal intelligence. The psychiatric interest in propounding such questions principally attaches to the reaction that the questions produce in the alien's mind, with due regard to their actual absurdity."[7]

Just as lawyers challenged blatantly discriminatory IQ tests (without success), East European governments protested the racist foundation of the Johnson-Reed Act. Some reformers, however, secretly welcomed the restrictions as a blessing in disguise. Jan Žilka of the Masaryk Academy of Labor in Czechoslovakia reflected that the new quotas "may have positive consequences for us at the end of the day." Žilka was not totally opposed to emigration. Like colonial activists in Austria-Hungary, he sought to redirect migration toward "culturally less-developed" parts of the world, where migrants would form compact colonies and "preserve their language and character."[8]

In reality, however, the flow of migrants from East Central Europe mostly shifted from North America toward destinations closer to home, especially France. Thanks to a low birthrate and chronic shortages of labor, France became the world's leading importer of immigrants between the wars, with an immigrant population of around three million by the early 1930s, fully 7 percent of the total French population. In 1931, according to French statistics, 507,811 Poles were living in France.[9]

Emigration also became a matter of growing international concern after World War I. The first postwar session of the newly formed International Labor Organization (ILO), held in October 1919 in Washington, DC, was devoted to the issue. The International Emigration Commission, comprising representatives from governments, employers, and workers from eighteen countries (including Czechoslovakia and Poland), met on August 2–11, 1921, in Geneva, where it adopted a program consisting of twenty-nine articles, including the principle of equal pay and social rights for foreign and native workers.[10] ILO leaders tended to view emigration as a utopian strategy for balancing out the world's population, diminishing unemployment, and preventing famine. The organization's optimism was not widely shared, however. As the ILO itself conceded, "countries both of emigration and immigration appeared to fear that in the troubles and confusion of the postwar period, large movements of the population might compromise their national future, and severely restrictive measures were adopted."[11]

These restrictions reflected the centrality of demography and population politics to interwar nation building. An unprecedented number of citizens had been slaughtered in battle during the First World War. Austria-Hungary lost at least 1,200,000 soldiers and 120,000 civilians in military actions, and another 467,000 to starvation or disease as the Spanish flu ravaged the population in 1918. These demographic losses, along with the pressing need for labor to reconstruct war-damaged societies, transformed human beings into what one emigration expert called the nation's "most valuable commodity."[12] Thanks to an expanding education and welfare system, meanwhile, governments invested unprecedented resources in citizens in the twentieth century. In the eyes of many social reformers, emigration not only robbed the nation of its rightful return on those investments but also threatened to strengthen foreign economies and militaries. In the twentieth century, citizens were no longer linked to their native soil as the property of feudal lords. Instead, they were bound to their homelands as a form of national patrimony.

Other demographic concerns also came to the fore between the wars. Beginning in 1918, when national homogeneity was linked to the positive values of national self-determination, democracy, and modernity, East European policymakers sought to rid their countries of unwanted national and religious minorities. The League of Nations itself began to seek new solutions to what was called the "minority problem" in Europe's former multinational empires. The preferred solution was to create minority protection treaties. These treaties guaranteed certain group rights to national and religious minorities (like the right to primary schools in their native language). The more radical "solution" was unmixing populations through population transfers or emigration. The international community experimented with both options between the wars. Beginning in 1923, over one million people classified as Greeks in Turkey were swapped for approximately 350,000 individuals from Greece's mainland and islands who were categorized as Muslims.

This unprecedented exchange of populations was carried out with the approval and support of the League of Nations. "Population transfer" is, of course, a euphemism that masks the violence of forcibly removing people from their homes and communities. Proponents of later expulsions—including that of millions of Germans from Eastern Europe and Palestinians from Israel after World War II—nonetheless cited the Greek-Turkish exchange as a model of a "humane" and "successful" transfer.[13]

For minorities without a nation-state, however, "transfer" or "exchange" was never a viable option. For these groups, the League saw emigration or resettlement as a potential alternative. In 1933, in the aftermath of massacres of Assyrian Christian refugees in Iraq, for example, the League considered resettling Assyrian refugees in Brazil or British Guiana. That plan was scuttled by lack of funds (and a belief that Assyrians could not tolerate tropical heat), but it set a precedent for later plans to resettle Jews in colonial territories. Population exchanges and resettlement schemes were justified as forms of humanitarian intervention. Resettlement would ostensibly serve not only emigrants themselves but the greater interest of "humanity" through the promotion of peace and stability in sites of former ethnic conflict, and through the "civilization" of colonial territories.[14]

In the former Habsburg lands, national minorities were supposed to be protected by minority protection treaties, enforced by the League of Nations. Without exception, however, the rulers of Habsburg successor states resented these treaties and did their best to undermine them, particularly since similar protections were not enforced in Western Europe.[15] While they stopped short of forcible expulsion, the governments of East Central Europe's new nation-states also attempted to use emigration policy as a strategy for getting rid of undesirable minority groups, effectively promoting "voluntary" population transfers through the back door.

In Czechoslovakia, only two-thirds of the population declared themselves to be members of the "Czechoslovak" nation on the census of 1920. Through the emigration of national and linguistic minorities and the return of nationally "reliable" and "productive" citizens from abroad, government officials aimed to transform a multinational state into a more homogeneous nation-state. In 1920, Czechoslovak officials praised emigrants returning from the United States as valuable "colonizing material," who could be settled in "unreliable regions" of the republic in order to alter the ethnolinguistic balance sheet. In Poland, likewise, officials hoped to settle re-migrants in the borderlands of western and eastern Poland "in order to colonize these areas as quickly as possible with strong and experienced Polish elements."[16]

This produced a paradoxical situation: the least "desirable" citizens from a nationalist perspective, members of national and linguistic minorities, actually enjoyed the most freedom of mobility. In Yugoslavia, migration policies encouraged the emigration of Germans, Bulgarians, Hungarians, and Muslim Turks, and obstructed the departure of Slovenes, Serbs, and Croats.[17] In Poland, new passport restrictions in 1920 hindered the emigration of Poles. But the Polish Interior Ministry simultaneously decreed that Jews should be encouraged to emigrate "in the interest of the Polish Republic."[18] Ukrainians were also free to leave interwar Poland. In the early 1920s, Józef Okołowicz, a founder of the Polish Emigration Society and former consul in Montreal, bluntly advised the Polish government to assist Ukrainian emigration to Canada as a strategy for "getting rid of elements that are enemies of or indisposed toward the Polish state."[19]

For equally cynical reasons, East European governments tended to look favorably upon Zionism and Jewish nationalism. In Czechoslovakia, for example, the state officially recognized Jews as a national community and offered Jewish citizens the option of declaring themselves members of the Jewish nationality on the censuses of 1921 and 1930. Czechoslovak officials (along with Zionists) hoped that German-speaking Jews would choose to identify as Jews rather than Germans. The Polish government also expressed its support for the Zionist cause throughout the interwar period, declaring its "special interest in the emigration of the Jews from Poland" as early as 1919.[20]

In their determination to create nationally homogeneous populations, East European governments also sought to reverse the prewar exodus to the West, encouraging "valuable" expatriates to return home. Czechoslovak officials hoped for at least 100,000 returnees from America alone.[21] Some emigrants did come back to Europe after the First World War. Vladimir Mlynec re-migrated to Slovakia as a child with his parents. He explained, "Father was always a *narodovec*—he wanted to go back home. Well, at that time, [Czechoslovak President] Masaryk came over here and he was kind of soliciting for citizens. . . . He said 'you know, you don't have to be in America, we can make America at home, you've got the opportunity to make America in Czechoslovakia.'"[22]

The Polish government was more ambivalent about return migration. While Polish nationalist associations and societies in the United States encouraged return as a patriotic duty, many Polish officials in Warsaw worried about the ability of re-migrants to adapt to life in war-devastated Poland. "Polish Americans are accustomed to better conditions. They are going to demand goods, machines, livestock and equipment, means of communication. We don't have any of that here," explained an official from the Ministry of Labor.[23]

Western observers tended to depict re-migrants as a "modernizing" force that would civilize and democratize Eastern Europe. A French consul in Danzig reflected in 1921, "In more than one village in the grip of economic depression and sterile political debates, these newcomers with fresh complexions and sharp eyes have become saviors."[24] The Polish economist Sigismund Gargas agreed that re-migrants from America were "a welcome gift to the newly established fatherland. They are bringing great experience of the most modern state system, they will doubtlessly be equipped with a great deal of technical knowledge. . . . [T]hey should generally possess substantial capital. . . . They will also bring home a true understanding of the meaning of national sovereignty."[25]

For a brief moment, it appeared that decades of movement out of Eastern Europe might actually be reversed. The First World War had virtually stopped all passenger travel across the Atlantic. Many migrants were eager to be reunited with family and friends after years of separation. In Poland, the government's emigration office registered 678,000 re-migrants between March 1918 and July 1922.[26] Czechoslovak officials counted around 200,000 re-migrants in the same period. In reality, however, the vast majority of these re-migrants were not fervent patriots eager to participate in postwar reconstruction. With the exception of elite political exiles, the decision to emigrate or return home was typically made on the basis of more mundane calculations. One Czech official even speculated that America's new Prohibition law was the decisive "push factor." "The majority of re-emigrants proclaim that 'it's better to earn less and at least be able to drink again.'"[27]

The nationalist narrative of triumphant homecoming was disrupted by another troubling reality: like Hordubal, many returnees felt and were treated like foreigners upon return. Some had never even lived in their purported "homelands." Many of the 100,000 Czechs and Slovaks who "returned" to Czechoslovakia from Vienna, for example, had actually been born and raised in the imperial capital. Smaller numbers of Volhynian Czechs also "re-migrated" from the Western borderlands of the USSR and Polish Silesia, where their families had lived for generations. The number of re-migrants from the West ultimately fell far short of government expectations. A paltry 42,000 out of over a million Czech and Slovak Americans chose to return from the United States between 1918 and 1922; in those same years, 40,884 Czechoslovak citizens departed for American shores.[28] Less than 200,000 individuals returned to Poland from America after the war, out of more than 2.4 million Poles counted by the U.S. census in 1920.[29]

These returnees often suffered a severe bout of reverse culture shock. New East European states were still recovering from shortages of food and basic resources. Czechoslovak re-migrants from Vienna tended to settle in southern Bohemia and southwestern Moravia, regions that were already overpopulated. Housing and employment were scarce, and the influx of re-migrants depressed wages.[30] The former vice-consul in the Polish embassy in New York, Mieczysław Szawleski, reported that re-migrants arrived in Poland full of optimism and hope, but were quickly disillusioned. In American cities, they had become accustomed to amenities like electricity and gas, warm running water, and easy access to meat, fruit, ice, and sugar. Women and children, he complained, were particularly numerous among the "malcontents," because of the "lack of conveniences and American entertainment" in Poland.[31]

In addition, returning migrants were often ignorant of local economic and social conditions, which made them easy targets for fraud. Local officials, not surprisingly, tended to blame Jews for such crimes. In April 1920, officials in Žilina, Slovakia, reported to the Office of the President of the Republic that fifty or sixty American Slovaks were arriving each day in the village. The re-migrants quickly "fall into the hands of the Polish Jews, who are everywhere," local officials lamented. Even those who did not blame Jews conceded that returnees faced many challenges. Disillusioned returnees ended up challenging rather than reinforcing triumphant narratives of national liberation and unity. "We met with Slovaks who returned to America with bitterness because no one cared for them, and given that they had supported the national liberation with their savings, they expected that it would at least be possible for them to gain a footing in their homeland," one official reported.[32] "Many of those who returned after the revolution faced confusing circumstances, were left to their own devices or untrustworthy advisers, lost everything they had saved abroad, and even degenerated morally," conceded a researcher from the Czechoslovak Foreign Institute in 1929. "In the first few years of our state's existence, everyone in America was saying: don't go back." This was a shame, since "we are a small nation. We need every soul— and wherever it is possible to preserve a soul it is our holy obligation to do so."[33]

Some observers blamed returnees themselves for their adjustment problems. They had allegedly become too "Americanized" to reassimilate. A guide for returning Poles denounced re-migrants who "returned home with dollars and all started to act like lords, and to waste money on servants and luxuries." These officials were not willing to concede the battle against emigration, however. They instead focused on quality of life, which they defined in terms of security and health, rather than material abundance. Returnees "admittedly recalled American amenities and big-city life" with nostalgia, the guide granted. "But all of them decidedly agreed about one thing, namely, that America had sucked away their health, nerves, and strength for work." Only upon return to Poland could an individual "enjoy a truly humane life."[34]

These themes dated back to the Habsburg Monarchy, but continued to resonate between the wars. True freedom could not be found through physical or social mobility, in the dance halls and movie theaters of American cities. Poles could be truly free only at home, enveloped by the security of the Polish family, community, church, and welfare state. In America, "our re-migrants lost

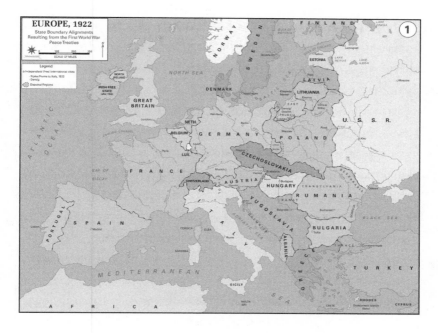

Eastern Europe's new nation-states, 1922.
Courtesy of the Department of History, U.S. Military Academy at West Point.

the best years of their youth and their youthful strength. Only the young and strong succeed there. And when one's strength begins to falter, when breath begins to shorten . . . the human being in America is thrown away like a used-up machine." In Poland, by contrast, citizens might not enjoy modern conveniences, but they could count on their families, communities, and the state to support them. Published testimonies drove the message home. Stanisław Szabot, aged forty, worked in America from 1912 to 1920 and again from 1924 to 1931, saving $11,200. When asked why he chose to return to Poland, he replied, "In America an elderly person is worthless." Jan Skorupa left for the United States in 1912, where he worked in the auto industry in Detroit. He came home in 1930 with $5,000. In spite of his good earnings in America, he did not hesitate to return to Poland. "Here I don't have some factory boss ruling over me. I am my own master," he insisted. In America, he was a servant; in Poland, he was free.[35]

Re-migration campaigns went hand in hand with intensified efforts to police the mobility of the nation's most favored citizens. New emigration laws introduced throughout East Central Europe were typically modeled on Hungary's 1909 legislation, the most restrictive in Europe. In Yugoslavia, the government introduced policies explicitly intended to make it difficult to obtain a passport. Romania banned emigration altogether.[36] Polish officials declared in a 1920 ILO survey that their goal was to ensure that "the smallest possible number of citizens leave the country."[37] In the early years of the republic, the Polish government banned seasonal migration to Germany entirely (that ban was only lifted in 1926), outlawed advertisements for foreign labor, established restrictive passport requirements, and negotiated bilateral treaties to protect migrants' social rights.[38] A 1936 law empowered the government to refuse to issue a passport if a citizen's travel abroad "jeopardizes serious state interests or threatens security, peace, or public order." That law remained unchanged after 1945, because it so perfectly suited the needs of the new Communist government.[39] These policies contrasted sharply with those of other traditional countries of emigration, including Italy, Spain, and Greece, all of which responded to the ILO survey by affirming citizens' "freedom to emigrate." Fascist Italy did not begin to restrict emigration in favor of formal colonial expansion before 1927, while Spain adopted an anti-emigration policy only with Franco's victory in the civil war.[40]

There was no easy consensus about emigration in interwar Poland, however. Poland did not actually pass a comprehensive emigration law until 1927, a reflection, in part, of divisions among Polish demographers and policymakers. While one school of population experts, mostly concentrated in academia, saw over-

population as Poland's primary challenge and wanted to encourage emigration, a competing group, concentrated in government ministries, focused on declining birthrates and underpopulation. In general, Polish authorities tended to view emigration as a necessary evil, and sought to control and direct it rather than ban it outright.[41]

In Czechoslovakia, by contrast, representatives of several political parties, including the Czechoslovak National Socialists (no relation to the Nazi party) and the Slovak People's Party immediately pressed the government to take decisive action against emigration. The Czechoslovak press also urged the government to restrict mobility. An April 1921 editorial in *Národní listy* asserted, "Our state and industrialists must fundamentally strive to reduce emigration as much as possible."[42] In 1922, Czechoslovak legislators responded with an emigration law that explicitly affirmed that emigration was an "individual freedom." At the same time, however, the government was empowered to limit that freedom, if emigration threatened the "life, freedom or property of emigrants," or in order to protect their "economic or moral interests." In addition, the state was entitled to restrict emigration in the name of "public interest" or in the economic or political interests of the state.[43]

The process of acquiring a passport in interwar Czechoslovakia was daunting enough to discourage all but the most determined. Czechoslovak citizens who wished to work in France, for example, were obliged to produce a baptismal certificate, birth certificate, certificate of residence, certificate of "good morals," a document demonstrating that they did not owe any taxes, proof of military service, and their marriage certificate, along with an actual passport application. Any parent leaving minor children behind had to demonstrate that he or she had provided for their support.[44]

Local police and passport offices enjoyed wide discretion to interpret and enforce these new laws. Skilled workers, particularly those in prominent Czechoslovak export industries such as glass-making, were often banned from emigrating, even if unemployed. Officials feared losing valuable skilled labor and worried that foreign firms would steal Czechoslovak trade secrets.[45] Women also found their mobility sharply curtailed after 1918. In one district in the Subcarpathian Rus, Czechoslovak officials refused to issue passports to women and children, unless they were traveling with or to a male guardian.[46] Throughout the 1920s, some Czechoslovak authorities even denied passports to women and children who planned to join husbands or fathers in the West. Women and children thereby became a form of human collateral. Decades later, socialist governments would make use of the same strategy.[47]

In the context of a growing international campaign to end the traffic in women, the movement of single women was particularly restricted. Any single woman traveling abroad was considered a potential victim of the "white slave trade" or a likely prostitute. In order to emigrate to Argentina or Brazil, single Czech and Polish women under the age of twenty-five were required to obtain an affidavit from a family member or employer who pledged to provide financial support and moral supervision. The Yugoslav government banned single women from traveling to Argentina without a close relative, while Polish women under the age of twenty-one could emigrate (to any country) only with the permission of a male guardian (father or husband).[48]

The enforcement of these rules was often arbitrary. One district passport office in Czechoslovakia systematically refused to issue passports to individuals who "could find work here if they made a genuine effort."[49] In other towns, potential emigrants were stymied by endless bureaucratic delays. Josef Novotný finally complained to the Ministry of Social Welfare after waiting three years (in vain) to have his passport application approved.[50] In Mijava, Slovakia, in 1923, all applicants for passports to South America were summarily turned down. The Royal Mail Steam Packet Company in London subsequently petitioned the Ministry of Social Welfare. The steamship company protested that in Czechoslovakia "citizens have the individual freedom to emigrate," insisting, "Government offices cannot randomly deny a citizen who cannot find employment here permission to search for work in some other country."[51] The Czechoslovak government disagreed. Rather than intervening on behalf of the emigrants, officials actually prosecuted the Royal Mail Steam Packet Company for illegally soliciting emigration.[52]

Interwar authorities were particularly intent on shutting down emigration agencies. As in the Dual Monarchy, blaming (Jewish) agents was far simpler than addressing the underlying causes of emigration. In 1923, an official in Mukačevo in the Subcarpathian Rus denounced the "large conspiracy of international agents who traffic in humans" for ongoing emigration. "The naïve and child-like souls of the local people do not help," the official lamented. "They want to go to America, and seeing as they can't do so legally, they allow themselves to be seduced into taking ill-advised steps by the promises of the Jews."[53] Not surprisingly, the growing number and complexity of migration restrictions after World War I only increased demand for the services of agents and smugglers.[54]

Illegal emigration became a lucrative business, and many migrants did fall into the clutches of dishonest migration brokers. Juraj Marcin and Juraj Hornyak from Slovakia claimed that they ended up in Brazil rather than in America thanks to the duplicity of an emigration agent. In June 1922, Marcin testified to Czechoslovak consular officials in Rio de Janeiro that he had decided to seek employment in America, and enlisted the assistance of a village pub owner. He paid 17,000 crowns and received a passport with the name Jan Stajer on it. When he finally arrived in Hamburg, he recounted, "I was put on a boat. I still thought I was going to the U.S. Only when the boat arrived at its port did I realize that it was going to Brazil." In desperate straits, Marcin requested financial assistance from the consul so that he could return home.[55]

Other migrants landed in Mexico or Canada, and then attempted to cross the border illegally into the United States with the assistance of smugglers. Michal Mičak of Vinna, Slovakia, was deported from the United States in 1923 for illegally crossing the Mexican–U.S. border. A local agent had promised to get him to America, he claimed. He traveled first from Slovakia to Prague, then on to Berlin, and finally to Bordeaux, paying almost six hundred dollars for the journey. After three weeks in Bordeaux, he boarded a boat that he believed (or so he claimed) would dock in Kentucky. Instead, he was deposited in Mexico, where he could not find work. He paid ten dollars to a smuggler to escort him over the border in Nuevo Laredo, where he was promptly arrested and deported.[56]

Of course, apprehended migrants had a strong interest in emphasizing their innocence and victimization at the hands of agents. The trope of the criminal agent was well established by the interwar years, and migrants were wise to invoke it. They played on the ambiguity between human trafficking (a crime committed *against* emigrants by exploitative agents) and illegal emigration (a crime committed *by* migrants, often with the help of agents) to their best advantage.

In its zeal to combat illegal emigration, Czechoslovak authorities intensified surveillance efforts, as well as the prosecution of agents. The Prague police appointed special undercover officers to monitor emigration in 1923. Their duties included "cleansing the train stations and the surrounding neighborhood of all unauthorized individuals," meeting trains to Prague from Moravia and Slovakia, and following emigrants and "suspicious" individuals.[57] Police officers apprehended emigration agents through a kind of racial profiling, as they routinely trailed "suspicious" Jews in train stations. By 1928, the department had compiled an index of six thousand suspected emigration agents.[58]

In one case, Ludvík Gros and Štefan Horvat were arrested for loitering around Prague's Wilson Train Station. "On 10 October 1922 we noticed some Jews with a few other people who looked like emigrants on Celetná ulice," the police reported to the Social Welfare Ministry. A dramatic chase ensued when the Jews "noticed that we were watching them, quickened their steps, and ran to Wilson Train Station, where they were apprehended." The men insisted that they had come to Prague to buy farm equipment. But when police searched them and found that they were carrying large sums of money and personal documents, they confessed. Both the Jews and the emigrants were arrested and returned home.[59]

Individuals caught in this web of restrictions expressed their desperation to emigrate in their passport applications. "As a worker I possess no property, and I don't have any family to whom I can turn, my mother is dead and my father remarried and is obligated to support his wife," appealed Ludwik Lalikur in 1930. "I have no work and I therefore have no choice but to seek a living abroad." He begged for permission to emigrate to France. Michal Kuprcak and Jan Jafernik likewise requested passports "because there is no work here for us and we are suffering from poverty and hunger."[60]

THE GOVERNMENTS of Eastern Europe eased restrictions on emigration only in response to the devastating unemployment of the Great Depression. Emigration policies actually became more liberal as East European governments drifted toward the right in the 1930s. They also focused more on the goal of channeling emigration toward colonization. As in the Habsburg Empire, the "colonies" envisioned by East European reformers were not to be acquired by force; the aim was rather to create enclosed settlements of emigrants in other states or empires. In 1936, the Czechoslovak government modified the 1922 emigration law. The recruitment of "colonists" from Czechoslovakia was now permitted with the Social Welfare Ministry's approval.[61] Around the same time, the Polish government began to liberalize its migration laws. In the 1930s, the Ministry of Foreign Affairs gained greater control of emigration policy in Poland. Its goal was also to create emigrant colonies that would remain in close contact with their homeland.[62]

Colonial aspirations built on ideas that had circulated in the Austrian empire before the war, as well as the examples set by Italy and Germany. In 1924, Jan Sykáček, a former diplomat, advocated that Czechoslovakia imitate Italy and Germany by creating enclosed Czechoslovak colonies in South America. "I have seen how other nations deal with this important question, especially the Italians and Germans. They work systematically in every sense, in that the motherland correctly understands the importance of colonies, from both a national and an economic perspective." Germany and Italy used their foreign colonies to "promote the motherland" around the world, according to Sykáček. "The motherland is in constant contact with them, and they are not held aloof as they are here in Czechoslovakia."[63]

As in the Austrian empire, however, officials continued to worry that East European workers might not be accorded the privileges of white Europeans in far-flung colonial settlements. In the 1920s, for example, French officials increasingly sought to recruit East Europeans to work in the French colonies. In 1927, a delegation of French and Czech authorities actually visited Corsica and then convened in Paris to discuss prospects for Czech and Slovak employment on the island. The French aimed to reassure their Czech colleagues that Corsica was safe for European habitation, citing low death rates and promising lush gardens and free wine to Czech workers.[64] Czechoslovak officials were unconvinced. They were even less enthusiastic about schemes to employ Czechs in Tahiti, where a colony of around ninety Czechoslovaks had already settled in June 1926. "The bad example of the natives, who live off fish and fruit and work only when they need money, negatively influences the immigrants, who often fall to their level," insisted a representative of the Czechoslovak Ministry of Foreign Affairs. "We do not recommend that our people emigrate to Tahiti or any other French Island under any circumstance. . . . The position of foreign workers there is the same as that of native workers and Chinese."[65]

In interwar Poland, meanwhile, a movement demanding the acquisition of formal colonies gained even more momentum. Colonial aspirations emerged in Poland as early as 1919, when a group called Polish Bandera began to promote popular interest in maritime navigation.[66] By 1930, the Polish Bandera had become the Maritime and Colonial League, a pressure group that raised funds for the navy and lobbied the government to pursue colonial interests. The league boasted 1,200 branches and 250,000 members as of 1934, and directly linked colonial demands to emigration, as well as to Poland's perceived crisis of overpopulation. Colonial advocates argued that emigration had been the primary "solution" to Poland's overpopulation crisis before World War I. But with the closing of international borders in the 1920s and 1930s, "another solution has arisen again . . . attaining our own colonial territories."[67]

In the wake of Mussolini's 1935 invasion of Ethiopia, Polish colonial advocates felt increasingly entitled to a place in the sun. "We Poles, like the Italians, are facing a great problem of accommodating and employing a large population increase," insisted the Maritime and Colonial League. "We Poles, like the Italians, have the right to demand that export markets as well as areas for settlement be opened to us, so that we may obtain raw materials necessary to the national economy under conditions similar to those enjoyed by the colonial states." In September 1936, Foreign Minister Józef Beck even formally appealed to the League of Nations for colonies—preferably those taken from Germany after World War I (he was unsuccessful). Popular pressure for Polish colonies culminated in the Maritime and Colonial League's "Colonial Days" festivities in April 1938, a series of nationwide parades and celebrations attended by around ten million Poles.[68]

Poland continued to lobby the League of Nations for colonies right up until the outbreak of World War II. A memo submitted in 1939 proposed that the League's colonial mandate system, which governed former Ottoman territories, be extended to Africa. The new African mandates would then be parceled out to European states according to "their capacity for colonization and their real economic and demographic needs." Of course, the Polish delegation insisted that Poland be placed at the top of the list. Poles had already "provided the proof" of their skill as colonizers, "by transforming the virgin forests and uncultivated plains of Brazil, Argentina, Canada, and Siberia into arable land," the memo asserted. "In particular the tenacity of labor, love of the land and pioneering spirit of the Polish peasant has rendered him invaluable." In response to British and French objections that redistributing African colonies would harm the "interests of indigenous populations," the Polish delegation invoked the brotherhood of white men. "There exist rural populations in Europe whose economic standard of living are particularly painful, and whose interests are worth at least as much as those of the black population in Africa. By closing off access to colonial territories to overpopulated nations, the great powers betray the interests of the white race. This treason endangers the solidarity and entente

"We demand colonies for Poland." Poster of the
Polish Maritime and Colonial League, 1938.
Courtesy of the National Museum in Poznań.

among peoples."[69] Not surprisingly, nations situated on Europe's
imagined margins seemed to have the most invested in maintaining the privileges of white Europeans—and in asserting their
membership in the club.

Emigration also continued to inspire new forms of social protection and economic reform in interwar Europe. These measures

could never be fully separated from the state's fundamental goals of surveillance and control, and from anxieties about Eastern Europe's civilizational status. In Czechoslovakia, land reform policies were intended to anchor small farmers and formerly landless peasants in their homeland—as well as to transfer wealth from "foreign" (i.e., German and Hungarian) nobles into the hands of "reliable" Czechs and Slovaks. Between 1919 and 1932, more than 450,000 families received farmland. Other initiatives brought new industries to regions heavily afflicted by emigration. Improvements in infrastructure, including the expansion of railroad lines and electrification, were intended to spur industry. The Czechoslovak government also constructed new schools, introduced tariffs to protect local wheat farmers, created government employment agencies, and sought to encourage dairy farming, tobacco production, and the silk industry. These investments were financed in part by the profits from Czechoslovakia's strong industrial economy—the ninth largest in the world between the wars—as well as by foreign investment.[70]

Throughout Eastern Europe, meanwhile, new agencies were established to monitor and protect emigrants. Poland founded the Emigration Office under the aegis of the Ministry of Labor and Social Assistance in 1920. The following year, the government created the Emigration Council, which included representatives from all relevant government ministries, parliament, and trade unions.[71] In Czechoslovakia, an entire division of the Ministry of Social Welfare was devoted to migration beginning in 1922. The Czechoslovak Foreign Institute (Československý ústav zahraniční), founded in 1928, was charged with cultivating ties to Czechs and Slovaks around the world. A department of the new Masaryk Academy of Labor meanwhile gathered experts to study emigration and "colonization" abroad. The Czechoslovak government also constructed a new sanitary inspection station in Svatobořice and a special barrack in Prague-Libeň, through which all emigrants were processed—a response, in part, to fears that Jewish transmigrants would infect the population of Prague with contagious diseases.[72] New state-led efforts to control emigration were complemented by those of expanding private or semiprivate philanthropic associations. In Poland and Czechoslovakia, the International Social Service, the Red Cross, the YMCA/YWCA, Polish Emigration Society, and the Association of Saint Rafael were among the most active champions of emigrant rights, advising and assisting emigrants locally on a case-by-case basis.[73]

All of these institutions were inseparable from the overarching goal of minimizing emigration. The Czechoslovak Foreign Institute, for example, was founded on the principle that for Czechoslovakia, a small nation, "the loss of every soul is twice as significant as it is for a large nation."[74] One of the institute's major initiatives was the creation of local counseling centers for prospective migrants. Emigration counselors were not neutral advisers, however. One representative of the Ministry for Social Welfare explained, "The primary mission of the local counselors will be to disseminate negative information about the bad conditions abroad."[75]

Jan Matušinský, a table maker, was a typical client. He wrote to the Foreign Institute looking for information about prospects in Argentina in 1929. In reply, he received a letter advising him to stay home. "We simply cannot encourage you, the father of a family, to move across the ocean in order to search for a job. As an unskilled worker, you would be poorly paid, you still don't speak the local language, you'll be working hard all day and won't have time to learn it, you will not earn enough money, and as your savings dissolve you will also become demoralized."[76]

Emigration reformers generally considered continental migration preferable to emigration overseas, since workers on the Continent were more likely (and sometimes required) to return home at the end of the harvest season, or after a few years' work. These migrants also enjoyed Europe's more protective labor laws. The Polish government, harboring resentments toward Germany and Austria, attempted to channel seasonal migration toward France in the 1920s. Through bilateral treaties, Polish authorities guaranteed that their workers in France (and, after 1927, Germany) would receive the same social benefits and pay as native citizens. Similar agreements regulated the treatment of Czechoslovak workers in France, Germany, and Austria. These treaties were considered an important form of protection for the domestic labor force, which would not be threatened by cheap competition from abroad.[77]

As the largest European employer of migrant labor between the wars, France was also the site of some of the most far-reaching programs to protect migrants' rights. According to Polish statistics, 625,391 Poles emigrated to France between the wars, and 217,787 returned home.[78] Beginning in 1927, however, the Polish government agitated against alleged violations of the French-Polish migration treaty, specifically with respect to pay and working hours, along with a purported lack of "moral oversight" of female workers. Rumors of abortions, infanticides, and prostitution among Polish migrant women in France, in particular, inflamed public opinion. The Polish government responded by capping the number of agricultural workers permitted to work in France at three thousand, requiring the French to take two men for every one woman, banning the emigration of single women under the age of twenty-one, and requiring women to be placed on farms near other Poles. In 1930, the Polish government threatened to prohibit female emigration to France altogether unless Polish-speaking inspectors were deployed to the countryside to monitor female migrants. In response, new Committees for the Protection of Female Agricultural Workers were established across France at

the departmental level. Departmental prefects chaired these committees, whose members included representatives from the Polish,
Czechoslovak, and Yugoslav consuls. The committees stationed
bilingual social workers in each department, where they were
charged with monitoring female workers, arbitrating conflicts,
and providing "moral support" (and surveillance).[79]

As the number of Polish agricultural workers in France
declined, the French government also intensified recruitment
in Czechoslovakia. As of 1932, there were around fifty thousand
Czechs and Slovaks working in France, divided equally between
industry and agriculture. That number would have been much
larger, however, had the Czechoslovak state not been so determined to limit emigration. Czechoslovak workers were at a disadvantage compared with migrant laborers from Poland, Italy,
and Belgium, who enjoyed "most-favored nation" status in France.
Workers from Czechoslovakia were entitled to the same wages
as French employees, but for the first six months of their twelve-
month contracts, health insurance had to be covered by their
employers rather than the government. They were also not entitled to French unemployment benefits. This was a source of serious
discontent among Czechoslovak workers and discouraged French
employers from hiring them.[80]

These inequalities were a direct product of the Czechoslovak
anti-emigration agenda. In the early years of the republic, Czechoslovak officials saw emigration as a temporary scourge. They did
not want to make emigration overly attractive, and therefore never
demanded complete equality between French and Czechoslovak
workers. By the end of the decade, however, it was clear that they
had miscalculated. The issue of emigration had not disappeared.
Beginning in 1928, Czechoslovak representatives sought to rene-
gotiate the terms of their accord with France, but it was too late.
By the time the parties made it to the negotiating table, the Great

Depression was under way, the market for foreign labor had collapsed, and xenophobia was on the rise in France.[81]

This is not to say that Czechoslovak workers were without rights. By the 1930s, an elaborate system had been created to monitor and protect East European workers in France, based on a combination of bilateral treaties and case-by-case mediation.[82] In 1936, for example, Rozalie Ondercikova appealed to the Czechoslovak consulate in Strasbourg. Rozalie was twenty-seven years old and divorced. In search of work and a fresh start abroad, she registered with the Slovak labor office in Bratislava and set out for France. She signed a one-year contract to work on Léon Grasser's farm in Dingsheim, in the Bas-Rhin, where she was employed as a "maid for all purposes." Upon arrival, Rozalie discovered that the work was physically taxing, that the farm was isolated, and that her employer constantly yelled at her in French, which she did not understand. She did not even have time to attend Sunday mass, since Sundays were devoted to cleaning out pig stalls and scrubbing kitchen floors. One Saturday morning in October, as Rozalie was cooking potatoes for the hogs' dinner, her boss began to scream at her. It was the last straw. Rozalie returned from the fields and declared that she was going to Strasbourg to file a complaint. Mr. Grasser slapped her in the face. The following week the conflict escalated. Rozalie attempted to leave the farm for Strasbourg, taking the key to her room with her. Mr. Grasser and his son attempted to wrestle the key from Rozalie's hands and knocked her to the ground. Grasser subsequently filed his own complaint with the local French labor office.

The French labor office assigned the case to a social worker employed by the local Committee for the Protection of Female Agricultural Workers, Hélène Lachaux. She advised Grasser to allow Rozalie to attend mass, and counseled Rozalie to "obey her boss."[83] But several months later, the situation had not improved.

In January, Rozalie left the farm for good, testifying that she "could not tolerate the abusive treatment continuously inflicted upon her by Madame Grasser." Lachaux investigated the case in the village. The Grassers, it turned out, were well known to mistreat their domestic servants. Rozalie was freed from her contract and allowed to seek employment elsewhere. In the future, Lachaux concluded, "we should absolutely refuse any request for foreign workers from Mr. Grasser." Her report was passed along to the Czechoslovak consulate, the Czechoslovak Ministry for Social Welfare, and the Bratislava employment office.[84]

Rozalie was in many ways no different from legions of other maltreated and overworked domestic servants. But the fact that her case reached the desks of social workers and diplomats in Paris, Prague, and Bratislava reflected a new paradigm of migration politics and social protection that emerged between the two world wars. What once would have been a local, private conflict became a minor international incident.

Overwhelmingly, however, foreign workers remained at a disadvantage in these disputes. Most workers filed complaints against their employers directly at the Czechoslovak consulates in Marseille, Strasbourg, Lille, or Paris. The consuls were not empowered to intervene directly. Instead, they were obliged to turn complaints over to the French Office for Foreign Labor, which conducted its own investigations. The Czechoslovak consul in Marseille reported in 1930 that the French Office for Foreign Labor was completely overwhelmed by workers' complaints. Investigations took months, if they took place at all. "It is clear that in these circumstances the protection of our workers against the exploitation of employers is simply illusory," the consul lamented.[85]

In 1937, Czechoslovak workers filed 107 complaints in the Strasbourg region. Only 6 of these disputes, or 5 percent, were resolved in favor of workers.[86] Czechoslovak officials were themselves invested in minimizing conflicts, particularly as unemployment rates at home soared in the 1930s. A guidebook for Czechoslovak workers headed to France, published by the Ministry for Social Welfare in 1931, warned workers not to file frivolous grievances. "Complaints should be made only in truly serious cases, never over quibbles. . . . There is no place for complaint because a migrant's fantasies about work in France are not fulfilled."[87]

In general, Czechoslovak and French authorities alike depoliticized employment disputes, attributing labor conflicts to linguistic barriers or problems of cultural and psychological adjustment. The Czechoslovak consul in Strasbourg noted, "A large number of complaints originate in problems related to the adaptation to a new environment, as feelings of homesickness arise, along with depression in cases in which the employee does not have the possibility to converse with anyone in his or her maternal language."[88] In reality, however, workers' complaints most often concerned basic labor issues: unpaid wages, overwork, and abusive treatment. Authorities generally responded by admonishing employees to work harder and complain less. Ignác Brázdovič was employed by the farmer Léon Baud in Évillers. He complained that he had not been paid his full wages. The consul, in reply, urged him to improve his behavior. A French Labor Office investigation had revealed that "from the 21st of July to the 6th of August you were drunk every day. . . . Mr. Baud found your bottle [of liquor], which you then broke in anger while threatening him. . . . A local field guard witnessed your drunkenness because he saw you passed out drunk on the local highway at 10 AM."[89]

The harsh treatment of Czechoslovak workers by French authorities is perhaps unsurprising, but the disciplinary stance of Czechoslovak representatives toward their own citizens calls into question the assumption that national kinship trumped class biases or diplomatic priorities. Czechoslovak consular officials often shared the social prejudices of French employers and officials toward the poorly educated agricultural workers they were charged to represent. They frequently had a greater interest in maintaining smooth diplomatic and economic relations between France and Czechoslovakia than in defending the rights of their compatriots.

Women were particularly vulnerable to both surveillance and abuse. A large number of the East European agricultural workers employed in interwar France were single women. For example, two-thirds of the Polish agricultural workers employed in the department of Indre-et-Loire were female. East European authorities were extremely concerned about protecting the moral and sexual virtue of these women, who were young and often away from home for the first time. Julie Šalmiková, aged eighteen, arrived in France in January 1938. That summer, she received a letter of reprimand. "The consulate of the Czechoslovak Republic in Strasbourg has been informed that you go out every evening and return late in the night. On July 14, 1938, you were out until 5 AM. You are consorting with three young men in Jussey, and your behavior is inciting scandal in the community," he warned. "If you are deported from France for your bad behavior, you should not expect this office to provide you with any assistance."[90]

In spite of such oversight, sexual abuse, rape, and pregnancy were among the occupational hazards faced by female workers on isolated farms. In 1934 alone, twenty-four unmarried Polish women gave birth in the department of Indre-et-Loire. Doctors in Tours reported that many other Polish workers showed up in the hospital with injuries attributed to overwork, and that they often appeared to be "physically and mentally depressed." Julie Duval, the local social worker for the Committee for the Protection of Female Agricultural Workers in Indre-et-Loire, received letters from East European women in her district complaining of hardships ranging from loneliness and overwork to rape and unwanted pregnancies. "Heaven, what sin have I committed to deserve such a bitter fate?" one young woman wrote. "If only I could rest a little on Sunday. . . . I pray to God not to go crazy. I take everything to heart so much that I don't sleep or eat. Since I have been here, I have not heard a single word in my language."[91] Weronika, a twenty-five-year-old farmworker from a village near Tarnów, wrote to Duval in desperation on behalf of her younger sister Józefa, who worked on a nearby farm:

> Dear Madame and mother to us all! First of all I want to thank you for my job here because I am well here and I am content, but I received a sad and painful letter from my sister. . . . They wanted to force her to become a whore, she tried to defend herself. . . . They beat her horribly and she was bleeding. . . . They locked her room and will not leave her alone. . . . Now they want her to work gain. . . . She has written to me in great suffering. . . . She wants to kill herself. . . . Dear Madame, you must do something about it and liberate her from this job because she came here to work and not to suffer.

It is safe to assume that the number of actual cases of sexual assault was much higher than those reported. Many women wrote to Duval only if they became pregnant as a result of a rape. Pregnant single women lost their jobs and feared social ostracism if they returned to Poland with a child. A young worker named Wiktoria wrote to Duval seeking help. "I came to Poland in 1928, I worked for an old widower. He promised to marry me, and wanted to sleep with me. . . . I could not defend myself, he raped me and now I have a six-month-old infant." She was alone in France without a job or any source of support. Such tales fed the flames of the anti-emigration movement back home in Poland, providing proof of the perils of work abroad. In a moment of frustration, Duval herself complained that "employers who are very kind to the French workers are much less so with the foreigners, who are seen a little like slaves attached to their home for a year."[92]

THE GREAT DEPRESSION intensified xenophobia throughout Europe and America, as immigrants were seen as a threat to native workers in a bitter competition for scarce jobs and resources. This meant tighter restrictions on immigration in the West, high unemployment, and an unprecedented flow of migrants back to Eastern Europe. Oral histories collected during the Depression by the Federal Writers' Project reflected the profound despair of many migrants, who had lived and worked for years in the United States, only to end up unemployed and impoverished in middle or old age.

"Well, what do you want to know? My life story, you say? I haven't much to tell," testified one Polish migrant in 1940.

> My living has been a mere struggle for bread. For years my parents wanted to till the soil, but never had a chance to buy any in the old country. When we came here, back in 1908, they tried to get a homestead, but all the good land was already taken up by that time. So when I was of age, I went to work on the railroads, washing cars.

In stark contrast to many of the oral histories collected in the 1980s and 1990s, his story had no redeeming ending.

> Sometimes I think life isn't worth a damn for a man like me. . . . I am not educated. My work is unskilled. I get little money, just enough to pay rent and buy food. I can't say

I am living a normal life. Look at my wife and my kids—
undernourished, seldom have a square meal. . . . Can you
blame me for taking to liquor? Of course, I haven't much
money for that neither. But a few of my friends treat me
sometimes . . . and that's the only time I forget how miserable I am.[93]

The American dream was a bitter illusion for many immigrants during the Depression. "Yes, I would love to live like some
people do—get married, have a nice home, get everything I need,"
recounted a Ukrainian immigrant who had settled in Newark in
1939. "But how can a man do that without an assured employment
or income? It just cannot be done. I live in a house not fit for rats
to live in. I am obliged to eat the cheapest food, which is never
quality food. As you see, I am wearing rags. And my future? Only
an undertaker can tell. . . . I tell you, life for me is one round of hell
after another."[94]

For some migrants, returning home to Europe seemed like the
best option. Writing in 1937, the International Labor Organization
observed that the Great Depression had produced "a virtual rever-
sal of migratory currents. Countries that have traditionally been
lands of immigration have been transformed into lands of emigration, and the typical countries of emigration have taken on the
form of countries of immigration."[95] Josef Kmet's father returned
from America to Slovakia during the Depression, taking young
Josef with him. "Well, it was the Depression, and my father—he
was afraid that he wouldn't be able to raise the family here [in
America], that it would be easier in Slovakia," he recalled. "You
know, you've got a little farm there, a little garden, so you can grow
some of your own stuff. Or maybe, I don't know, kill a chicken or
maybe a rabbit."[96]

The Depression began to upset the migration balance sheet in

1931–32. In Poland, there were more repatriates than emigrants beginning in 1931, when only 64,000 people emigrated (down from 178,000 in 1929), and 80,000 returned to Poland. Czechoslovakia also saw a dramatic decline in emigration that year, from 40,000 emigrants in 1930 to 17,400 in 1932.[97] In 1931, the U.S. Immigration Commission even offered to pay for the repatriation of migrants who had arrived within the last three years and were receiving public assistance.[98] These "journeys of despair" alarmed social workers on both sides of Europe and the Atlantic. Suzanne Ferrière of the International Migration Service in France lamented, "The process followed in the U.S. is being copied all over Europe, and it becomes worse every month. Be it expulsion, or repatriation, every country in Europe now tries to get rid of its unemployed foreigners. The situation is appalling."[99] George Warren, director of the American branch of the International Migration Service, observed in 1931,

> This flow of individuals and families back to Europe . . . is perhaps satisfying to the economist, to the politician, and to the man in the street who visualizes more elbow room here, more jobs for citizens, lighter relief burdens for our communities and a reduction in those elements of our population supposedly contributing to our more recent forms of criminal activity. But to the social worker sensitive to the social considerations surrounding this migration, to the shattered hopes and the atmosphere of defeat and despair in which these returns are made, questions immediately arise as to the intangible and immeasurable losses created by this disruption in family life.[100]

The return of migrants to Poland and Czechoslovakia from France during the 1930s was particularly contentious. "The situation of these exiles is miserable," reported a French correspondent in Katowice in December 1931. "They have worked for many years in France. They paid for social security and unemployment insurance. Today they are returning penniless. They are coming through the train stations of Upper Silesia and Pomerania by the thousands. These re-migrants offer a terrible spectacle of misery and desperation."[101] East European authorities deplored the moral, political, and social impact of destitute returnees. "Failed" migrants were often a burden to their families, the community, and the state, officials lamented. They came home "like beggars and tramps, in a state of great poverty, often with ripped clothing and infested with lice. People who emigrated full of hope that they would improve their social situation are returning as beggars loaded with debts. . . . Men who were once independent will now be dependent (on charity) until they die."[102]

Both the Polish and the Czechoslovak press devoted extensive attention to the plight of return migrants in the 1930s, drawing a stark (but predictable) lesson from their experiences: treaties were meaningless, and emigration led to ruin. The *Kuryer Codzienny* even published a poem by a Polish worker, Czeslaw Mondryk, who returned from France during the Depression, bitter and impoverished:

> *Poland! After years of emigration in search of bread*
> *We have returned en masse, hungry, without a złoty,*
> *Looking like vagabonds and beggars . . .*
> *In exchange for our trouble, for our struggle*
> *We get no recognition, but an order of expulsion!*
> *Workers, beware!*
> *Don't believe in conventions, in treaties with foreign states—*
> *They are filled with nothing but lies!* [103]

French officials estimated that between 1932 and 1934, 20 percent of Polish workers left France, close to 64,000 people.[104] Officials in the French Labor Ministry denied rumors of systematic deportations, insisting that the government was merely trying to "facilitate" the return of migrants to Poland.[105] To workers themselves, however, the distinction between "facilitating repatriation" and "deportation" often seemed arbitrary.[106] East European diplomats intervened on behalf of their citizens with little success. A memo from the Polish embassy in Paris objected, "It is clear that the administrative expulsion of Polish workers en masse, in a period of crisis . . . is contrary to the letter and spirit of the treaty between Poland and France." The repatriations did not stop, however. Return migration from France to Poland reached a high point in 1935, when 35,451 Poles left France, and only 1,360 arrived.[107]

In protesting these repatriations or deportations, racial anxieties once again came to the fore, as East European journalists and workers compared the plight of migrant workers to that of slaves. The *Kuryer Codzienny* declared in May 1934, "We know that the workers who went to France were attracted there by promises of paradise on earth, but that they were quickly disillusioned. We know that Polish workers in France have frequently been treated as white slaves, that they have been subjected to injustice and violence."[108] *Venkov*, the newspaper of the Czechoslovak Agrarian Party, saw the ongoing expulsions as proof of the need to curb emigration once and for all. "It is no longer possible to export merchandise or men," the editors insisted. "We must therefore live and generate enough bread and work at home."[109]

A tragic symmetry ultimately defined the arc of emigration and repatriation in interwar Eastern Europe. Whereas the re-migrants of the early 1920s embodied the utopian hopes invested in the construction of new nation-states, the desperate repatriates of the Depression era signified the brutal collapse of those dreams. Their return coincided with the collapse of democracy itself in East Central Europe, as right-wing and fascist governments increasingly seized control in the region. To many, the plight of destitute returnees seemed to corroborate decades of existing anti-emigration sentiment. Their fate furnished compelling evidence that emigrants were powerless, that diplomatic treaties were meaningless, and that national sovereignty—at home and abroad—was tenuous.

CHAPTER FOUR

The First Final Solution

I n November 1938, Count Jerzy Potocki, the Polish ambassador to the United States, sat down for a frank conversation at
the U.S. State Department. The subject was the "Jewish problem." The situation of Jews in Germany and Austria was growing
increasingly desperate. Tense negotiations were under way between
Nazi authorities, Western diplomats, and international organizations to facilitate Jewish emigration from Germany and Austria.

The Polish government found the situation terribly unfair.
Why, Potocki demanded, were the Nazis being rewarded for their
ruthless policies of persecution? Poland also wanted to be rid of its
"excess" Jews. The emigration of Jews from Poland, he insisted, was
an urgent necessity that "could not be ignored by other countries."[1]
The U.S. ambassador to Poland, A. J. Drexel Biddle, attempted to
reassure his colleague that the Americans were on the same page.
"A solution of the Jewish problem in a global sense was a matter
for our generation to settle," Biddle agreed, since future generations could not be counted on to deal with the issue "with the same
degree of tolerance, objectivity and liberalism as our own."[2]

The lines between rescue and removal, between emigration and expulsion, and between humanitarianism and ethnic cleansing were already hazy in 1938–39. By the time the Third Reich began its assault on Eastern Europe, a conviction had spread well beyond the borders of Nazi Germany that the peace of Europe depended on finding a solution to what was widely referred to as the "Jewish question" or "Jewish problem." To be sure, the plight of refugees fleeing Nazi Germany was seen as a massive humanitarian crisis. But it was also seen as a precious opportunity. Isaiah Bowman, Franklin Delano Roosevelt's most trusted adviser on refugee policy, insisted that humanitarian interests alone could not guide the resettlement or refugees. "The whole enterprise ought to be conceived not as an emergency measure for a population in flight but as a broad scientific undertaking, humanitarian in purpose, orderly in its functioning, and essentially serving the self-interest of those who receive populations."[3]

Europe's refugee problem was, in short, a crisis too good to waste. For population experts like Bowman, along with many government leaders, the massive dislocation of people before and during the Second World War represented an opportunity to strategically rebalance the world's population and to remold national demographics. International and local humanitarian organizations, working on behalf of refugee welfare, proved instrumental in carrying out these visions. For Bowman, Biddle, Potocki, and Roosevelt, the solution to the "Jewish question" was clear. The organized emigration of East European Jews, preferably to someplace in South America or Africa, represented a forward-thinking and "orderly" alternative to chaotic deportation and flight. It was a strategy for responding to Europe's refugee crisis without increasing Western immigration quotas. And it was a step toward the creation of a more peaceful and prosperous world. These ideas were not invented by Western diplomats or humanitarian workers and imposed on Eastern Europe. Rather, they "trickled up" into the realm of international diplomacy and humanitarianism from the East European contexts in which emigration had long been seen as a "solution" to large-scale social, political, and demographic problems.

Jews, socialists, and other "enemies" of the Third Reich had been desperately seeking refuge from Nazi Germany since Hitler's seizure of power in 1933. The refugee crisis became an international issue only gradually, however. By 1938, it could no longer be ignored. In April of that year, a Nazi decree effectively shut Jews out of the German economy and paved the way for the seizure of their assets. Then, on November 11, 1938, the naked violence of the Kristallnacht pogroms shattered any remaining illusion of physical security for Jews in the Third Reich. The pogroms were intended to provoke the flight of Jews from Nazi territory, and they achieved that goal. Around 33,000 Jews fled Nazi Germany and Austria in 1938, and another 77,000 did so in 1939.

The number of Jews seeking to escape Europe expanded with the Third Reich. The *Anschluss* of Austria in March 1938 brought an additional 192,000 Jews into the Reich's clutches. More than 6,000 people a day were soon lined up outside the U.S. consulate, where, from nine in the morning until ten o'clock at night, officers conducted interviews to determine which candidate deserved one of the only 1,413 spots per year permitted by immigration quotas. In September of 1938, Hitler occupied the Sudetenland, prompting the flight of most of its 28,000 Jews. Finally, the dismemberment of the remainder of Czechoslovakia in March 1939 and the conquest of Poland in September 1939 brought millions more Jews into the Nazi orbit. Not only were these Jews threatened with the loss of their citizenship, livelihood, and lives, but their prospects for escape were dismal. Already in 1938–39, thousands of Jewish refugees were suspended in legal and physical "no-man's lands" between states, as officials literally shoved them back and forth across state lines.[4]

An estimated twenty thousand refugees from Nazi Germany sought safety in the first Czechoslovak Republic between 1933 and 1938. The *Anschluss* of Austria brought a new wave of Jewish refugees to Czechoslovakia, where they hoped to find sanctuary in one of Europe's sole remaining democracies. Tragically, however, anti-Semitism and anti-German sentiment often overlapped and reinforced each other in Czechoslovakia. Czech anti-Semites had long resented Bohemian and Moravian Jews for their alleged attachment to the German language and culture. When refugees began to pour into Czechoslovakia from Austria, many Czechs made no distinction between Nazis and the German-speaking Jews, Social Democrats, and Communists who fled Nazi persecution. They were all simply "Germans" and unwelcome in the state.[5]

Otto Eisler, an engineer born in Opava, Bohemia, before World War I, had grown up in the Bohemian lands, where he still had relatives and friends who were willing to support him. After the *Anschluss*, he applied for asylum in Czechoslovakia, but his application was rejected. "Not only does he not speak the state language, but his behavior and appearance suggest that he would be an ungrateful guest in our state. He is a typical unscrupulous merchant-Jew," advised the Czech consul in Vienna. Eisler was eventually deported from Vienna to Theresienstadt, where he perished on April 7, 1943.[6]

With the Nazi annexation of the Sudetenland on October 1, 1938, the refugee crisis darkened. More than 160,000 Jews, socialists, and Communists fled or were expelled from the Sudetenland to the Czech interior in 1938.[7] These refugees were almost all Czechoslovak citizens, but they garnered little sympathy from the Czech government. Following the dismemberment of Czechoslovakia at Munich, a right-wing, anti-Semitic coalition led by the Agrarian Party's Rudolf Beran established the Czech Second

Republic, a short-lived authoritarian regime that lasted only until the Nazis occupied the remainder of Czechoslovakia on March 15, 1939. In a telegram to the U.S. secretary of state on October 12, 1938, the American special envoy to Czechoslovakia, Wilbur John Carr, reported that Beran's government had issued a blanket order to deport all non-Czech refugees within forty-eight hours. Neill Malcolm, the League of Nations high commissioner for refugees, attempted to negotiate with the Czech government to suspend the order for two weeks, but "this request was flatly and finally refused." The situation quickly became desperate. "The suicide toll among refugees mounts but it is impossible to convey the figures as the Czech radio station has stopped mentioning these cases," Carr reported. The Czechoslovak government thereby deprived many Jews of their citizenship well before the Nazis imported the Nuremberg Laws to Czechoslovakia.[8] By November 1, 1938, around twenty thousand Jews from the Sudetenland had fled to the Czechoslovak interior and been expelled back into Nazi territory.[9]

Many refugees were trapped in the cracks between state borders. On November 12, 1938, a month after the Third Reich invaded the Sudetenland, Nazis drove Josef Metzger and his family over the demarcation line between the Sudetenland and the rump state of Czechoslovakia. Metzger, his wife, and three children were all Czechoslovak citizens and could prove their legal residence in the Czech interior. They should have been entitled to return there. But border guards used the pretext that his thirteen-year-old daughter lacked a passport to force the entire family to return to Nazi territory. Within hours, the Germans deported them back to Czechoslovakia. After being shunted back and forth across the frontier several times, the entire family was finally detained in a border station while Czech and German officials negotiated their fate.[10]

Those who did gain admission to the Czech interior often

received a cold welcome. In December 1938, the Prague police department recommended that Jewish refugees be interned "in the interest of public safety." The police department also expressed the hope that international humanitarian organizations would soon reach a decision that would enable Czech authorities to "collectively deport them [the refugees] from the territory of the Czechoslovak Republic." Provincial authorities in Prague likewise recommended the "rapid internment of all of these unwanted and difficult-to-control emigrants."[11]

Similar scenes played out across Eastern Europe in the autumn of 1938. In March 1938, the Polish government had passed legislation that stripped most Polish Jews living outside Poland of their citizenship. Three days before the measure took effect, on the night of October 28, Nazis rounded up seventeen thousand Polish Jews living in Nazi Germany and attempted to deport them to Poland. Poland promptly closed its borders. Like Czechoslovak refugees from the Sudetenland, these Polish Jews were rendered stateless by the Polish government before the Nazis occupied Poland. Thousands of Jews were suspended in the no-man's land between the Polish-German border near *Zbąszyń* that November. Many were separated from family members on the other side of the border. They were housed in miserable conditions in tents, barracks, condemned military stables, or simply outdoors, exposed to the elements.[12]

Other Jewish refugees were stranded in an outdoor purgatory between the Hungarian-Slovak border. Following the First Vienna Award of November 2, 1938, when Hungary gained territory from Slovakia, the Slovak government expelled two thousand Jews to Hungary. Hungary refused to admit them, and the refugees lived on the border for weeks in hastily erected camps. Marie Schmolka of the HICEM in Prague reported, "More than 300 refugees found themselves in an open field for one week, in a temperature which went as low as 20 degrees below zero during the daytime and 50 degrees below zero at night. They built scanty huts and roofs from maize stalks and dug pits in which they placed their children."[13]

East European governments were not alone in punting unwanted refugees across borders. In the most infamous case, the SS *St. Louis* was transformed from a lifeboat into a floating detention center for almost six weeks in 1939. The ship, which was transporting 937 desperate refugees from Nazi-occupied Europe, was refused at both Cuban and American ports between May and June, and eventually forced to return to Europe. Suicide patrols monitored the decks at night to prevent passengers from throwing themselves overboard or trying to swim to shore.

Closer to home, the Danube River harbored its own mini-*St. Louis*. On April 16, 1938, Jewish residents of the Burgenland in Austria were driven from their apartments, robbed of their possessions and identity papers, and dumped on a Danube island that belonged to Czechoslovakia. The Czechoslovak government deported them on the same day, to another "no-man's land" between the borders of Czechoslovakia, Austria, and Hungary. The refugees spent three days trapped between the bayonets of border guards from three states. Finally, the Jewish community of Bratislava devised an impromptu solution. It rented a tugboat that was stationed on the Hungarian coast of the Danube, and took the sixty-eight refugees on board. No country would allow the ship to land, however. The refugees remained on board for three months, while Jewish organizations attempted to find a sanctuary for them. For Schmolka, a Czechoslovak Zionist, the plight of these refugees demonstrated the urgent need for a Jewish state. "These Jewish men and women on the tugboat that can land nowhere are a symbol of our situation in the diaspora, and their transfer to Palestine, the only solution, will also become a symbol of the solution to the Jewish problem at large."[14]

IN THIS DESPERATE CONTEXT, a strange consensus emerged about the answer to the "Jewish question." Humanitarian activists, Western leaders like FDR, East European Jews (including Zionists and many non-Zionists), East European diplomats, and Nazis themselves came to agree that large numbers of Jews would need to emigrate from Europe. The motivations, goals, and politics of the individuals and groups invested in Jewish emigration in the 1930s all differed starkly, however, as did their relative power locally and internationally. For the Nazis, emigration entailed a brutal policy of segregation, expropriation, and deportation. For many Jews, it was a desperate response to violence, poverty, and persecution. What united these different groups, however, was a preoccupation with facilitating the emigration of Jews from Europe at a time when most of the world's borders were closed to immigration. All of these visions for Jewish emigration were also shaped by the longer history of emigration, population, and colonial politics in Central Europe.

The politics of exit was particularly complex within the Jewish community itself. Most Zionists did not believe that all Jews could or should emigrate from Europe. They were rather torn between the desire to achieve a demographic majority in Palestine and concerns that overly rapid settlement would overwhelm the economy and undermine the entire movement. Many were convinced that the success of the Zionist project depended precisely on selectively recruiting the right *kind* of settlers (even as they disagreed about the qualities of the ideal pioneer). This meant that Zionists were generally committed to a struggle on two fronts: the long-term dream of creating a new Jewish home in Palestine, and a concurrent goal of protecting and establishing Jewish collective rights (framed as "national" rights) in Europe. The departure of some

Jews to Palestine was supposed to enable others to stay, with more secure political and cultural rights. This discussion was largely theoretical, however. Zionists had little power to determine the pace of emigration to Palestine, since the British government controlled the number of certificates issued.[15]

Many Jews, Zionist and non-Zionist alike, were clamoring to escape interwar Poland, in any event. Around 400,000 Jews emigrated from Poland between 1921 and 1938 (thanks to high birth-rates, the Jewish population nonetheless hovered at around three million). By the end of the 1930s, several hundred thousand more Polish Jews had registered with Zionist and non-Zionist emigration societies, indicating their desire to leave. The decision about *where* to go was often more pragmatic than political.[16] Barrett Rubin, who emigrated to the United States from Poland in 1929 at the age of four, recounted that his father had applied for visas to both Palestine and the United States. "From what I understand, he was waiting on both. And we got the visa to the United States and about a week or two later we got the visa to Palestine, but he chose to come to the United States because he had three aunts living here. . . . My father . . . hated the fact of the anti-Semitism in Poland. . . . He just wanted to get out of there, and he wanted his family out of there."[17] Likewise, for many Jewish humanitarian workers and organizations, trying to help Jews leave Europe was a pragmatic response to the growing menace of anti-Semitic violence and persecution.

Even if there was widespread agreement that many Jews needed to leave Europe in the late 1930s, there was no consensus about where they should go. The United States, Britain, and France, traditionally lands of asylum and immigration, all adopted a NIMBY policy.[18] In the United States, immigration had been severely restricted by the quota system since 1924. Then, in 1931, in the context of the Great Depression and massive unemployment, the

U.S. State Department began to use a strict interpretation of the "likely to become a public charge" clause to reduce immigration even below the small numbers allowed by the quotas. As a result, even after the Nazi seizure of power in 1933, the German quota was rarely filled.[19]

Although President Roosevelt expressed public sympathy for the plight of the refugees, he did nothing to interfere with these State Department procedures until 1938. After the Kristallnacht pogroms that November, Roosevelt announced that the German and Austrian quotas would be merged and that refugees would be accepted up to quota limits, but he did not push to increase the quotas. That was a clear concession to American public opinion. As late as 1938, a Gallup poll revealed that 77 percent of Americans opposed allowing substantial numbers of refugees to enter the United States. Around 250,000 Jewish refugees nonetheless reached the United States between 1933 and 1944—thanks largely to the determined activism of organizations like the American Joint Distribution Committee (JDC) and advocates for refugee rights like Secretary of Labor Frances Perkins.[20]

In France, refugee policies fluctuated with the ever-changing governments of the 1930s. Immediately after the Nazi seizure of power, German refugees crossed the border to France with relative ease, but this ended in 1934–35 with the sharp rise in unemployment and the inauguration of the conservative Bloc National government of Pierre-Étienne Flandin and Pierre Laval. In 1936–37, the left-wing Popular Front government offered some reprieve to refugees—normalizing the status of German refugees who had arrived before 1936 and exploring colonial settlement possibilities. The amnesty was not, however, applied to refugees from Eastern Europe or to those who came after 1936. Then, in 1938, under Édouard Daladier, a new crackdown on refugees took effect, this time based on fears of political subversion—namely, that Jewish refugees were Communists who threatened to drag France into a war with Hitler. By 1939, approximately fifty thousand Jewish refugees had entered France in spite of these policies, but most enjoyed only a brief respite from persecution, since foreign Jews were the first to be deported by the Vichy regime beginning in 1942. While 25 percent of French Jews survived the Holocaust, between 41 and 45 percent of foreign Jews living in France were murdered.[21]

The United Kingdom insisted throughout the war that it was not a country of immigration, treating the refugee issue as a question of national interest. The British government therefore attempted to select those refugees who would best bolster the British economy. Like the French, British authorities also hoped to prevent refugees from settling permanently in the United Kingdom. Around ninety thousand refugees were ultimately admitted to Britain between 1933 and 1939; another eighty thousand escaped Europe (legally or illegally) to Palestine from Germany, Austria, or the Czech Republic between 1933 and 1941, in spite of British efforts to limit emigration there.[22]

Given these limitations, many refugees pinned their hopes on destinations in Latin America, Africa, and Asia. Zionists had, of course, been advocating the creation of a Jewish homeland outside of Europe for decades, and had also long advertised their potential contribution to colonial projects. At the Sixth Zionist Congress, in 1903, the British Zionist Israel Zangwill speculated, "If Britain could attract all the Jews of the world to her colonies she would just double their white population. . . . [W]ith all of Judea helping us . . . we could create a colony that would be a source of strength, not only to Israel but to the British Empire . . . a colony that would co-operate in extending civilization from Cairo to the Cape."[23] The congress rejected proposals for a Jewish colony in Africa in 1905, but activists affiliated with Zangwill's territorialist movement continued to seek other settlement possibilities for Jews around the world.[24] This longer history of territorialism and colonialism shaped the possibilities for Jewish emigration as the refugee crisis of the 1930s intensified. Yet even outside of Europe, countries like South Africa and Brazil aimed to restrict Jewish immigration in the 1930s, further narrowing possibilities for escape.[25]

In 1938, Roosevelt called the world's leaders to Evian to try to address the Jewish refugee crisis. In order to get delegates from thirty-two countries to the negotiating table, however, he promised that no country would be asked to increase its immigration quotas. The Evian Conference infamously produced almost no concrete offers to shelter refugees. Its one accomplishment was the establishment of a new intergovernmental organization, called the Intergovernmental Committee on Refugees (IGCR), whose mission was to continue searching the world for a refugee haven.[26]

Unlike the League of Nations High Commission for Refugees (established in 1922), the IGCR was empowered to negotiate directly with the Nazis to establish "conditions of orderly emigration." The organization's first director was the American lawyer and diplomat George Rublee. Rublee opened negotiations with Hjalmar Schacht, president of the German Central Bank, and then with Helmut Wohltat of the German Ministry of Finance. The agreement they hammered out would have placed an estimated one-fourth of Jewish assets into a trust fund (around 1.5 million reichsmarks) that could then be used to purchase German equipment and goods to be taken abroad for settlement purposes. The remaining three-fourths of Jewish property and wealth would go to the Reich.[27] Not surprisingly, the plan was extremely divisive among Jewish agencies and the Allies themselves, since it effectively sanctioned the large-scale confiscation of Jewish property— and presumed that the Nazis were negotiating in good faith. The French senator Henry Bérenger ridiculed IGCR leaders for going "to Berlin every week or so to salute Hitler's—or is it Goering's—

behind." The World Jewish Congress meanwhile objected to any plan that "rewarded the Nazi regime with economic advantages in return for its policy of expropriation and expulsion."[28]

British and French diplomats were also concerned from the outset that any scheme in which the German government profited from Jewish emigration would create a moral hazard throughout Eastern Europe. Once the international community got into the business of facilitating Jewish emigration, they feared, Poland, Romania, and other East European countries would also demand international assistance with their own "Jewish problems."[29]

These fears were well-founded. In Poland, ever since the death of the Polish leader Józef Piłsudski in 1935, the government had taken an increasingly right-wing and anti-Semitic turn. An epidemic of pogroms erupted across the country beginning in 1935, along with anti-Semitic boycotts and decrees restricting Jewish participation in trade and the professions. Between March 1935 and January 1937, according to the JDC, 118 Polish Jews were killed and 1,350 were wounded in more than three hundred separate incidents of anti-Semitic violence. The violence was typically well organized, and appeared to be tolerated by both local authorities and highly placed members of the Polish government.[30]

At the same time, Polish officials were actively seeking out a territorial or colonial solution to their own "Jewish problem." By the mid-1930s, all of the major Polish political parties with the exception of the Social Democrats were actively promoting Jewish emigration.[31] In 1936, the Polish Senate discussed the issue. One speaker bluntly proclaimed, "Three and one half million Jews are too many for Poland, and one million of them should emigrate." On December 11, 1936, the Polish representative to the League of Nations, Tytus Komarnicki, demanded that the League help Poland reduce its Jewish population. He cited the "necessity of emigration for the Jewish masses . . . who can only with difficulty assimilate to the social evolution taking place in contemporary Poland." The Catholic press joined the campaign for what was referred to as the "evacuation" of Jews from Poland.[32]

Advocates of Jewish emigration in Poland tended to depict emigration as a "natural" flow toward demographic equilibrium. By naturalizing emigration, Polish officials depoliticized it. The Jewish flight from Poland, they insisted, was not a result of Polish anti-Semitism or politics; it was a force of nature. The Polish Foreign Ministry's information service thus insisted in 1938 on the need to "restart normal Jewish migratory currents, which are the result of natural economic and demographic processes." The Polish government also deflected responsibility for Jewish emigration by depicting it as an international problem, demanding an international solution, rather than a local problem caused by Polish anti-Semitism.[33]

In 1937, Polish hopes of exporting Jews reached a high point when Marius Moutet, French minister of colonies under Léon Blum's Popular Front government, announced his support for refugee resettlement in Madagascar.[34] The announcement was greeted with enthusiasm in Poland, and the government rushed to send a three-member team to Madagascar to survey prospects for Jewish settlement. The French government, alarmed by the overzealous Polish response, quickly qualified its offer. It had envisioned a small-scale settlement of a few hundred refugees already in France, not the mass expulsion of Polish Jews.[35]

The Polish-French Madagascar plan was shelved completely once Moutet was replaced as colonial minister in January 1938. That was partly because colonial authorities, along with French settlers and representatives of the Malagasy population, were opposed to it. The French newspaper Journal de Madagascar protested that Madagascar should not become "the 'human trash bin' for all of Europe's undesirables." Of course, this was not the end of the Madagascar plan; it was soon revived as the Nazis' own preferred solution to the "Jewish problem" until the end of 1940.[36]

Polish Jews generally saw the Madagascar plan for what it was—an effort, in the words of the Polish-Jewish (and pro-Zionist) newspaper *Nasz przeglad*, "to throw the Jews out of the civilized world." Polish Jews across the political spectrum denounced what they called "emigrationism" in the late 1930s. When the revisionist Zionist leader Vladimir Jabotinsky called for the "evacuation" of Polish Jews in the Polish conservative daily *Czas* in September 1936, it actually hurt the Zionist cause, setting off a maelstrom of protest from the Jewish press and political parties.[37] Anti-Zionist parties and groups such as the Jewish-socialist Bund, so-called assimilationists (including Communists), the Orthodox Agudas Israel and the diaspora nationalist Folkspartey were particularly incensed by calls for mass emigration. But the majority of Polish Zionists also objected to the notion that Jews could or should be "evacuated" en masse from Poland. They continued to insist on the need to protect the equal rights of Jews as citizens within Poland and maintained that any emigration should be gradual. In 1937, the annual convention of the Zionist Federation of Congress Poland passed a resolution denouncing the Polish government's emigration plans. Representatives of Polish Jewry also emphasized that if emigration was necessary, that was a function of the general crisis of overpopulation in Poland. The Bund leader Henryk Erlich thus insisted in 1937, "We Bundists do not deny the need for masses of Jews to emigrate, but we do deny that that need applies to Jews only."[38]

Neither Jewish protests nor the scuttled Madagascar plan deterred Polish authorities, however. Schemes to encourage the emigration of Polish Jews continued to circulate in Polish government circles in 1938 and 1939. Michael Glaser (also known as Michal Głazer), a Polish-Jewish diplomat, authored several proposals for Jewish emigration in the late 1930s. It was necessary, he held, to find "an integral and total solution—one which will settle the matter once and for all."[39] Specifically, Glaser called upon world leaders to come together and create an international plan by which "Poland can be relieved of this burden and of the center of inflammation by the removal of the excess Jewish population under a scheme of planned emigration. Such action will not only be highly advantageous for Poland, for the Jews inhabiting that country, but also for the world."[40]

The Evian Conference and the creation of the Intergovernmental Committee on Refugees in 1938 seemed to answer Glaser's call, as well as the hopes of the Polish government. Polish diplomats immediately lobbied the organization to include Polish Jews in any emigration scheme negotiated or sponsored by the IGCR.[41] But even as the Polish government insisted on the urgent necessity of Jewish emigration, policies on the ground made it difficult for Jews to leave the country. The largest interwar organization devoted to assisting Jewish emigration from Poland was the Jewish Emigration Society (JEAS, Żydowskie centralne towarzystwo emigracyjne w Polsce), affiliated with the Hebrew Immigrant Aid Society (HIAS). By November of 1937, Leon Alter, the director of JEAS, reported "a particularly intense demand for emigration that is taking on the character of a psychosis" among Polish Jews. The Polish government, however, hindered emigration in practice, by restricting the amount of capital Jews could take out of the country (in what amounted to a policy of systematic expropriation). These restrictions often left Jews unable to pay the fees demanded by countries of immigration. "At the moment we find ourselves before problems of exceptional severity," Alter lamented. "While our emigration committee is trying not to allow any possibility for emigration to escape, we must simultaneously resist all attempts to provoke a massive, chaotic, forced emigration."[42]

Czechoslovakia was widely seen at the time (and has been since) as an island of "Western," democratic values in East Central Europe, the only state not to fall victim to fascism. The state's leaders energetically promoted this image throughout the interwar years.[43] As we have seen, however, Czechoslovakia was also no haven for Jewish refugees by 1938. Even there, many began to suggest that emigration was the best "solution" to the "Jewish question."[44] In October of 1938, shortly after the Nazi occupation of the Sudetenland, the Czech newspaper *Národní osvobození* published an editorial by Professor Jan Kabelík of the University of Olomouc. Kabelík urged the Czechoslovak state to facilitate the emigration of all Jews from Czechoslovakia "for humanitarian and selfish reasons." Jewish and German emigration, he insisted, would bring economic relief to the country, since "every emigrating German or Jew means a job for a Czechoslovak."[45]

Many ordinary Czechs shared his opinion, including opponents of the Nazis. In March 1939, only a week after the Germans occupied what remained of Czechoslovakia and created the Protectorate of Bohemia and Moravia, a Czech antifascist wrote to a friend in England informing her about events at home. That friend, Doris Campbell, was at the time the foster mother of seven-year-old Milena Roth, a Jewish child who had escaped Czechoslovakia on a Kindertransport only months earlier. Campbell had met Milena's mother, Anka, in 1930 at an International Girl Guides' Jamboree and maintained contact ever since. Now she was trying to help Milena's parents emigrate to England. H.T. advised Campbell not "to get unduly worried" about the fate of Milena's family. "You would not be doing your country a very good service by taking these people in," he insisted. H.T. believed that the "Jewish question" could be solved only through mass emigration. "I really think personally, and my opinion is shared by many, that the whole question will have to be solved radically,

and that some portion of land will have to be given to them somewhere in the world, where they can at last live as a nation, among
themselves, occupying all positions, being servants and road
sweepers and smiths and everything, and not only businessmen
and bankers."⁴⁶

Romania also hoped to solve its "Jewish problem" by means
of emigration. As in Poland, anti-Semitic legislation and violence
proliferated in 1930s Romania. The government issued restrictions on Jewish participation in trade and industry as early as 1934.
Anti-Semitic measures multiplied with the rise of the fascist Iron
Guard and the right-wing National Christian Party, led by Octa-
vian Goga and Alexandru Cuza. In 1937, Goga became prime minister and rapidly issued a series of anti-Semitic decrees, barring
Jews from the civil service, closing Jewish newspapers, and confiscating some Jewish-owned property and land. A January 1938 law
required Jews to submit to a "review" of their citizenship, with the
goal of denaturalizing those who had become citizens after 1918.
More than 270,000 Romanian Jews were rendered stateless.⁴⁷ In
January 1939, Franklin Gunther Mott of the U.S. State Department
reported that "the attitude of the Rumanian Government is . . .
that this surplus population of non-citizen Jews must go," elabo-
rating that "the Rumanian government facilitates their emigration
in every way except in the transfer of funds, while obstructing the
emigration of ethnic Rumanians."⁴⁸

Romanian diplomats also requested international humanitarian assistance to deport Romanian Jews. In March 1939, Romanian
ministers demanded that the IGCR "devise some practical method
for the emigration of at least a small percentage of Rumanian
Jews." In response, a U.S. State Department official reassured his
Romanian colleagues that "the long range program of the Committee very definitely proposed migration of minorities from other
. . . East European countries."⁴⁹ In fact, the IGCR and Western allies

anticipated the need to resettle Jews from across Eastern Europe from the outset. In the words of Theodore Achilles of the U.S. Department of State, "The problem of refugees from Germany, great as it is, is merely a small part of the problem presented by the existence of seven million unwanted Jews between the Rhine and the Russian frontier. . . . A basic solution of the larger problem would unquestionably be a major contribution to European stability and world peace, worth using heroic measures to achieve."[50]

President Roosevelt was on the same page. He envisioned an ambitious transfer of populations that would solve both the immediate refugee crisis and the East European "Jewish problem" over the long term. "It must be frankly recognized that the larger Eastern European problem is basically a Jewish problem," he maintained in January 1939.

> The organized emigration from Eastern Europe over a
> period of years of young persons at the age which they enter
> actively into economic competition, and at which they may
> be expected to marry, is not beyond the bounds of possibility. The resultant decrease in economic pressure; the actual
> removal over a period years of a very substantial number of
> persons; the decrease in the birthrate and the natural operation of the death rate among the remaining older portion
> of the population should reduce the problem to negligible
> proportions.[51]

Roosevelt appointed the geographer Isaiah Bowman, then president of Johns Hopkins University, to lead the search for an appropriate refuge. Bowman had previously served on the U.S. delegation to the Paris Peace Conference in 1919, and was head of the American Geographical Society from 1915 to 1935. In the years 1938–42, Bowman directed a project at Hopkins to research possibilities for refugee resettlement around the globe. The goal of the project, in Roosevelt's words, was to locate "uninhabited or sparsely inhabited good agricultural lands to which Jewish colonies might be sent."[52]

Bowman and his team surveyed settlement sites on five continents, and his reports circulated widely in government and humanitarian circles. Not coincidentally, however, he did not seriously consider the United States as a potential destination (aside from a cursory examination of Alaska). Bowman firmly believed in eugenics and in natural racial hierarchies. He actually introduced a new Jewish quota at Johns Hopkins in 1942 and also banned African American undergraduates from the university. He was personally convinced that the United States had reached its "absorptive capacity" with respect to Jewish immigrants—even as he lamented declining birthrates among white, middle-class Americans.[53]

At the international level, then, the most critical years of the Jewish refugee crisis before World War II were spent searching the globe for a new refuge, dumping ground, or homeland for European Jews. The Madagascar plan remains the most infamous resettlement scheme, since the Nazis themselves favored it. But the IGCR, in cooperation with British, American, and Jewish agencies such as the JDC and the World Jewish Congress, considered a range of territories for potential Jewish resettlement. British Guiana, Angola, the Dominican Republic, Northern Rhodesia, Alaska, and the Philippines were among the most widely discussed possibilities. At huge expense, and in a nakedly colonial tradition, intergovernmental and humanitarian organizations dispatched teams of experts in agricultural science and tropical medicine on fact-finding missions to these far-flung destinations. They wined and dined dictators; surveyed the climate, soil, and "natives" in supposedly "underpopulated" lands; and speculated about whether urban Jews could be transformed into farmers who would "civilize" colonial outposts.

These fact-finding missions took place at the intersection of two long-standing debates about race: whether white people could thrive in the tropics and whether Jews were white.[54] The relative "whiteness" of Jews emerged as a central preoccupation in the emigration and refugee policies of the late 1930s. If Jews were white, in the racial logic of the time, they might not be able to withstand hard agricultural labor in a tropical climate. If Jewish refugees were not quite white, they might not be welcome in places like the Dominican Republic, where the dictator Rafael Trujillo was desperately seeking an influx of white settlers. In practice, the answers to these questions were unstable even across small distances of time and space. In Brazil, for example, Jewish immigrants were privileged as nonblack and discriminated against as nonwhite at the same time; a secret circular banned Jewish immigration to Brazil in 1937, but more Jews arrived there in 1938 than ever before, thanks in part to pressure from the United States and a competing, philosemitic view of Jews as economically useful.[55]

British Guiana was among the more serious candidates for Jewish resettlement. Colonial governors there were supposedly more enthusiastic about the prospect of Jewish immigration than French colonial rulers in Madagascar. The British government also seemed amenable, at least initially. Not coincidentally, Whitehall declared its openness to Jewish settlement in British Guiana one week before releasing the May 1939 White Paper announcing that Jewish emigration to Palestine would be limited to 75,000 for the next five years and would subsequently be regulated by Arab authorities.[56]

Julius Savit, a Jewish-American social worker and activist, was an ardent supporter of settlement in Guiana. In his report "Guiana as a Refuge," he praised the many advantages of the trop-

ics for Jewish settlement. Jews were "a tropically adaptable people by nature," he claimed. "If we consider further that the Jews
migrated from Egypt to Palestine, then were driven to Rome and
sunny Spain and that they have lately again succeeded in Palestine, we can hardly escape the conclusion that they are within the
orbit of that part of white mankind which is capable of adapting
itself to the tropics." As an added benefit, the alleged Jewish "aver-
sion to excessive use of liquor" would enable them to tolerate the
hot weather.[57]

Joseph A. Rosen of the American Joint Distribution Committee was also enthusiastic about the Guiana plan. He acknowledged
that Guiana suffered from poor soil, a lack of transport facilities, an unfavorable climate, and the risk of tropical diseases, but
insisted that it was "precisely on account of these disadvantages"
that mass Jewish settlement was possible. "Practically all of the
less primitive and more desirable or more suitable countries are
either occupied by existing local populations or are controlled by
governments who are not willing to open them for settlement by
refugees."[58] There were also critics of the Guiana plan, however—
especially among those who saw Jews as too "white" to thrive in
the subtropical climate there. Dr. Morton Kahn of Cornell Medical College, recently returned from three years in British Guiana,
asserted, "The menaces to life, particularly malaria, are so great in
number that it would be murder to settle white men there."[59]

In February 1938, the IGCR dispatched its own subcommittee of
colonial experts to British Guiana. On the eve of the expedition, the
committee chairman, Dr. Edward Ernst of the Pan-American Sanitary Commission, reported back to IGCR headquarters, "Tomor-
row we fly into the jungles, to stay maybe four or five weeks. We
have everything, hammocks, mosquito nets, two cooks, saddles for
horses up at Rupinimi, cigarettes, Scotch, and hard-tack. . . . Off
the record, it don't [sic] look good!"[60] The IGCR's British Guiana

subcommittee ultimately recommended beginning with a modest settlement of three to five thousand people. While this would not solve Europe's "Jewish problem" in its entirety, the settlement would serve an important experimental purpose, paving the way for future colonies. "It is essential to have experimental proof on a considerable scale that white people can perform relatively hard physical labor in this climate," the committee explained.[61]

Even this modest "experimental" plan was never realized, however. From the beginning, British authorities had insisted that any scheme for refugee emigration would have to be financed by outside sources. Then, in July of 1939, in a conversation with the U.S. State Department official Robert T. Pell, the IGCR's chairman, Lord Winterton of Britain, declared that the British government had no intention whatsoever of permitting the "mass settlement" of Jews in British Guiana or any of its colonies. At most, it would agree to tiny scattered colonies of 50 refugees here and there, "not forming a homogeneous mass of Jews." The change of heart was linked to fears that Guiana would set a precedent for Palestine, and that Jews might attempt to move from Guiana back to Britain after the war. Plans to erect a small experimental colony of 250 to 500 refugees in the autumn of 1939 were interrupted by the war.[62]

A similar fate befell plans to resettle Europe's Jews in Angola, the site most favored by Isaiah Bowman and Roosevelt. The IGCR hoped that the territory could be purchased for the purpose of Jewish settlement from the Portuguese government. As it turned out, Portugal had no interest in divesting itself of its colonial holdings and opposed Jewish settlement on any territory under its control. An official from the Portuguese embassy in Washington bluntly declared that there was "no Jewish problem in Portugal because Portugal had expelled the Jews in the Middle Ages."[63]

Racism may have thwarted visions of Jewish colonization in Madagascar, Guiana, and Angola. Ironically, however, racism also

opened the door to Jewish settlement in the Dominican Republic, which made the only concrete offer to admit Jewish refugees at
the Evian Conference. Generalissimo Rafael Trujillo's offer, motivated by his desire to increase the number of "white" settlers in the
Dominican Republic, is one of the most striking examples of how
humanitarianism and ethnic cleansing became entangled in the
years leading up to World War II.[64]

Trujillo first offered to admit European refugees to the Dominican Republic in 1935. He repeated his offer at Evian, declaring
his willingness to accept up to 100,000 refugees on short order. A
fact-finding delegation headed by the JDC's James N. Rosenberg
visited the island between March and April 1938, and President
Roosevelt endorsed the plan in October of that year. The JDC and
the Agro-Joint, established by the JDC in 1924 to resettle Jews in
the Crimea in the USSR, jointly organized and funded the project.
In December 1939, they created the Dominican Republic Settlement Association (DORSA) to carry it out. Rosenberg, the former
leader of the Agro-Joint, became DORSA's president; James Rosen,
the former director of the Agro-Joint's Crimean settlement project
on the ground, was named vice-president.[65]

Generalissimo Trujillo initially seemed an unlikely humanitarian benefactor. In 1937, only a year before the Evian Conference,
he had brutally massacred fifteen thousand Haitians. Now he was
seeking an influx of white settlers to replace them. He was also
hoping to curry favor with the West after his reputation had been
tarnished by the massacres.[66] "The primary desiderata in the eyes
of the Dominican Government are assimilable agricultural immigrants of near white race, obtainable at a minimum of expense,"
reported R. Henry Norweb, an American diplomat stationed in the
Dominican Republic.[67] Upon signing the settlement agreement,
Trujillo expressed his joy that the settlement would "bring to our
soil racial elements both capable and desirable."[68]

The Dominican settlement was established in Sosúa on a territory of about 26,000 acres. The land was a gift from the general himself. It had once housed a banana plantation (which had failed) and therefore possessed minimal infrastructure.[69] In spite of the lofty offer to accept 100,000 refugees, however, the colonists never numbered more than 500. The first 37 settlers arrived in Sosúa in May 1940, when war had already blocked European borders, sealed its ports, and rendered transportation across the Atlantic nearly impossible. The U.S. State Department was also partly responsible for choking off the flow of refugees to Sosúa. Although Roosevelt and the State Department initially supported the project, State Department officials quickly began to drag their feet when it came to issuing the necessary transit visas, fearful that the settlers would try to return to the United States and suspicious of potential "fifth columnists" and spies. After July 1941, the State Department ceased issuing transit visas altogether.[70]

Proponents of the Dominican settlement nonetheless seized on the trope of the colony as an experiment to argue that its significance transcended its size. The DORSA vice-president Joseph Rosen predicted that after the war, millions of people would be forced to seek new homes. The goal of DORSA was to determine concretely whether Europeans could do hard physical labor in subtropical conditions, as well as "whether they can be established there on a sufficiently high standard of living, considerably above the standards of the native laboring population, and be able to maintain these standards without continued help from the outside."[71] James Rosenberg agreed in 1940 that Sosúa's purpose was to prepare the ground for future Jewish colonization. "Whatever the outcome of the present war, students of world conditions are agreed that in the coming years there are bound to be mass movements of populations from overcrowded, war-torn countries in Europe. If those enslaved people can find new life in such fertile

Jewish settlers at Sosúa, Dominican Republic,
living in an agricultural settlement established
at the invitation of President Trujillo.
Courtesy of the American Jewish Joint Distribution Committee Archives.

undeveloped lands, some part, at least, of the world's sickness may be cured."[72] Humanitarianism, colonialism, and population transfers would go hand in hand.

The settlement was also supposed to contribute to the general goal of Jewish productivization. It would transform Jews into workers and farmers, proving their desirability to other potential lands of refuge. Writing for the New York German-Jewish newspaper *Aufbau*, Pat Frank affirmed this message after a 1941 visit to the colony. "This settlement is the 'test-tube' for colonization in the sparsely settled regions of the Western hemisphere and a source of real hope for the despairing," he proclaimed. "The theory that Jews do not make good agriculturalists does not hold in Sosúa. Things are growing under the hands of Jewish white-collar workers as if they were in a greenhouse. I saw 20 Jewish cowboys herding Sosúa's cattle with all the aplomb of Nebraskans, except for the cowboy's 'yippee.'"[73]

In order to raise money for the scheme—and bring the negotiations with Trujillo to a successful conclusion—JDC and IGCR officials conspired in the fiction that Trujillo's offer to admit Jews to the Dominican Republic was a purely humanitarian act. They were also obliged to promote an image of Trujillo himself as a benevolent and enlightened dictator. Following a visit to the Sosúa colony, N. Chanin of the *Jewish Daily Forward* reported that Trujillo was "conducting the domestic and foreign affairs of his country with intelligence and understanding. . . . Although he is a dictator, one can hardly feel the burden of dictatorship."[74]

In fact, the JDC was well aware that many of Trujillo's political enemies, including politicians, labor leaders, and students, had "disappeared" after his seizure of power in 1930. The Dominican parliament existed to rubber-stamp his policies, the labor movement had been suppressed, and there was no freedom of the press.[75] But Trujillo had promised Jewish refugees freedom from persecution, and democracy was out of fashion everywhere in the 1930s. Rosenberg personally was clearly seduced by the general's charm. While observing, "The Generalissimo is all-powerful," he insisted that he had "gone beyond being a military chieftain" and was "tackling large economic problems and improving the life of the Government." In his diary, he described one intoxicating evening of entertainment at Trujillo's estate:

We were ushered right into the reception held near the swimming pool at the rear of the house . . . outside there, in the light of the full moon and the surf less than 100 feet away, a perfect evening. . . . What a setting! . . . The roar of the surf was near. There were about 200 or 250 people at the party. A large orchestra; exceptionally good music. . . . I have never seen such continuous and overflowing hospitality.[76]

The irony of being saved by a racist was not lost on the colonists. In the words of Luis Hess, one of the settlers in Sosúa,

The person who wanted to help us was not a humanist. But did we have a choice? Hitler, the German racist, persecuted us and wanted to murder us. Trujillo, the Dominican racist, saved our lives. . . . We were in the awkward position of having to be thankful to a dictator. . . . I was grateful to Trujillo. If a murderer saves your life you still have to be grateful to the murderer.[77]

The intersection of racism and humanitarianism in the Dominican Republic project was perhaps extreme. It was nonetheless typical in the larger context of East European emigration politics in this period. In Poland in 1939, for example, the Jewish activist Majer Pollner wrote a tract in which he speculated that Western colonial powers would open their territories to Jewish settlement in order to combat the "inevitable danger of flooding by the yellow race." Jews, in other words, would be seen as desirable settlers by virtue of their relative whiteness.[78] Debates about the relative merits of Jewish colonization in Argentina, Angola, or Palestine ran parallel to long-standing discussions about the possibilities for Austrian, Polish, or Czech settlement in Brazil, Tahiti, and New Orleans. Jewish settlement plans were likewise inextricable from European imperialism and its hierarchies, even when they took shape in response to racial persecution. These resettlement schemes generally effaced the presence of native inhabitants with the assertion that the lands to be settled were "underpopulated" or "undeveloped."[79] Opponents of Jewish settlement outside of Europe were no less anxious than their Czech and Polish peers about the imagined dangers of racial mixing and degeneration. Hans Klein, an Austrian territorialist, opposed Jewish settlement in the tropics in 1937, on the basis of his conviction that Jews would be reduced to colonial labor. "They will sink to the level of Coolies and their wives will mix with the Negroes!" he warned.[80]

The majority of the resettlement plans so extensively researched and debated on the eve of World War II saved few lives. Most Jews who successfully escaped the Nazi empire found refuge in Palestine, the United States, or Great Britain—not Guiana, Angola, Madagascar, or the Dominican Republic. And for most of the international community, investigating and plotting fanciful emigration schemes substituted for the kind of action that would have saved lives, like lifting quotas and issuing visas.[81]

HUMANITARIANISM AND ETHNIC CLEANSING also intersected at a more local level in the late 1930s and the 1940s. In November 1938, Czechoslovak authorities established the Czech Institute for Refugee Welfare under the aegis of the Ministry for Social Welfare. This institute was charged both with assisting the tens of thousands of Czech refugees flowing into the Czech rump state and with facilitating the emigration of Jews and other national minorities. In January 1939, it even sponsored a mission to Rhodesia in the hope of resettling Jewish and German refugees from Czechoslovakia there (another far-fetched refugee resettlement project that went nowhere).[82]

The director of the refugee institute was Lev Zavřel, former chief of the Czechoslovak Ministry for Social Welfare's emigration division. The institute's emigration department actually assumed the functions (and absorbed the staff) of the interwar emigration department, with one crucial difference. In interwar Czechoslovakia, the goals of emigration policy had been to prevent the emigration of Czechs and Slovaks and to protect the welfare of Czechoslovak emigrants abroad. Now its goals were to encourage and assist the emigration of Jews and Germans and to rob them of their property on their way out.

The Institute for Refugee Welfare is best known for administering the £4 million gift from the British government to Czechoslovakia to facilitate refugee emigration (the so-called Stopford action), which is credited with getting up to twelve thousand Jews out of Czechoslovakia before the war began.[83] The Stopford gift entitled each emigrant to receive up to £200 pounds (or the equivalent in the currency of their destination country) as well as help with transportation costs. Emigrants who had additional funds available were allowed to exchange up to 50,000 crowns, subject to a "tax" not exceeding 30 percent of the total. The confiscated funds were supposed to be used to pay for the emigration of other, more destitute refugees.[84]

After World War II, former employees claimed that the refugee institute had always been a resistance organization, illegally and secretly engaged in anti-Nazi activity. "The Institute worked in a spirit of faith in a better future and in resistance to all of the evils committed throughout all of the long years of the occupation," proclaimed Ružena Pelantová in a 1945 essay. According to Pelantová, the institute had also remained entirely under Czech control throughout the war. "The Institute for Refugee Welfare . . . was one of the only small state agencies that remained solely in the hands of Czech officials and where German oversight was only very superficial," she insisted.[85]

But under the banner of humanitarianism, the Czech Institute for Refugee Welfare also systematically worked to cleanse Czechoslovakia of Jews and Germans and to confiscate Jewish businesses and homes in order to transfer them to the hands of Czech refugees. The institute thereby carried out a central goal of interwar emigration policy, encouraging the emigration of national minorities and protecting the interests of Czech migrants. Like the IGCR at the international level, it seamlessly blended a humanitarian mission with the pursuit of a nationally homogeneous state.

The Institute for Refugee Welfare began to encourage and organize the emigration of Jews—including Czechoslovak Jews—several months before the Nazis occupied what remained of Czechoslovakia and created the Protectorate of Bohemia and Moravia on March 15, 1939. In January 1939, an institute memo explained that in addition to 10,000 to 15,000 foreign Jewish refugees in Czechoslovakia, there were thousands of Czechoslovak Jews "who will want to emigrate and will have to emigrate."[86] With the Nazi annexation of the Protectorate there was little change in the personnel or policies of the institute. Lev Zavřel remained at the helm and professed his eagerness to work with the Nazi regime to solve the "Jewish problem." "As leader of the emigration department of the Institute for Refugee Welfare, I want to work in full agreement with the interests of the Reich and the Protectorate, and in the closest possible cooperation with the German authorities, particularly the Gestapo, toward the solution of this problem," he declared in June 1939.[87]

A major task of the institute was to locate housing and employment for the thousands of Czech refugees from the Sudetenland and territories lost to Hungary, Poland, and Slovakia. In June 1939, a few months after the establishment of the Protectorate, Zavřel ordered local Czech officials to proactively seek out Jewish homes and businesses that could be confiscated and transferred into the hands of homeless or unemployed Czech refugees. Local officials were required to report each month on the number of Jewish businesses and apartments successfully transferred into Czech hands. Zavřel suggested that local officials put Jewish business owners directly in contact with individual refugees and that the two parties attempt to negotiate a "voluntary" agreement for the quick sale of Jewish property to the Czech refugees.[88]

Czech refugees quickly got wind of the opportunity and began to write directly to the institute to request Jewish businesses, jobs, and homes.[89] Local officials reported varying degrees of success in carrying out the order, however. Reading between the lines, some may have been hesitant to take the initiative in confiscating Jewish property. Other district officials declared that local Czechs had already claimed all of the Jewish businesses, so none remained for refugees.[90] Authorities in Roudnice nad Labem reported that they had approached all of the twenty-eight Jewish shop owners in their district and asked them to "voluntarily" sell their businesses to Czech refugees. The shop owners refused to cooperate. "All of the business owners declared that they would not voluntarily transfer their businesses, since their successful businesses were the fruit of a lifetime of hard work, there was not yet any legal order for the confiscation of Jewish property, and their stores were the only means they had to make a living." The officials requested "further instructions."[91] Zavřel replied that if "voluntary" negotiations between Jewish business owners and refugees "did not achieve their goal," cases should be referred to Czech provincial authorities, which had been empowered by a Protectorate decree of June 21, 1939, to seize Jewish property.[92]

New opportunities to transfer Jewish property into Czech hands arose with the creation of the Terezín concentration camp–ghetto in November 1941. In early spring 1942, Reichsprotektor Reinhard Heydrich ordered that all Czech residents of the garri-

son town of Terezín be evacuated to make room for the incoming Jewish inmates. The Institute for Refugee Welfare, responsible
for relocating these Czechs, quickly sought to resettle them in the
homes and businesses of deported Jews. Once again, the institute
was proactive, sending requests to district officials around Prague
for lists of Jewish apartments and businesses. Czech citizens of
Terezín themselves petitioned the Interior Ministry to be allocated Jewish homes and shops. As of April 1942, the institute had
secured seventy-five Jewish homes for refugees in Prague alone,
but continued to seek out more Jewish homes and businesses in the
areas surrounding Prague.[93]

Was the Institute for Refugee Welfare a "humanitarian" organization to be credited with rescuing Jews? Or a collaborationist
organization that facilitated the expropriation and deportation of
Jews from Czechoslovakia? It was arguably both at the same time.
This was no paradox. Like their colleagues at the international
level, the institute's employees amplified the logic of interwar
emigration politics. That logic saw the emigration of undesirable
or "surplus" minority groups as a means of solving political and
social problems, and as an opportunity for the social advance-
ment of nationally "desirable" citizens. In the end, there was a very
thin line between the rescue, deportation, and expropriation of
Czechoslovakia's Jewish population, just as there was an ambigu-
ous frontier between rescue and removal at the international level.

THE CONTINUITIES BETWEEN the emigration policies of
the interwar era and refugee experiences during the Second
World War were not only ideological in nature. The networks
established through decades of emigration—long-lost siblings,
cousins, and uncles in Palestine or the United States, in particular—became lifelines years later. Seymore Zryb's father emi-

grated to America in 1927 and brought the rest of the family over to join him in 1935. Seymore was ten at the time. He never knew why his father had decided to leave Poland, but he knew that the decision had saved his life. "Somehow he had a sister living in Brooklyn and she must have talked him into coming here or something. The reason for his leaving, I don't know. . . . It was a stroke of genius, I suppose."[94]

Those *without* such connections or networks often resorted to searching the New York City phone book, appealing to the charity of random people with the same last name (or even without the same name).[95] Above all, refugees sought an "affidavit" from an American citizen—a guarantee of financial support. "One often hears the joke here (which is dead serious) that the biggest Jewish holiday is 'Affidavit Arrival Day.' I am therefore appealing to you so that I can also celebrate this holiday," wrote Otto Braun of Prague in one such letter. Braun got lucky: his American stranger happened to be Isidore Popper, a surgical instruments importer in the Bronx who signed thirty-two affidavits for Jews in Czechoslovakia and Austria, many total strangers. And yet, Affidavit Arrival Day was far from a guarantee of survival, because the U.S. quota for Czechoslovakia was 2,700 per year (compared with 27,000 for Germany). By 1938, the waiting list was two to three years long. Popper's own brother, sister, and their children all secured affidavits: he even hired an expensive immigration lawyer to expedite their cases. Their quota numbers never came up. They were all deported and murdered in Auschwitz, with the exception of a nephew who survived as a Kapo.[96] "What is a man without papers? Rather less, let me tell you, than papers without a man!" Joseph Roth observed in 1937. The deadly paper walls erected in the West created what Roth called a "metaphysical afflication" for European Jews. "You're a transient and you're stuck, a refugee and a detainee; condemned to rootlessness and unable to budge."[97]

The laws used to expropriate Jewish emigrants also built on interwar precedents. The so-called Reich flight tax (*Reichsflucht-steuer*) had actually been established in 1931 in Germany, by the republican Weimar government, as a way to deter emigration and preserve foreign currency. The law provided for the confiscation of 25 percent of emigrants' wealth by the state if the emigrant earned more than 200,000 reichsmarks per year.[98] That law was extended by the Nazi regime, and gradually radicalized to become an instrument of systematic plunder. In the fiscal year ending March 31, 1939, the Reich collected 343,625,521 reichsmarks from the flight tax, compared with 1,938,000 reichsmarks in 1931–32. As of April 1939, the only valuables emigrants could legally take from the Third Reich were their wedding bands, two four-piece sets of cutlery per person, a silver wristwatch or pocket watch, and no more than 200 grams per person of other silver articles.[99] When the Nazis extended the flight tax to the Protectorate of Bohemia and Moravia, they justified it with the same arguments that had supported emigration restrictions for decades. Refugees had benefited from the state's "investment" in their education and welfare. They therefore "owed" the state a tax when leaving, in order to pay back that investment.[100]

These continuities should not tarnish genuine humanitarian efforts—many of which saved thousands of Jewish lives. To the refugees whose lives were saved by the opportunity to populate the Dominican Republic, the rationale behind the visa mattered very little. Jewish refugees could not afford to reject offers of asylum on principle. Refugees and humanitarian organizations were relatively powerless compared with the government authorities that issued visas, and compared to the Nazi regime itself.

But in order to understand why so little was done to save Jewish refugees, even once the immediate menace to their lives was apparent, it is necessary to understand the logic of population politics in the 1930s, itself an outgrowth of decades of emigration policies. That logic envisioned the large-scale emigration of Jews as a "humanitarian" solution to the "Jewish problem" in Europe. Well before the Nazis occupied Eastern Europe, moreover, many Polish, Czech, Romanian, and Hungarian officials and citizens had been hoping (and planning) for the evacuation of Jews from their territory. It is therefore hardly surprising that there was so little organized protest when Hitler fulfilled these fantasies.

As the intentions of the Nazis became apparent, the moral imperative to help Jews emigrate from Europe became increasingly pressing. And yet the long-term convergence of population politics and emigration policies was also a trap in the 1930s. The ideal of emigration as a "solution" to social and political problems shaped the possibilities available—both to refugees and to those who sought to assist them. It not only determined the (very limited) opportunities for escape and survival available to individual Jewish refugees; it also determined, in many cases, who escaped and who didn't. Emigration schemes almost universally privileged some groups and individuals over others. If the ideal of humanitarianism might seem to dictate that the most vulnerable individuals be saved first (the weak, the sick, the elderly, the young), it was very often those seen as the most robust who actually got out. "Dr. Trone asked me if I was afraid of hard work. He chose me because I was young and strong," recalled Heinrich Wasservogel, one of the lucky few selected to pioneer the Sosúa colony.[101]

Emigration schemes continued to capture the imagination of policymakers throughout the war, guided by the same blend of colonial thinking, population politics, and humanitarianism. In 1940, American delegates to the International Labor Organization's conference in Havana speculated about the situation when the war finally ended: "We shall have on the one hand large numbers of people who will be seeking a new area of the earth's surface in which to live and work and on the other hand areas in the Western Hemisphere where the soil is fertile and economic opportunities exist. The problem . . . will be, and is, to bring together soil and the man who is to till it."[102] Out of war, human misery, and mass displacement, they hoped, a new and better world would be born.

CHAPTER FIVE

Work Will Set You Free

On April 18, 1945, as the Soviet army advanced on Berlin, the French prefect of Meurthe-et-Moselle in Lorraine had more immediate concerns. The Nazi occupation of Alsace-Lorraine had left human traces: thousands of Polish slave laborers imported to cultivate land expropriated from French farmers. Much to his frustration, the Poles refused to continue working after the Nazi defeat. "These deportees are distinguished by their flagrant laziness, as they systematically refuse all work," he complained. The presence of an American military base nearby was not helping matters. Polish women preferred to do domestic work for American soldiers—for which they were compensated with goods profitably sold on the black market. In addition, the prefect asserted, "Too many of these young women complement the family revenue through prostitution."

The prefect threatened to intern the Polish laborers in concentration camps, but this hardly motivated them. "The Poles, warned of the creation of such a camp, did not manifest any more enthusiasm for work. Their misconduct in all domains continued all the more," he reported. Worse still, the displaced Poles seemed in no hurry to return home. They even appealed to local charities, "vehemently" demanding "clothing, beds, tables, chairs, furnaces and everything else necessary for what appears to be their permanent installation here." Local police subsequently attempted to round up 383 Poles for deportation back to Poland. They managed to capture only 16; the rest had been warned in advance and managed to escape. In this town, Poles were welcome only insofar as they made a seamless transition from slave labor to migrant worker.[1]

AT THE END OF the Second World War, millions of unsettled people clogged Europe's battered roads and bombed-out train stations. Demobilized soldiers and prisoners of war crossed paths with ethnic Germans as they fled the Red Army or were expelled from their homes. Liberated concentration camp inmates shared bunks with former forced laborers. Parents searched for the children they had lost in the chaos of flight or deportation. Most had one goal: to get home as quickly as possible.

The vast majority of the unsettled, called displaced persons, or DPs, in United Nations parlance, hailed from Eastern Europe. By September 1945, Allied military authorities and the United Nations Relief and Rehabilitation Administration had provided assistance to around 7,270,000 displaced Soviet laborers and POWs, 1,610,000 Poles, 1,807,000 French, 696,000 Italians, 389,000 Yugoslavs, 348,000 Czechs, and 285,000 Hungarians. During the spring and summer of 1945 alone, over 10,000,000 DPs made their way home by train, truck, or foot.[2]

Immediately after the liberation, thousands of Jewish refugees also trekked back to Eastern Europe to search for surviving relatives and reclaim their property. They did not typically receive a warm welcome. Neighbors who had appropriated Jewish homes, furniture, and businesses often had no intention of returning the loot. A June 1946 pogrom in Kielce, Poland, left 40 Jews dead and many more wounded, hastening the flight of at least 200,000 Jews. Ironically, most of the survivors found temporary refuge in the American zone of occupied Germany, from which they hoped to get to Palestine.[3]

Other East Europeans refused to return home for personal or political reasons. Some had collaborated with the Nazi regime and were afraid of being tried as traitors. Simply being taken prisoner by the Wehrmacht was seen as an act of treason by the Soviet government. Others objected to the newly installed Communist regimes in the East. Many simply wanted to join relatives abroad or make a fresh start someplace new. With the Communist seizure of power in Eastern Europe, another wave of refugees headed toward occupied Germany and Austria. Almost all of the one million refugees who remained on German soil a year after the liberation were from Eastern Europe.

Millions more were forcibly uprooted from their homes after the war ended. The removal of Germans from the East had begun in the death throes of the Third Reich. As the Red Army advanced, Germans fled or were evacuated westward. At the Yalta Conference in February 1945 and the Potsdam Conference in July 1945, the Allies laid the foundation for further population transfers. They also agreed to Soviet demands for Polish territory east of the Curzon line, compensating Poland for the loss with a large chunk of eastern Germany. Some three million Germans were expelled from Czechoslovakia, and another seven million fled or were expelled from Poland.

The Potsdam agreements decreed that these expulsions were to be carried out in an "orderly and humane" manner, but neither order nor humanity was in evidence. Germans from Czechoslovakia and Poland, most of whom had been settled in the region for generations, were generally gathered into concentration camps to await deportation. They were deprived of their property, stripped of their citizenship, and forced to wear armbands designating them as Germans. Before being shipped "home to the Reich" in cattle cars, they were subjected to forced labor and starvation rations. Many were beaten, raped, or tortured; hundreds were simply shot and dumped into mass graves.[4]

These expulsions formed part of the broader current of ethnic unmixing in Eastern Europe after the war. Around 1,500,000 Poles who lived on the Soviet side of the Polish-Soviet border were deported west, while 482,000 Ukrainians were "repatriated" to the Soviet Union. Another 140,000 Ukrainians were forcibly resettled in Poland's western territories in a violent wave of deportations between April and June 1947. Some 89,000 Slovaks were swapped with at least 70,000 Hungarians across the Hungarian-Czechoslovak border. Homogeneous nation-states, the Allies believed, would make Europe a more peaceful, democratic place.[5]

THE UNSETTLED MILLIONS tramped through landscapes of dust and rubble. Arriving in Cologne in July 1945, the British official and writer Stephen Spender reported, "My first impression on passing through the city was of there being not a single house left. There are plenty of walls, but these walls are a thin mask in front of the damp, hollow, stinking emptiness of the gutted interiors." The city's physical destruction, he claimed, mirrored the psychological state of its residents. "The ruin of the city is reflected in the internal ruin of its inhabitants, who, instead of being lives that can form a scar over the city's wounds, are parasites sucking at a dead carcass, digging among the ruins for hidden food."[6]

In Eastern Europe, the Nazi occupation had left obscene trails of destruction. In Yugoslavia, 25 percent of vineyards, 50 percent of livestock, and 60 percent of roads had been ruined. Polish cities were virtually uninhabitable. The Nazis had razed more than 85 percent of Warsaw, the nation's capital, along with 55 percent of Gdansk, the country's major port. Only one in six farms could harvest crops, and 75 percent of railway tracks were damaged.

The destruction of infrastructure was dwarfed by the loss of human lives. Poland lost approximately one in five of its pre-war citizens to the war; Yugoslavia one in eight, the USSR one in eleven—a staggering twenty million people. The casualty rate in Western Europe paled in comparison: France lost less than 2 percent of its population, the United Kingdom less than 1 percent, and the United States a mere one-third of 1 percent. Stalin expected to be compensated for this sacrifice in blood with control of Eastern Europe. This was in fact a fait accompli, since his armies were already stationed on the ground in most of Eastern Europe by the time the postwar settlement was negotiated.[7]

Reconstruction was the first priority of European leaders in both the East and the West. It was an immense task, to be sure, but they considered it an opportunity as well as a challenge. Destruction brought with it the chance to remake populations, cities, and states in a new image. Europe's refugees were particularly instrumental to both the reconstruction and the reinvention of European societies after World War II. They forced policymakers to answer difficult questions about how citizenship would be defined in a postfascist world. What criteria would be used to include or exclude migrants, refugees, and citizens in Europe's postwar states?

Allied leaders began to address these questions well before the war ended. In 1943, they created the United Nations Relief and Rehabilitation Administration (UNRRA). The agency was called (and soon became) a "United Nations" agency, but it preceded the founding of the actual United Nations in 1945. UNRRA's charge was to dispense immediate relief to refugees and to help them get home as quickly as possible. As Cold War divisions solidified, however, fewer migrants were willing to return to Eastern Europe. In 1947, UNRRA was replaced by the International Refugee Organization (IRO), which concentrated on resettling refugees who would not or could not return to their countries of origin.[8]

Once again, government leaders and international organizations imagined emigration as a utopian solution to the world's problems. J. Donald Kingsley, director general of the IRO, was convinced that overpopulation in Europe had been a major cause of the rise of fascism in Europe. The ongoing presence of millions of refugees in Europe threatened the Continent's future security, in his view. "One of the foremost threats to the maintenance of a democratic system and of peace is the existence for any extended time of large pools of human misery in the midst of plenty," he claimed in 1951. "Mussolini and Hitler were, to a very large degree, the products of such misery." Kingsley envisioned the mass departure of refugees from Europe as both a humanitarian solution to the refugee crisis and an impetus to "development" and progress. "The millions of 'surplus' men, women, and children who now burden the relief rolls and lengthen the queues of the unemployed across the face of Europe, could and would contribute enormously to the wealth, the strength, and the progress of the free world if means could be found to transport them to those broad areas where their talents and skills are in great demand." Under his direction, he hoped, the IRO would transform "fretfully idle" East European refugees into productive workers and citizens who would rebuild the "free world."[9]

AS KINGSLEY'S WORDS suggest, the movement of people from east to west after World War II was once again embedded in a broader discussion about the meaning of freedom and free labor. It was a debate that seemed particularly urgent in the aftermath of the war, as Europeans grappled with the legacy of slavery on

European soil. During the war, the words "Arbeit macht frei"—
"Work will set you free"—hung above the iron gates of Auschwitz.
After the war, these words became a potent symbol of Nazi cyni-
cism and cruelty. In Eastern Europe, the Nazi conscription of Slavs
into forced labor confirmed the worst fears of policymakers about
emigration, justifying new and more draconian restrictions on
mobility after the war ended. Western officials and humanitarian
workers meanwhile depicted forced labor in Hitler's Germany and
"slavery" in the socialist East as signature abuses of human rights
by "totalitarian" regimes.[10]

Many humanitarian workers and government officials worried
that former forced laborers and concentration camp inmates had
been irreparably damaged by wartime trauma. Refugees—like the
Polish workers staked out in Alsace-Lorraine after the war—often
seemed resistant to work and suspicious of all authority. Social
workers, psychologists, and policymakers feared that Europe's refugee camps would become sites of criminality, prostitution, and
psychological disarray.[11] Yet they also saw displaced persons as a
potential resource. Properly rehabilitated, they were the construction workers who could rebuild bombed-out city buildings, the
agricultural laborers who would replant the earth, and the children who would repopulate decimated nations.

In particular, an imagined connection between political freedom and free labor shaped the politics of refugee relief and resettlement after World War II. European relief workers and government
officials insisted that work was essential to the reconstruction of
European societies at large and to the rehabilitation of individual
refugees. East European refugees ostensibly needed to relearn the
virtue of self-government in order to become productive citizens.
The American Federation of International Institutes thus insisted
in 1949 that East European refugees required a gradual "education
for freedom." "For those who experienced capture, imprisonment

in camps, were driven to work as slave laborers, then rescued only to be again located in camps and there live a dependent and regimented existence . . . a too complete plunge into uprooted liberty becomes a frightening experience," the federation insisted. "The fast moving currents of American life become too much for their unpracticed powers of independent decision."[12]

But humanitarian workers suspected that many former forced laborers lacked the self-discipline necessary for free labor or democratic citizenship. In 1948, an IRO social worker accompanied a group of DPs on their voyage from Germany to their new homes in Canada and the United States. The DPs were required to work on the ship, presumably to pay their way across the Atlantic. But on the first day, out of one hundred emigrants assigned to work, only twelve turned up. Refugee women allegedly refused to scrub ship compartments and decks. "On each transport there are of course quite a few people who really work well and hard during the whole trip," the frustrated escort reported. "Unfortunately these hard-working people are usually outnumbered by those who are just too plain lazy to work." She ultimately resorted to compulsion. On future voyages, DPs who refused to work on board were denied meal tickets.[13]

This pattern repeated itself. Even as the Western Allies denounced Nazi practices of forced labor, they resorted to various degrees of compulsion to put refugees to work.[14] As early as November 1945, DPs were required to work for their keep in the French zone of occupied Germany. In the British zone, labor was mandatory for DPs beginning in 1947. Those who refused to work could be prosecuted and lose their welfare benefits.[15] As of 1948, the IRO required displaced men between the ages of sixteen and sixty-five and women aged sixteen to fifty-five to work. Henceforth, refugees who "make no serious effort to support themselves" would not be entitled to IRO assistance.[16]

Since forced labor had been discredited as a "totalitarian" evil, Allied authorities and humanitarian workers tended to portray work as a therapeutic activity. Work would set refugees free from their own traumatic pasts and give them hope for the future. Work was also supposed to save refugees from the perceived vices of camp life: gambling, alcoholism, promiscuity, and trading on the black market. The 1945 UN "Report on Psychological Problems of Displaced Persons" suggested that while "forced work has a familiar and unpleasant flavor for displaced people," assignments such as peeling potatoes, doing laundry, and constructing barracks could produce therapeutic wonders. These tasks would teach refugees how to establish "effective working relationships with others," as well as how to share "social responsibility" and to acquire "a sense of social purpose and worth."[17]

From a purely pragmatic perspective, the ability to work often determined a refugee's prospects for resettlement. Most emigration schemes for DPs privileged individuals with specific occupational skills. The problem was that a significant number of displaced persons did not have the skills demanded by host countries. Many had spent the prime years of their youth in hiding, in exile, or in concentration camps. Some had received no education or vocational training at all.

The UN and other voluntary organizations attempted to address this problem by organizing vocational training programs in refugee camps. These programs were intended to serve two purposes: warding off refugee "idleness" and "demoralization," and preparing refugees for new lives abroad. The preamble of the IRO constitution stipulated that one of the organization's primary missions was to provide refugees and displaced persons with "useful employment in order to avoid the evil and anti-social consequences of continued idleness."[18] IRO vocational training centers thus sought to "inculcate in the Displaced Person an appreciation of the dignity of work" and "to restore and/or maintain their morals" as well as improve their chances of resettlement.[19]

By July of 1948, the IRO had established seven residential vocational training centers and eight subsidiary centers in the American zone, along with sixteen training centers in the British zone. Not surprisingly, the training programs tended to promote traditional gender roles. In the wake of the wartime disruption of "normal" family life, anchoring men in the workplace and women in the home was itself supposed to heal wartime trauma. While vocational courses for men focused on construction, mechanics, and farming, women were encouraged to study homemaking, nursing, garment making, and typing.[20] Women were also supposed to find psychic relief in housework. Cooking and cleaning in refugee camps, UN workers insisted, would provide "useful outlets for women's domestic interests that will have an important rehabilitative effect."[21]

Fears about DP "idleness" meanwhile reflected relief workers' specific concerns about impaired masculinity. Camp life, they believed, posed a severe threat to the masculinity of refugees who were deprived of their roles as breadwinners. Social workers worried that idle men were likely to spend their time drinking, playing cards, engaged in black-market activity, or worse.[22]

Jewish philanthropic organizations made special efforts to provide Jewish refugees with vocational training. These programs reflected the specific concerns of the Jewish community in the aftermath of genocide. The largest and most ambitious programs were run by ORT (Obshestvo Remeslenofo zemledelcheskofo Truda), originally founded in Russia in 1880 to provide Jews with vocational and agricultural skills. After the First World War, ORT expanded its activity throughout Europe, the United States, and Canada. During the Second World War, the organization continued to offer vocational courses for Jews interned in the Warsaw ghetto until its liquidation.

ORT was reborn in occupied Germany after the Nazi defeat. The first courses were up and running in the Landsberg DP camp, in the American zone, in the autumn of 1945. Jacob Oleski, former director of the ORT school in Kovno, led the program, which was staffed by a number of East European Holocaust survivors. By 1947, ORT had established seven hundred schools throughout Europe, training over 22,634 students. Like UN training centers, ORT courses aimed to go well beyond the teaching of vocational skills, however. They were also intended to serve higher causes, including the collective regeneration of European Jewry and the psychological rehabilitation of traumatized survivors. In the tradition of other "productivist" efforts to reorient Jews professionally, ORT was determined to transform Jewish youth into farmers and workers rather than into merchants or professionals.[23]

Zionists, meanwhile, took steps to train the pioneers who would settle Palestine. In the words of Samuel Gringauz, president of the Congress of Liberated Jews in the American zone, "The importance of the school centers is in the fact that they . . . inspired an ideology which will become the foundation of the national rebirth of the Jewish people."[24] Jacob Oleski also hoped that vocational work could alleviate the psychological suffering of individual refugees. "We must give camp residents a purpose. They must have the feeling that everywhere there are things to do," he insisted. "This is the only way we can prevent our fellow sufferers from letting their minds atrophy and become even more demoralized. . . . It is only through productive, creative work that we can lessen our anger at having lost so many years."[25]

Most refugees were eager to support themselves and restart their lives. They did not necessarily seize the opportunity to receive vocational or agricultural training, however. Many refugee youths, who had been deprived of schooling during the war, were hungry for higher education. Others were exhausted from years of forced labor and frustrated by the mandate to accept menial jobs. American immigration authorities urged social workers to remind refugees "at every opportunity" of "the fact that all honest work is respected in America and there is no stigma attached to either manual labor, farm work, or domestic service."[26] In defense of its policy of discouraging higher education, an IRO manual explained, "Experience has shown that reception countries prefer skilled workers and put up barriers against the immigration of persons with higher educational diplomas and/or university degrees."[27]

Humanitarian workers themselves tended to pathologize refugees who resisted manual labor. Louise Holborn, the IRO's historian, attributed low enrollments in IRO vocational courses to refugees "of low intellectual level, who had become accustomed to idleness and were apathetic or antagonistic to the discipline and hard work required."[28]

American social workers claimed that they were doing refugees a disservice if they catered to their educational or professional ambitions. "If we assume that the man is physically able to work and is not 'mentally ill' . . . but the newcomer refuses it—and yet we continue assistance—we are supporting him in an 'unreal' situation—and continuing a pattern of dependency," argued Beatrice Behrman, a social worker affiliated with the United Service for New Americans, in Baltimore. Persuading recalcitrant refugees to embrace free labor often required a degree of compulsion, however. "Proper use of authority is sometimes a valid approach—since it may be the only thing the individual understands."[29]

The expectation that refugees would accept any work offered rendered them vulnerable to exploitation. In a letter to the IRO, Lillian Taylor of Lapeer, Michigan, described the "free labor" that awaited refugees in her town. After reading an article in the local newspaper about a family of Estonian DPs newly settled in Lapeer, she paid them a neighborly visit. "I found them on Kenneth Anderson's muck-farm; a man and wife and 17-year-old daughter from the camp Bad Geislingen. . . . The man—past middle age— knew nothing about farming, and apparently did not want to farm. Only the daughter spoke English. They could not have landed in a more desolate, god-forsaken spot." The family's new home con- sisted of a single room in the attic above the kitchen, which they shared with another family. There was no heat. The only furniture was two cots and one dresser, not counting the old batteries and tires heaped in the corner.[30]

Economic logic generally set the limits of humanitarian sol- idarity in postwar Europe. The employment contracts offered to refugees were often highly restrictive, designed to keep them in low-paid or undesirable jobs for as long as possible. Belgium's "Operation Black Diamond" imported 32,000 DPs as miners, but required them to work a full two years in the mines before they were allowed to seek employment elsewhere. As of 1949, 8,000 had returned to refugee camps in Germany, unable to tolerate the harsh conditions.[31] Other employment programs were similarly restrictive. Britain's "Westward Ho!" program enabled 82,000 migrants from Eastern Europe to emigrate to the UK, but confined refugees to employment in mining, textiles, agriculture, or domes- tic service, rather than allowing them to move freely between jobs or professions.

The French government, with its ongoing anxieties regarding population growth, was initially among the most eager to recruit DP labor. The French military commander Pierre Koenig imme- diately recognized that East European DPs "represent a human and labor resource that we will have a high interest in using to the advantage of our country," and he urged French authorities to recruit the best workers. In 1948, the French government even set up its own vocational training courses for refugees in the French zone of occupied Germany.[32] Conditions for foreign workers in postwar France were notoriously poor, however, and that hampered recruitment efforts. Ultimately, the IRO resettled only 38,107 East European refugees in France between July 1, 1947, and December 1950. The bulk of refugees were headed to the New World. In the same period, the United States received 238,006 refugees, Israel 120,766, Australia 170,543, and Canada 94,115.[33]

IN NEARLY EVERY SCHEME, recruiters scrambled to select those considered to be the cream of the refugee crop. In 1946, Pierre Pflimlin, the French minister of population, warned that when choosing migrants from Europe's DP camps, it would be necessary "to go to the greatest lengths possible in investigating the human value of the candidates." While insisting that France "would not for a second consider sacrificing to some kind of racial prejudice," he did not consider all refugees equal. "We need to give preference to welcoming foreigners who come from countries neighboring ours, which are close to us with respect to their ethnic character, their customs and their language, and whom will assimilate more easily than others."[34]

As Pflimlin's words make clear, the racial hierarchies that had governed interwar and Nazi immigration and emigration policies did not disappear after the war, even as policymakers rhetorically sought to distinguish their migration policies from those of the past. Instead of focusing on race, they tended to discriminate on the basis of the supposed economic productivity or cultural "assimilability" of refugees. Both work ethic and assimilability, however, were typically seen as a function of race or nationality rather than of individual character.

There was an ironic twist to this story. For decades, East European officials had restricted emigration because of anxieties that their citizens would be reduced to the status of nonwhite, colonial labor. After World War I, the United States had drastically restricted East European immigration in the name of protecting American racial stock. But now, after World War II, East European refugees were often considered more desirable immigrants precisely because of their perceived "whiteness," as they were ranked favorably in relation to postcolonial migrants and Jewish refugees.

French population experts were particularly careful to distinguish their postwar immigration and nationality policies from the racist credos of the Nazis. In 1945, the demographers Alfred Sauvy and Robert Debré wrote, "The idea of a 'pure race,' of 'the protection of the purity of the race' is nothing but a political polemic, with no foundation or value." The goal of French immigration policy was therefore "not to conserve the purity of a race that doesn't exist" in the Nazi tradition but rather "to preserve the best qualities in the French type and character" by choosing the most assimilable immigrants possible.[35]

From the beginning, however, French authorities walked a fine line as they parsed a purported distinction between racial and civilizational hierarchies. This balancing act had a long history in the French Empire, and reflected immediate concerns about the rise of North African immigration in postwar France. At the end of the Second World War, the empire was reconstructed as the "French Union," and former colonial subjects, including Algerian Muslims, acquired the right to travel freely between Algeria and France. In the years 1946–54, the number of Algerians in metropolitan France increased from 22,000 to almost 212,000. By 1968, that number had grown to over 500,000.[36]

This influx of North African migration alarmed French demographers. "Islam is separated from [French civilization] by a massive gulf that renders the fusion of the two populations difficult, and without a doubt, undesirable," Debré and Sauvy specified.[37] A year later, France's new National Demography Institute published a detailed study of North African immigration authored by Louis Chevalier. Chevalier emphasized cultural rather than racial barriers to integration, distancing himself from Nazi rhetoric. Yet he insisted that the cultural imprint of Islam was so profound that assimilation was a lost cause: "Much more than a faith, much more than a religious practice, much more than a community pride, Islam is a manner of being, of feeling, of understanding, in sum, a temperament, a psychology that creates a profound refusal of all assimilation behind all the secondary appearances of Europeanization."[38] While migrants from Northern and Southern Europe earned the highest approval ratings in France, East Europeans ranked above postcolonial migrants. "The Italians are considered the best. Then come, in order, the Spanish, the Portuguese, the Poles, the Yugoslavs, the Africans, and the North Africans," concluded one Parisian study of public opinion on immigration.[39]

In Britain, East European DPs also gained stature after World War II, thanks to their comparative whiteness, as growing numbers of ex-colonial subjects arrived in the British metropole.[40] The UNNRA worker Kathryn Hulme described the process by which DP camps began to clear out in the late 1940s. Every emigration scheme had its own set of discriminatory exclusions, many based on race, age, or gender. "Brazil wanted mainly agricultural workers eighteen to forty years of age, all nationalities and religious groups accepted, with the exception of Jews and persons of Asiatic origin. . . . New Zealand sought two hundred orphans for adoption into private homes and three hundred single women under forty to work in mental hospitals." A minor international scandal broke out in 1947, when the Canadian industrialist and member of parliament Ludger Dionne requested one hundred young Catholic women to work in his shoe factory in Quebec and made it clear that he would accept only certifiable virgins.[41]

The United States also practiced racially selective humanitarianism. As late as 1950, Asian refugees were excluded from
immigrating to the United States altogether.[42] In 1948 and 1950,
the American DP acts enabled over 400,000 European refugees
to enter the United States. This legislation was, however, openly
discriminatory, specifying that 30 percent of the new Americans
had to be agricultural workers (which excluded most Jews), and 40
percent had to come from territories annexed by the USSR. Prot-
estant refugees from the Baltics (Latvians, Estonians, Lithuanians)
were the most prized immigrants. While visiting Germany, Con-
gressman Frank Chelf of Kentucky lauded Balts as "unmistakably
intelligent, industrious, energetic," adding that they "showed every
sign of having come from good stock and good breeding."[43] The DP
acts of 1948 and 1950 did eventually enable around 100,000 Jewish DPs to enter the United States, in spite of these restrictions, in
part because aid workers on the ground in Europe interpreted the
requirements liberally. But race, religion, and nationality all played
a role in determining who obtained an American visa.[44]

THE MULTINATIONAL TURF of the refugee camp ultimately
pitted refugees against one another in a brutal competition for
visas, jobs, and new homes. This competition was particularly
fierce in postwar Austria, a country at the symbolic and geographic
heart of Cold War Europe. In 1951, the *Ost-West-Kurier*, a newspaper in Bremen, decried the degrading mistreatment of Austria's
"prisoners of the postwar." These "prisoners" were not former concentration camp inmates or forced laborers. They were the ethnic
Germans who had been the beneficiaries of Hitler's empire. "In
the entire Western world, there is today no group of human beings
who have been sentenced to live with so few rights as the so-called
Volksdeutsche in Austria," the newspaper's editors proclaimed.

"300,000 people, whose homes and property have been torn from them through the expulsions, all too often by their closest neighbors, endured a hard journey to Austria, where they believed upon arrival that it could be something like a greater Heimat for them. Because only three decades ago, they too were Austrians."[45]

In 1945, Austria was a reluctant host to approximately 1,432,000 refugees, including DPs and ethnic German expellees; more than three-fourths of them quickly repatriated or settled after the war's end. The so-called DPs were generally either East Europeans brought to Austria as forced laborers during the war or Jewish survivors. The expellees tended to be Germans from nearby Czechoslovakia or Yugoslavia.[46]

The fraught encounter between expellees, Austrians, and DPs in Austria after World War II was shaped by the peculiar relationship of Austrians to both the Nazi and the Habsburg past. In the Moscow Declaration of October 1943, the Allies had famously anointed Austria the "first free country to fall victim to a Hitlerite aggression." The declaration also stated, however, that Austria "has a responsibility she cannot evade for her participation on the side of Hitlerite Germany," and warned that "the final settlement will inevitably take account of her own contribution to her liberation." This declaration was a strategic (and failed) attempt to incite Austrian resistance to Nazi rule. As the Nazi Reich crumbled, however, Austrian politicians held tight to the protective mantle of victimhood.[47]

This required the invention of a new, distinctly "Austrian" national identity, unsullied by association with Hitler's Germany. Provincial and local identity, Catholicism, Alpine landscapes, opera, Baroque architecture, images of imperial glory, choirboys, and dancing horses all featured prominently in the construction of this new Austrian identity.[48] But postwar Austrians also wavered precariously between attempting to differentiate themselves from their neighbors in Germany and continuing to define Austrian-ness in German ethnolinguistic terms.

Austria's official status as a victim of Nazi aggression absolved the Austrian government of the immense legal and financial obligations toward German expellees that the Allies had imposed on occupied Germany. The Austrian government had no obligation to shelter *Volksdeutsche*, to naturalize them as Austrian citizens, or to provide them with basic social rights and benefits such as the right to work or to social insurance. In short, expellees were initially considered no different from and treated no better than any other "foreigners" on Austrian soil. Unlike other postwar refugees, however, expellees did not enjoy the protection or assistance of international humani-tarian organizations such as UNRRA and the IRO. They were subject to restrictions on mobility, housing and employment discrimination, reduced rations, and barriers to admission into Austrian universities. They were also denied welfare benefits and citizenship rights. As of July 1949, nearly fifty thousand *Volksdeutsche* expellees remained in camps owing to persistent housing shortages.[49]

The treatment of *Volksdeutsche* refugees as second-class citi-zens generated protest in both Austria and Germany, thanks to the growing political organization of expellees themselves. Even as they deployed a universal language of "human rights," however, expellee activists in Austria made claims on the Austrian state in nationally exclusive terms. They demanded political and social rights based on their status as former citizens (or the children of citizens) of the Austro-Hungarian Monarchy. In a petition to the Austrian president in December 1949, Sigmund Gorski wrote,

In great distress I am appealing to you in the name of all Germans from the Bukovina. . . . All of us who have been hard hit by the events of the war and have been forced to flee to your country have not only been impoverished and disowned—we are also without any financial means. Our parents were all citizens of the former k.k. Monarchy, of the crownland Bukovina. Their achievements in terms of culture and patriotism should be well known to you. For that reason alone it is incomprehensible to us why we have been treated so harshly.[50]

Many expellees rejected the tainted label *Volksdeutsche* altogether, instead anointing themselves *Altösterreicher*, or old-Austrians, in an effort to underscore continuities between the former Austrian empire and the Second Republic.[51] According to editors of *Die Presse*, "From a moral and national perspective, the fact of the matter is that all of these *Volksdeutsche* from the regions of the former Austro-Hungarian Monarchy are old-Austrians." Austrians therefore had a moral duty to welcome German refugees "with feelings of brotherhood . . . and to help them to find a new *Heimat* here."[52]

Writers in *Wegwarte*, a right-wing newspaper representing Sudeten German expellees in Austria, likewise insisted in 1949,

The demands of these old-Austrians for full recognition of their Austrian citizenship . . . are fully justified unless one wants to break with both history and tradition and claim that the current Austria has nothing to do with the old Austria. The Republic of Austria is however both materially and technically the legal successor of the old, greater Austria. A centuries-old common cultural tradition, our shared education, lifestyles, the architecture of our homes, churches, and cultural institutions, all are closely bound together, and have spiritually, racially, and psychically coalesced to make what is called an Austrian.[53]

The resurrection of Austro-Hungarian citizenship seemed, in principle, to efface or bypass the racial hierarchies of the Third Reich, but those hierarchies remained potent beneath the surface. At the same time that 300,000 *Volksdeutsche* made their homes in postwar Austria, hundreds of thousands of other East European DPs, especially Yugoslavs, Hungarians, Czechs, Romanians, Ukrainians, Poles, and Jews from the former Habsburg lands, also descended (or remained) on Austrian soil after the war. The consolidation of Communist power in Eastern Europe brought new waves of refugees from Hungary, Czechoslovakia, and Yugoslavia into Austria's DP camps. As of January 1948, some 164,000 refugees, awkwardly labeled "non-German-speaking foreigners" by Austrian authorities, were housed on Austrian soil under the protection of the IRO, including 24,791 Jews.[54]

Like the German expellees who sought refuge in postwar Austria, these DPs were often former citizens (or the children of citizens) of the Habsburg Empire, and could typically claim regional ties to the Austrian provinces. Unlike the *Volksdeutsche*, however, they were never considered old-Austrians or entitled to Austrian citizenship or social rights based on their Habsburg heritage.

Like other European governments after World War II, Austrian officials judged refugees on the basis of their economic "usefulness" and their perceived ability to assimilate. And like other officials and humanitarian workers across Europe and beyond, Austrians typically saw both "work ethic" and assimilability as a function of ethnicity.[55] In a 1947 meeting between Austrian officials and British occupation authorities, Interior Minister Oskar Helmer announced that Austria's first priority was to see that "all of the inhabitants of the DP camps disappear," since these refugees "do not work" and represent "only a burden to Austria." Austria was eager to be rid of "non-German-speaking foreigners, who are not assimilable," he declared. [56]

Expellees themselves strategically defined themselves as hard-working, culturally and economically valuable migrants—in direct opposition to Slavic refugees and Jews from Eastern Europe. Their cause, unlike that of the non-German DPs, was gradually taken up by the Austrian press and government. In liberated Austria, "the behavior of the *Volksdeutsche* was in keeping with their old southeast German colonial tradition," *Der Fortschritt* claimed. "They became agricultural laborers, construction workers, and domestic servants . . . the reconstruction of Austria . . . would not have been possible without the contribution of the *Volksdeutsche*."[57] A group of American émigrés called the American Aid Society for the Needy and Displaced Persons of Central and South-Eastern Europe echoed these claims in a petition to the Austrian embassy. "These Volksdeutsche refugees worked industriously to rebuild Austria, while all of the other DPs lived like parasites at the state's expense," the petition insisted.[58]

These appeals gradually commanded a response. The defeat of the Communist Party in Austria's November 1945 elections brought to power a grand coalition government more favorable to *Volksdeutsche* interests, led by Leopold Figl of the Austrian People's Party (a successor to the interwar Christian Social Party). Then, in 1949, the Verband der Unabhängigen (VdU), a right-wing "independent" party, was founded with the support of many former Nazi party members and returning POWs. The party began to agitate on behalf of expellees, effectively forcing the hand of the two major parties.[59]

In 1948, meanwhile, American occupation authorities transferred responsibility for *Volksdeutsche* in the American zone to the Austrian government, and the British and French quickly followed suit. As of 1951, the Austrian Interior Ministry assumed direct responsibility for all of Austria's refugee camps, including those housing non-German DPs and Jews. Outright conflict between

Austrian police, local Austrians, and refugees escalated. Police officials in Innsbruck reported in 1952,

> Complaints about the behavior of the so-called displaced persons are justifiably becoming ever sharper. It cannot be denied that along with a number of refugees who really need the right to asylum and who behave as guests in our country, there is a large percentage of adventurers and do-nothings, who are running the black market. The demands of the population to gather these "displaced persons" together in unified camps and place them under strict supervision are becoming ever louder.[60]

In 1953, the Jewish voluntary organization Agudas Israel lobbied the Austrian government to ease the process of acquiring citizenship for Jewish refugees who remained in Austria, "under consideration of the circumstances that led the concerned individuals to lose their homes." At the very least, the group requested that Jewish refugees receive the same treatment for naturalization accorded to Sudeten German expellees.[61] Between 1945 and 1952, the Austrian government naturalized only 23 Jewish DPs, while over 150,000 *Volksdeutsche* and 35,000 other non-German-speaking DPs received Austrian citizenship.[62] The Interior Ministry summarily rejected the appeal. Austrian officials countered that Jewish refugees were economically superfluous and "in many cases demonstrate a poor capacity to assimilate. . . . In Austria there is no shortage of independent craftsmen or traders, so there would be no economic advantage to the naturalization of Jewish refugees. The policy of the Austrian government agencies with respect to this group of refugees, who can be assimilated only with great difficulty, is to force them to emigrate."[63]

Volksdeutsche meanwhile succeeded in their quest to secure a privileged status among the stateless in postwar Austria. An Austrian federal law passed on June 18, 1952, rendered *Volksdeutsche* expellees equal to Austrian citizens with respect to employment rights, the right to establish businesses and to enter trades. Further legislation in June 1952 guaranteed expellees equal access to other state welfare and unemployment benefits.[64] The rate of naturalization for expellees also steadily increased in the early 1950s. The Austrian Chancellor's Office reported that 225,000 "old-Austrians" had become Austrian citizens by March 1954.[65]

The same opportunity was never afforded to non-German DPs or Jews. In a 1950 memo to the International Red Cross, Interior Ministry officials complained that since 1945 the Austrian government had unwillingly spent 283,546,382 schillings for the care of these refugees. "In view of these costs it will appear understandable that Austria wishes to reduce the problems stemming from the DPs to a minimum and to implement a final solution to the DP problem. From the Austrian perspective this goal can only be realized through the evacuation of the difficult-to-assimilate non-German-speaking DPs."[66]

WITH THE CONSOLIDATION of Cold War rivalries, the process of sorting refugees—and transforming them into migrant workers—became even more complicated. A new world emerged after World War II in which official recognition as a "refugee" brought new forms of privilege and protection, including the right to asylum and to international legal and social assistance. These privileges were doled out selectively, however.[67] The IRO's 1947 constitution introduced the first rigid distinctions between political and economic refugees. Henceforth, individuals were considered refugees (and entitled to IRO assistance) only if they expressed "valid objections" to repatriation based on actual experiences of persecution, or "fear based on reasonable grounds of persecution because of race, religion, nationality, or political opinion."[68] The 1951 Geneva Convention anchored this distinction in international law, defining a refugee as an individual

> who owing to a well-founded fear of being persecuted for reasons of race, religion, nationality, membership of a particular social group or political opinion, is outside the country of his nationality and is unable or, owing to such fear, is unwilling to avail himself of the protection of that country; or who, not having a nationality and being outside the country of his former habitual residence as a result of such events, is unable or, owing to such fear, is unwilling to return to it.[69]

This definition embedded emerging Cold War precepts into new understandings of human rights. It explicitly privileged political freedoms and civil liberties over economic rights. Yet at the same time that government authorities discriminated between economic migrants and "genuine" political refugees, they continued to scour refugee camps for cheap migrant labor.

In the immediate aftermath of the Second World War, classification as a "displaced person" and entitlement to humanitarian assistance had little to do with *how* or *why* a person was uprooted. Any Allied citizen displaced abroad before December 20, 1945, was considered a displaced person and entitled to UN assistance. The cutoff date was later extended in the American zone, enabling Jewish refugees who fled from Eastern Europe after the war to enter UNRRA camps. The only migrants excluded from receiving assistance were Germans and those found guilty of collaboration with the Axis. As Cold War tensions escalated, the U.S. government became more interested in fighting communism than in punishing Nazi collaborators. Even refugees who had been members of the German army or Baltic and Ukrainian units of the Waffen-SS were soon eligible for resettlement in the United States. They simply had to argue convincingly that they had been drafted into the Wehrmacht by force, or even that they had voluntarily enlisted out of anti-Soviet convictions rather than hostility to the Allies.[70]

Once the IRO established a legal distinction between "bona fide" political refugees and economic migrants, the situation changed. It was no simple task, Louise Holborn recalled, "to select genuine refugees and displaced persons among the huge mass of uprooted humanity." The IRO's Review Board for Eligibility Appeals, which began to hear cases in early 1948, adjudicated contentious cases. The board, which consisted of a chairman and twenty-eight members, rendered 36,742 decisions between 1947 and 1951, developing into "an organ having the character of an investigator, psychologist, and judge," according to the board's chairman. Out of 8,082 cases heard by the appeal board in 1948–49, 2,141 decisions were reversed.[71]

While acknowledging that the very nature of Communist regimes blurred distinctions between economics and politics, the IRO eligibility guide maintained that "clear and exclusively economic considerations are, of course, no use whether they advert to bad conditions at home or bright hopes in the western world." For example, an individual seeking asylum because his farm or small business was confiscated by the Communist regime was treated as an economic emigrant. "If, however, loss of political rights is alleged and substantial then a valid objection is possible."[72]

Eligibility guidelines also distinguished between "active" and "passive" dissidence. In order to claim valid objections to returning home, refugees had to demonstrate not only that they disagreed with the government but also that they had *acted* on anti-Communist convictions. "The absence of agreement with the governmental policy or ideology is not sufficient," eligibility guidelines specified. The distinction between the "active" and "passive" dissident tended to privilege men over women, since women were rarely seen as "active" political agents.[73]

The review board's decisions reveal that from the beginning the very category of the political refugee was designed for men. Most important, a woman's entitlement to refugee status, like nationality and citizenship in many countries at the time, followed that of her husband or of the "head of family," defined as "the eldest male or the eldest breadwinner depending on circumstances."[74] IRO guidelines explained that this provision was intended to protect family unity and to protect wives who lost their citizenship through marriage to a foreigner. It created bizarre situations in practice, however. Aurelia Holterman, a Polish Jew, was denied assistance by the IRO after she married her husband, Waldo, a non-Jewish German. The review board's decision explained that whereas "a refugee who takes a German wife may find some difficulty to enter the German economy . . . a wife living with a German husband must be considered as absorbed in the German economy" as his dependent, and was therefore "no longer the concern" of the organization.[75]

In another case of mixed marriage, Arthur Beckers submitted a passionate (and ultimately successful) appeal after he and his Jewish wife, Gitta, were denied refugee status. Beckers had converted to Judaism before he married Gitta in 1922. Shortly afterwards, the couple emigrated to Brazil. When their son fell ill in 1935, they returned to Germany, unaware of the extent of Nazi anti-Semitism. Beckers used his birth certificate to prove that he was Aryan, which in turn protected his wife (since German Jews in mixed marriage were typically spared from deportation). But their son was deported to a concentration camp in 1941 and murdered. Because he was married to a Jew, Beckers lost his job and was forced to perform agricultural labor while his wife was subjected to forced labor. Gitta's entire family was exterminated. The IRO nonetheless refused to recognize the couple as refugees because Arthur was not Jewish and "had not been in a concentration camp himself." In his petition to the review board, he protested, "That the loss of an only son in this terrible manner cannot be ascribed to the father as 'persecution' is quite incomprehensible to me."[76]

On the other hand, a German woman who married a refugee was automatically recognized as a refugee, unless she was considered a war criminal. Anna Elisabeth Dybczak, who joined the Nazi party in 1940 and worked as a typist for the Wehrmacht, thus acquired IRO assistance through her marriage to a Polish DP. Here too, the assumption that women were apolitical guided the IRO's decision making. The review board concluded, "The Appellant did not perform any function which could be construed as upholding the Nazi regime and . . . her membership of the Nazi party was merely of a formal character."[77]

Because women became refugees through marriage, those who appealed to the review board on their own behalf were generally single, widowed, or divorced. Even unmarried women, who theoretically should have been assessed as individuals, were often granted or denied refugee status on the basis of the political activity of male family members. In determining whether an individual woman had "valid objections" against returning to her homeland, officials typically considered whether or not she had male family members at home. If a woman's brothers and father were persecuted or were themselves refugees, this counted in her favor. If she had male family members who were living "unmolested" behind the Iron Curtain, review board members tended to doubt a woman's claim to have a "reasonable" fear of persecution.

Lenke Fuszessery, a Hungarian, fled to Austria in the summer of 1948. She claimed that she was persecuted in Hungary because she could not get work as a teacher unless she joined the Communist Party. The review board rejected her appeal largely on the grounds that her father remained in Hungary "unmolested," continued to receive a monthly pension from the government, and had not been required to join the party himself. "Petitioner appears to be an opportunist. The Board is not convinced that petitioner has formed political opinions," the ruling declared.[78]

The case of Maria-Marica Tomazic was an exception that proved the rule. A twenty-eight-year-old Slovene from Yugoslavia, she fled home in May of 1945. Initially the IRO rejected her application because "both parents, who are farmers, and a brother, now in the Army, live at home and are not molested." In her appeal, Maria-Marica contested the decision, insisting that she had political opinions independent of her father and brothers. She had been opposed to communism since her youth because of her participation in Catholic youth organizations. As soon as Communist partisans gained influence in her region during the war, she joined a group of five young women who spread anti-Communist propaganda. She now received letters from her mother warning her not to return to Yugoslavia. Maria-Marica invoked her traditional role as the only daughter and expected caregiver of her aging parents in her appeal. "My parents are elderly. . . . I am the only daughter who could now be of the greatest assistance to my mother," she explained. "What mother would not like to have her daughter with her . . . ? Indeed, if my mother could be sure that nothing bad would happen to me in my homeland, she would certainly ask me to go home immediately."[79] She successfully appealed her case with the legal assistance of the Papal Mission for Refugees from Yugoslavia.

East European wives of Nazi collaborators meanwhile capitalized on the assumption that women were apolitical. Maria

Mosonyj was excluded from IRO protection when it was discovered that her husband was secretary of state during the fascist Szálasi regime in Hungary. On appeal, however, her refugee status was restored because she convinced the board that she had not "shared in or profited by her husband's activity."[80] Another woman, whose husband had been arrested and imprisoned as a war criminal, insisted that she had been completely unaware of her husband's collaboration with the Nazis. "I never asked him about politics, as I was not interested," she explained.[81]

The fate of female refugees also depended on whether they conformed to traditional gender roles. Austrian border guards, for example, frequently granted or refused asylum to refugees coming from Yugoslavia on the basis of snap judgments of their appearance or moral character. Border guards accepted several women as refugees because they appeared "unspoiled and upstanding" or made a "refined impression." They rejected others for smoking, wearing makeup, appearing "totally spoiled in a moral sense," or being "unsuitable for physical labor." In 1954, one thirty-year-old Slovene woman fled to Austria and reported that she was continuously physically and emotionally abused by her husband. She was deported back to Yugoslavia on the grounds that she had "left behind her husband and four children." In another case, a twenty-two-year-old woman was denied asylum and forcibly returned to Yugoslavia in 1956 for being involved with a married man in Austria. "Granting her asylum would be a state endorsement of adultery. Her deportation therefore seems urgently necessary," a border official maintained.[82]

As time went on, refugees learned the rules of the game. A few were naïve enough to confess outright that they were economic emigrants, like Anton Veverka, a Czechoslovak citizen who crossed the German border in 1948. He told the IRO review board that he was unwilling to return to Czechoslovakia, because he wished "to settle overseas and learn new languages and see new places." Another migrant from Romania, Josef Bitto, testified that he "wanted to emigrate like everyone else at IRO expense with his wife."[83] But after an extended stay in a refugee camp, and with the assistance of anti-Communist national committees, religious, and philanthropic organizations, many refugees learned how to successfully perform the role of refugee. Drina Babic, for example, was initially denied refugee status for lack of valid objections. On appeal, though, she testified that "she would return only in a coffin as long as the present regime lasts," adding that as a Catholic she wanted her daughter to be "brought up in a God-fearing country." Put in these terms, her appeal was successful.[84]

As refugees became more sophisticated, however, officials also became more cynical. This meant that appeals that sounded too formulaic aroused suspicion. Border guards and IRO eligibility officers increasingly rejected applicants whose stories did not sound "authentic" or "genuine" enough. Stanislowa Garcarek, a sixty-two-year-old woman who refused to return to the USSR, was denied asylum because "the stereotyped wording of her appeal, which is identical to many others, is an indication that it does not sincerely express petitioner's own ideas."[85] Here too, the assumption that women are less capable of independent political thought may have undermined her case.

Although IRO review board members grew more cynical with the passage of time, they also tended to define "valid objections" more generously. This was partly a function of escalating Cold War tensions, and partly a result of the growing demand for migrant labor in the West. By 1949, the IRO rejected only "the few who are naïve enough to admit that they are economic migrants," owing to pressure from the Truman administration, which wanted to admit larger numbers of migrants from Eastern Europe to the United States for political reasons.[86] Many women whose fears of persecution were deemed illegitimate in 1947 or 1948 were accepted as refugees a year or two later. When Slavka Boras, a refugee from Yugoslavia, first claimed that she feared persecution on political and religious grounds, she was turned down. On appeal in 1949, the board concluded, "Although the board does not consider that an illiterate peasant woman with her background would be an object of persecution in the sense of IRO definitions . . . her convictions are sufficient," and she was accorded refugee status.[87]

Local economic conditions also informed asylum policies. Beginning in the late 1950s, as the West German "economic miracle" increased demand for labor, the definition of the "political" refugee became more elastic. Simply living in the East was recognized as grounds for claiming political persecution, based on the precept that everything was political in a "totalitarian" society. Beginning in July 1961, only weeks before the sudden construction of the Berlin Wall cut off the massive flow of emigrants from the East to the West, West German laws acknowledged that a desire for a better standard of living could itself constitute a valid "political" motivation for emigration.[88]

In Austria, however, it became more difficult to obtain asylum as time went on. In order to be accepted as a "bona fide" political refugee there, a migrant had to be willing to do low-paid labor. In a letter of protest, the Yugoslav committee in Salzburg complained that Yugoslav refugees arriving in the British zone of Austria were typically thrown into prison for two to three months before they were granted an asylum hearing. They were then "distributed" to Austrian farmers and forced to work eighteen hours a day for meager pay, subsisting on a diet of "bad bread and vegetable soup." The refugees protested that this constituted a continuation of Nazi practices of forced labor.[89]

Austrian security officials inadvertently substantiated these claims. One border guard explained, "A refugee who comes to

Refugees at El Shatt in Egypt, the United Nations Relief and
Rehabilitation Administration's camp for displaced Yugoslavs.
Library of Congress, Prints & Photographs Division, FSA/OWI Collection.

Austria . . . must be prepared to accept any job offered. . . . The
fact that refugees refuse to work on farms suggests that we are not
really dealing with refugees." Before 1955, when British occupation authorities had the final say, almost no one was actually sent
back to Yugoslavia. Once Austria regained its sovereignty in 1955,
however, a growing number of applicants for asylum in Austria
were summarily deported. There were enough "Austrian workers
of equal quality available," the Interior Ministry explained in a 1955

circular. Between August and December of that year, 169 out of 325 refugees were sent back to Communist Yugoslavia.[90]

Then, in 1956, East European refugees once again became a major international issue, as some 180,000 Hungarian refugees descended on Austria in the aftermath of the failed Hungarian uprising. At first, Austrians tended to welcome the refugees with open arms. They presented the newly sovereign Austrian state with an opportunity to represent itself as a great power and as a democratic and peaceful land of asylum. In time, however, as greater numbers remained in camps and settled into life in Austrian towns and cities, Hungarian refugees were saddled with the same negative stereotypes that had plagued other refugees from Eastern Europe since the end of World War II. They were accused of being work-shy freeloaders and opportunists, who had overstayed their welcome and abused the generosity of their hosts.[91]

Although Austria did not deport Hungarians, Austrian diplomats and government officials made it clear from the outset that their hospitality had an expiration date. Hungarian exiles were strongly encouraged to move on to other countries for permanent resettlement. In a 1957 speech, Interior Minister Oskar Helmer proclaimed, "It is no longer acceptable that by virtue of its geographic position, Austria is condemned to bear the major burden of the refugee problem."[92]

In the aftermath of the Hungarian crisis, the number of individuals who fled across the border from Yugoslavia also multiplied. In 1957, around a quarter of Yugoslav applicants for asylum were rejected and issued deportation orders.[93] The reasons for rejection remained arbitrary and inconsistent. One Yugoslav refugee was turned back on the grounds that "if all of the anti-Communists flee, who will remain behind in the country to fight the Communists?" Most asylum seekers were turned away simply because Austrian authorities insisted that they were "economic" and not "political" migrants. The criteria for distinguishing between the two remained obscure, however. A refugee who "made a good impression and has worked hard" and one who had "worker's hands" were granted asylum. A less fortunate candidate was rejected on the grounds that he was a "heavy smoker who has not worked much."[94]

Across Western Europe after World War II, policymakers and humanitarian activists attempted to distance themselves from both the Nazi past and the socialist East. They officially repudiated Nazi racial policies and rhetoric, denouncing the evils of forced labor under Nazism and communism. But the doors to citizenship remained far from open, as racial hierarchies did not disappear overnight. Instead, they were translated into subtler, more malleable (and ultimately more effective) idioms of economic productivity and cultural assimilability. Officially, political persecution was a refugee's ticket to the West in the early Cold War. In reality, asylum remained contingent on an individual's perceived assimilability and value as a worker. The ideal refugee of the early Cold War era was ultimately not so different from the ideal emigrant from the Habsburg Empire: a miner, factory worker, or farmer who understood that work would set him free.

CHAPTER SIX

The Freedom Train

On September 11, 1951, Czechoslovak newspapers reported that innocent Czechoslovak citizens had suffered a vicious "terrorist attack." That afternoon, a regional train departed the small town of Cheb in northern Bohemia for Aš, a border town twenty-five kilometers away. Over a hundred people were on board, including many railroad workers and high school students on their daily commute. As the train approached its destination, passengers realized something was amiss. The train was accelerating rather than slowing down. At first, everyone thought that the brakes had malfunctioned. Then the train sped through Aš and throttled across the heavily fortified border that separated Communist Czechoslovakia from West Germany. As it finally sputtered to a halt in the American zone of occupied Germany, it became clear that the change of route was no accident: the train had been hijacked by a group of young Czechs determined to breach the Iron Curtain.

"The Freedom Train," as it was quickly dubbed, was only one of many hijacked, borrowed, or stolen vehicles to pierce the Iron Curtain in the early Cold War. The train's conductors were immediately celebrated as Cold War heroes in the West. The Council of Free Czechoslovakia, an organization of anti-Communist émigrés in the United States, congratulated the emigrants and welcomed them to the ranks of exiles: "Your ingenious and splendidly executed flight from our homeland . . . is telling evidence of your devotion to freedom and democracy. September 11, 1951, will be recorded as the day when resourcefulness and courage found a new method of fleeing Communist slavery," the bulletin proclaimed.[1]

The Czechoslovak press, meanwhile, denounced the "terrorists, organized and provided with money and weapons by American agents," who had kidnapped innocent passengers and taken them hostage. Upon arrival in Germany, the Communist Party newspaper *Rudé Právo* alleged, the involuntary emigrants were held captive on the train for two days and then bribed to remain in Germany with American cigarettes, chocolate, and promises of lucrative employment. Fortunately, these enticements could not seduce the patriotic Czechs to betray their country. "Every last one of our citizens rejected the American offers," *Rudé Právo* boasted. The proud Czechs purportedly refused food from their captors and demanded their immediate return home to Communist Czechoslovakia. The kidnapping and the theft of the train and its passengers, the paper insisted, was "a typical example of the gangsters' methods used by the Americans against the Czechoslovak state."[2]

In reality, twenty-seven of the Czechoslovak passengers chose not to return home; the other eighty were repatriated to Czechoslovakia two days later, on September 13. One couple had been en route to Cheb to search for an apartment when they suddenly found themselves in West Germany. "My wife and I were among the 27 persons who decided at once to remain in the free world," the husband testified. "We said to each other that we simply had to avail ourselves of this miracle although we were not at all prepared for such a sudden emigration."[3]

Karel Ruml, aged twenty-three in 1951, helped organize the escape. He decided to leave Czechoslovakia after being arrested and interrogated by the Communists in 1950. On the train, his task was to guard the handbrake that could stop the train in its tracks:

> We could see the machine-gun towers, the minefields with the barbed wire around, all the beautiful sights of a police state. . . . It was so close then, from that point to the border, there wasn't much time to think of anything else. This enormously fat policeman approached me and tried to push me away from the brake, whereupon I jammed the gun in his stomach and tried to use him as a barrier between myself and his colleagues who were behind him, praying to God that I wouldn't be forced to pull the trigger. But the guy turned cowardly like all the defenders of totality and didn't do anything, just stood there giving me a horrible look of hate. I could smell his breath smelling of beer and onion . . . and that's how I crossed the border.[4]

"Escapees" like Ruml became living symbols of totalitarian oppression in the 1950s and beyond. Their dramatic stories, heavily publicized in the Cold War West, underscored an association between mobility and freedom. More than ever, Western authorities decried "slavery" and "captivity" in the socialist East.[5] Socialist propagandists, meanwhile, insisted that emigrants were traitors, criminals, or materialists who had been seduced into "wage slavery" in the West. Although this Cold War rhetoric around emigration echoed that of previous decades, the policies it justified were far more radical. Now, for the first time, East European governments resorted to deadly force to keep emigration in check.

The first total ban on emigration in Czechoslovakia was not a Communist innovation, however. It was the brainchild of a democratically elected, republican government. As early as 1945, three years before the Communists seized power, the Czechoslovak government issued passports only for "necessary" travel abroad. In a December 1945 meeting on emigration, Czech officials planned to limit travel and emigration as much as possible, citing the need to retain labor for reconstruction.[6] A government decree in January 1946 authorized still more severe restrictions. While interwar passport laws had empowered the Czechoslovak government to impede travel abroad if it *harmed* the state's interests, such travel was now permitted only if it *served* the interests of the republic. By the end of 1947, the Czechoslovak Republic had banned emigration entirely, along with all travel abroad for private purposes, including tourism or visiting family members.[7]

Czechoslovakia's legislation was typical of the policies adopted after World War II in East Central Europe. Across the Eastern bloc, new socialist regimes radicalized existing anti-emigration policies and fortified their borders, typically only allowing (or forcing) members of national or religious minority groups to emigrate. By 1955, ten years after the Communist takeover, Polish borders were reinforced by 1,100 kilometers of barbed wire fence and 1,314 watchtowers.[8] Yugoslav citizens were also trapped in their own state until the government introduced liberalizing reforms beginning in 1963–64. Because travelers could easily defect, travel to nonsocialist countries for leisure or business was strictly limited across the Eastern bloc, until the post-Stalin thaw that began in 1956. Even travel within Eastern Europe was difficult before the thaw, as an atmosphere of intense xenophobia conflicted with lofty proclamations of socialist "friendship" and "internationalism."[9]

The exception that proved the rule was East Germany. As in other Eastern bloc countries, in East Germany escape to the West was considered an act of treason (the crime even had a special name, *Republikflucht*, or flight from the republic). It proved impos-

A boy sitting on the shoulders of another in West Berlin looks
over a section of the unfinished wall, August 23, 1961.
AP Photo/Werner Kreusch.

sible to control the exodus from the German Democratic Republic,
however. Even after the frontiers of the state were fortified in 1952,
the divided city of Berlin provided a leaky porthole between East
and West. Between 1945 and August 1961, when the construction of
the Berlin Wall put an end to the exodus, a total of 3.5 million East
Germans decamped for the West. Half of the migrants were youth
under the age of twenty-five, a fact that particularly troubled East
German officials.[10]

To a certain extent, postwar restrictions on emigration in Eastern Europe were an outgrowth of Sovietization. There had never
been a golden era of free movement in Russia. Prohibitions on emigration dated back to the era of Peter the Great, when emigration

was technically illegal and Russian subjects were required to carry internal passports. After a brief period of liberalization during the Russian Revolution and the Civil War, the Soviet regime closed its exits for good in 1922. The regime was never fully able to control its vast borders, but emigration was consistently considered an act of treason in the USSR.[11]

Given the long history of anxiety about emigration within East Central Europe, however, it would be a mistake to see postwar emigration restrictions as a Soviet imposition. Echoing decades of anti-emigration rhetoric in East Central Europe, socialist propaganda continued to justify restrictions on mobility as a form of humanitarian protection. Now more than ever, East European officials linked emigration to the West to slavery, exploitation, and moral ruin. As Polish displaced persons in Germany emigrated en masse to America, Canada, or Australia under various labor recruitment schemes, the Polish Red Cross protested, "The recruitment of refugees and displaced persons for labor recalls a slave market, even though slavery has been abolished since Lincoln."[12]

In the West, meanwhile, the anti-Communist press increasingly defined freedom in terms of a holy trinity of free movement, free labor, and free enterprise. But this commitment to the right to exit was itself rather new. In 1945, after all, Harry S. Truman and Winston Churchill had agreed to Stalin's demands for the forcible repatriation of Soviet citizens, leading to tragic scenes. In Dachau on January 19, 1946, at the site of the former Nazi concentration camp, American troops had to use tear gas to force Soviet POWs from their barracks. After being thrust outdoors, the soldiers fell to the snow and pleaded with their captors to shoot them rather than send them home. Ten POWs succeeded in killing themselves, and twenty-one were injured before the group was turned over to Soviet authorities for repatriation.

It was not an isolated incident. Many Soviet POWs feared that they would be imprisoned or executed if they returned home, since Soviet authorities had declared surrender an act of treason. Others simply opposed the Soviet government or hoped for a new life abroad. As a result, many displaced Soviet citizens posed as Poles or Ukrainians to escape repatriation, since these groups were not forcibly returned to the USSR. Soviet DPs were not entirely wrong to fear return: an estimated 6.5 percent of the 2,272,000 DPs who had returned to the USSR as of March 1, 1946, were handed over to state security agencies and probably executed, while another 14.4 percent were conscripted into labor battalions. Responding to mounting protests and escalating Cold War tensions, U.S. authorities finally suspended forced repatriation to the USSR in early 1946.[13]

Then, in 1948, at the dawn of the Cold War, the United Nations Declaration of Human Rights elevated freedom to emigrate to the status of a "human right"—but only after a serious fight in the UN General Assembly. Not surprisingly, Soviet delegates opposed the clause, insisting it should guarantee only the right to leave one's country "in accordance with the procedure laid down in the laws of that country." An American delegate replied that the Soviet amendment would render the right to exit meaningless. "During the discussion on the other articles, it had been recognized that in certain circumstances individuals had to be guaranteed protection, even against their own government," he argued. "To state that freedom of movement should be granted only in accordance with the laws of each country would be equivalent to limiting the fundamental rights of the individual and increasing the powers of the state." The Soviets were ultimately outvoted, with seven delegations supporting the Soviet amendment, forty-four opposing it, and thirteen abstaining.[14]

By the early 1950s, daredevil "flights to freedom," celebrity defections, and stories of families divided by the Iron Curtain had firmly consolidated a rhetorical distinction between a "free world" in the West and a "slave world" in the East.[15] During the Cold War, East European governments finally triumphed in their decades-long battle against emigration. But as they resorted to increasingly repressive and deadly measures to achieve that goal, they lost the larger struggle to define freedom itself.

THERE WAS A SIMPLE REASON that Eastern Europe's new Communist governments were so determined to prevent emigration after the Second World War: they needed human capital to rebuild war-devastated societies. As in 1918, the return of migrants who had emigrated during previous regimes was particularly important to state legitimacy. Returnees were once again heralded as symbols of national and social liberation. "For more than 100 years, our compatriots have departed for every corner of the earth, in search of a living to support themselves and their families, because they could not subsist at home," explained Bedřich Steiner of the Czechoslovak Foreign Institute. "After the liberation in 1945, the first priority of the government was to enable this diaspora to return home."[16]

Postwar repatriation campaigns were directly linked to the simultaneous process of ethnic cleansing, as millions of Germans and other minorities were forcibly expelled from their homes and deprived of their citizenship and property. In the eyes of postwar governments, repatriates and re-migrants were desperately needed to replace wartime casualties, to occupy the jobs, homes, and farms of expelled minorities, and to do the hard labor of reconstruction. "Today, following the expulsion of the Sudeten Germans . . . there are plenty of excellent opportunities here and an insufficient number of workers. We must therefore make the greatest effort to bring the largest possible number of our compatriots back to their homeland," declared Andrej Novicky of the Czechoslovak State Planning Office.[17] In addition to more than 600,000 displaced persons who returned to Czechoslovakia from Germany after the war, about 200,000 re-migrants—mostly labor migrants who had emigrated in the 1920s and 1930s—responded to the call to return home between 1945 and 1949, whether out of curiosity, opportunism, or a genuine desire to contribute to postwar reconstruction.[18]

Poland had lost a staggering number of workers, children, and citizens to the Nazi death machine, and postwar re-migration and repatriation campaigns took on even greater significance there. Between 5.6 and 5.8 million citizens, more than 16 percent of the state's total population, had perished under Nazi occupation, including 3 million Jews. The Polish state lost another 7 million Germans to flight and expulsion. To heal these demographic wounds, the Polish government attempted to recall the non-Jewish Polish diaspora after the war ended. During the spring and summer of 1945, the United Nations and allied military authorities repatriated 1.61 million people to Poland.[19]

To the fury of the Polish government in Warsaw, however, hundreds of thousands of Poles refused repatriation. Many hailed from the Polish territory East of the Curzon line that had been annexed by the USSR. Others were vehemently opposed to the new Communist government in Warsaw. Some simply wanted to seek new opportunities elsewhere. Out of 773,248 DPs receiving United Nations assistance in June 1946, over half were registered as Poles (though many of these "Poles" were certainly Soviet Russians, Ukrainians, or Baltic refugees trying to avoid forced repatriation). In German refugee camps a virtual civil war erupted between Polish supporters of the new Communist regime, who promoted repatriation as a national duty, and their anti-Communist opponents (supported by a Polish government-in-exile in London), who encouraged resettlement.[20]

In the eyes of Communist officials in Warsaw, refusal to return to Poland was an act of egoism at best, cowardice and treason at worst. Poles who remained abroad were doomed to a life of servitude and exploitation, the party claimed. "Whoever does not return . . . sentences himself to a life of hopeless exile, to miserable vegetation in foreign lands," declared a government publication for DPs in 1946. "Do you want to become servants to foreigners, to wash dishes in their restaurants, to become charwomen and mistresses, messengers and watchmen?" Those who refused to return were allegedly criminals, collaborators, or soulless individuals who had "lost every scrap of feeling for their country and who . . . do not like the idea of a hard life in a Poland that is being rebuilt out of ruins."[21]

As these polemics suggest, anti-emigration propaganda was often highly contradictory. Socialist authorities wavered between portraying emigrants as hapless victims of Western propaganda and denouncing them as dangerous traitors and criminals. They oscillated between depicting labor in the West as an exploitative form of "slavery" and chiding migrants for choosing Western consumer comforts over the hard, patriotic work of postwar reconstruction. And they denounced Western materialism in the same breath that they attempted to lure migrants home with promises of luxurious homes, furniture, and property expropriated from Germans.

Miners were particularly valuable, and Czechoslovak authorities made special efforts to woo them home. A government decree issued on July 31, 1945, promised re-migrants employment, housing, and social benefits equal to those that they had enjoyed in the West. Returning miners were also guaranteed new homes, amply outfitted with furniture, linens, and clothing. All of these goodies had been recently confiscated from the Czechoslovak Germans being expelled "home to the Reich" in retaliation for their role in the Nazi occupation.[22]

In the summer of 1945, a group of three hundred Czech miners and their families in France answered the call to return home. The miners had all emigrated to France in the 1920s and 1930s, seeking economic opportunities there. For the most part, they had done well. Most owned a home, a garden populated by a goat or two, rabbits, and a few cats and dogs. They earned the same wages as their French co-workers. Now they liquidated their affairs in France, sold their homes and chickens and furniture. In Czechoslovakia, the government promised, everything would be new and better.

The first sign that things might not go as planned came on departure day, when the re-migrants were packed onto a transport full of Sudeten German collaborators being deported back to Czechoslovakia by the French. When the train reached Pilsen, the first stop on Czechoslovak soil, the soldiers who met them did not distinguish between them and the Germans. They handled the re-migrants roughly and seized their money and documents. All of the passengers, including women and children, were left standing outside on the train platform in the pouring rain without food. The downpour soaked and ruined their clothing and bedding. After thirty-two hours, the soldiers finally loaded the miners and their families back onto the train to Prague, and transported them to their new home in Most, in northern Bohemia.

Before the war, over thirty thousand German miners and around twenty thousand Czechs had populated the mining towns of northern Bohemia. With the Nazi defeat in 1945, most of the German families were expelled or fled the advancing Red Army. Those Germans had owned pretty villas and spacious apartments. All were lavishly equipped with furniture, bedding, and dishes. All awaited distribution to the newcomers. But before the re-migrants from France arrived, local Czechs and carpetbaggers from around the country rushed to get dibs on the loot. By the time the miners got to Most, the pickings were slim. The re-migrants received chairs with three legs and insect-infested homes with broken windows and no running water. The entire fortunes of the expelled Germans had mysteriously disappeared. The returnees became bitter and disillusioned. "We happily left our good jobs abroad, in order to put our strength in the service of the republic," they protested. "But no one ever imagined what awaited us. At every step of our journey we encountered more enmity than the Germans. . . . We are very unhappy here, and the majority of us would like to return abroad."[23]

Their experience was typical. Postwar East European governments, still in a process of economic and political reconstruction, could rarely keep the promises they made to re-migrants. By February 1946, the Czechoslovak government had already reneged on its initial pledge to provide re-migrants with employment and housing equal to that in the West. Returnees were informed that they should henceforth expect employment and housing only according to "the available possibilities." In January 1947, officials further reduced expectations: re-migrants were now instructed that they would have to accept jobs in construction, mining, or forestry, regardless of their qualifications.[24]

Disappointed and bitter returnees made their grievances known. These returning emigrants, who were supposed to embody socialism's promise, quickly came to undermine new socialist regimes as they challenged narratives of socialist superiority.[25] A year after returning to Czechoslovakia, Jarmila Hassen found herself living in a single decrepit room without heat or cooking facilities, still unemployed in spite of the government's promise of a job and housing. "It is self-evident that repatriates cannot sleep under bridges when they return to their homeland. It is self-evident that they must immediately work when they have no one else to support them," she complained. Like many other re-migrants, Hassen compared her standard of living in Czechoslovakia with that in the West, and found it wanting. "If I were in Austria, America, or England, I would certainly get regular unemployment benefits.... How is it then possible that in a people's democracy a person can be without employment or a home?"[26]

Polish officials were also intent on repatriating Poles from France, since they were often valuable miners and skilled workers. There were around 500,000 Poles living in France at the end of the war. They included workers who had emigrated to France before World War II, forced laborers conscripted by the Nazis, and refugees who had fled the Nazi occupation.[27] The problem was that the French government was equally determined to retain skilled Polish workers. As early as May 1945, Polish Communists demanded the mass repatriation of Polish miners from France, and insisted that the French government stop recruiting Poles from refugee camps in occupied Germany.[28] French authorities ignored these demands, instead bribing Polish miners to remain in France with free labor permits, extra family benefits, quick naturalization, and housing subsidies. "The best specimens," elaborated a confidential French memo, should be offered special benefits in exchange for "repopulating and revalorizing the abandoned French countryside."[29]

In fact, the French government had little to worry about. Between 1945 and 1949, only 56,400 Poles in France chose to return home.[30] Reports flowed back to France that those who did return soon regretted it. In 1947, Guy Monge, French vice-consul in Wroclaw, received letters and visits each day from Poles desperate to return to France. "They are all re-migrants from France lured by the excessive promises of Polish propaganda and extremely disappointed upon arrival in Poland with the quality of life they found there." Although he wanted to help them return to France, it was extremely difficult, he lamented. "The door that has slammed shut behind them will reopen only with great difficulty, since exit passports and visas are granted only in exceptional cases." By 1951, repatriated Poles were attempting to return illegally to France. Several were recaptured and sentenced to eighteen months of forced labor.[31]

THESE NEW RESTRICTIONS on mobility occurred in concert with ethnic cleansing. As in interwar East Central Europe, the goal of emigration policies was to keep national minorities out and "desirable" citizens in. The larger the number of Jews and Germans who were expelled, the more urgent it seemed to prevent everyone else from leaving. It was, however, no simple task to sort out desirable and undesirable citizens, given a long tradition of bilingualism, national indifference, and intermarriage in Eastern Europe.[32] "Viennese Czechs," for example, were encouraged to "return" to Czechoslovakia en masse after World War II. But many of them had been born and raised in Vienna and seemed suspiciously German to local Czechs. The Czechoslovak government therefore created a classification system closely modeled on Nazi procedures of racial classification (the so-called Volksliste), as well as long-term traditions of national classification in Habsburg Central Europe. A five-member committee in Vienna investigated applicants' "origins, knowledge of their maternal language, record of school attendance . . . census records, education of children in the family, membership in emigrant societies, behavior during the occupation and attitude toward their homeland" in order to determine whether the individuals concerned were desirable Czechs or undesirable Austrians. Applicants were classified into three groups: Card A was reserved for those "who demonstrated only positive traits," while Card B was issued to applicants who were demonstrably Czech but had some kind of flaw on their records. For example, an applicant who had served in the Wehrmacht, but could prove that he had not done so voluntarily and had "behaved perfectly as a Czech in all other ways," would be issued the B Card. Finally, individuals of questionable nationality who had nonetheless "behaved flawlessly with respect to national and political loyalty" received certificates of "validation." By the end of 1945, the committee had issued more than twenty thousand identity cards. Many of the applicants were small businessmen and women— bakers, café and bar keepers, hairdressers, shoemakers—hoping to be allocated businesses or homes expropriated from expelled Germans. Anna Pabstová, a hairdresser, was looking for a shop in Kutná Hora. Although she had been born in Austria and was an Austrian citizen, she had lived in Czechoslovakia most of her life and wanted to return as a citizen after the war. She received an A Card and was allowed to re-migrate.[33]

But re-migration did not necessarily have a happy ending. Even once fully certified Czechs and Slovaks arrived "home" to Czechoslovakia, many encountered so much hostility that they immediately returned to Vienna. The re-migrants were often seen and treated like Germans by local Czechs. A 1945 petition signed by thirty-nine re-migrants from Vienna protested, "We are the ones who suffered the brunt of German domination the longest. We are the ones who remained true to our language and our nation abroad. . . . We are not gold diggers, we don't expect anything for free, we want to work and to help with the development of a free Czechoslovak Republic."[34]

Officials also struggled to distinguish between Czechs and Sudeten Germans stranded in DP camps. Intermarriage, which was extremely common, further complicated matters. While

Czech men married to German women were generally permitted to return to Czechoslovakia, Czech women married to German men were typically excluded. The double standard reflected both patrilineal citizenship laws and the assumption that German men were more politically and nationally threatening than German women. Until July 1946, Czech women married to German men could not legally repatriate except with special permission.[35]

Given the state's desperate need for labor, a re-migrant's potential usefulness to the economy could tip the scale in doubtful cases. In general, valuable "experts" were exempt from expulsion. In 1946, a large group of Czech miners from near Bremen joined the re-migration convoys. Many had lived in Germany for decades and were married to German women. Some could not speak Czech at all. In spite of their dubious Czech credentials, the Czechoslovak government was eager to claim them. The Czechoslovak Foreign Institute ordered the local population of Falkenov, where the workers were resettled, not to harass the miners simply because they could not speak Czech. "We remind you that the reason for the expulsion of the Germans is not their linguistic difference, but their insufficient will to be constructive and loyal citizens of the ČSR."[36]

In Poland, likewise, an individual's usefulness to the state could mean the difference between losing and keeping one's citizenship. Hundreds of thousands of bilingual Silesians who had been classified as ethnic Germans by the Nazi regime were reclassified as ethnic Poles after the war, through a massive process of ethnic "verification." The classification of these individuals as Poles helped justify the Polish state's claim to land annexed from Germany after World War II.[37]

Jews, however, were rarely welcomed home. As "undesirable" citizens from a nationalist perspective, they ironically enjoyed more freedom of movement than their non-Jewish compatriots. The line between voluntary and forced emigrations remained blurry, however. Out of a prewar population of 354,342 Jews, approximately 30,000 had survived the war and returned to postwar Slovakia by November of 1946. In the Bohemian Lands, the Jewish population numbered 24,395 in June 1948.[38] In an April 1946 conference on emigration in Prague, one Czech official specified that while Czechs and Slovaks should be prohibited from emigrating except in "exceptional circumstances," Jews should be encouraged to leave, since "these are often physically and financially damaged individuals, in whom we have no interest."[39]

Immediately after the war ended, some Czechoslovak Jews were actually forcibly expelled from Czechoslovakia as Germans. In May 1945, the Czechoslovak Interior Ministry sent a memo to the Jewish community in Prague, specifying that any Jew who had registered as a German on the 1930 census was no longer a Czechoslovak citizen, since all Germans had been officially stripped of their Czechoslovak citizenship by the Beneš decrees. All citizens of Czechoslovakia had been required to declare their nationality on the 1930 census. Those census records were now being used to determine the citizenship status of millions of people. Around forty thousand Czechoslovak Jews who were German-speakers and identified with the German language and culture had registered as Germans in 1930.[40]

These Jews were now to be "regarded as German citizens" and subject to all punitive measures that applied to Germans, including loss of property and citizenship and deportation.[41] Almost a year later, a representative of the United Nations in Prague reported with dismay that "Czechoslovak authorities are still making no distinction between Jews and pro-Nazi Sudeten Germans and are therefore insisting on their expatriation to Germany." It was only in September of 1946, with the expulsions well under way, that the government formally changed this policy.[42]

In Hungary, likewise, returnees encountered ongoing

anti-Semitism, and many concluded they had no future in Hungary. Around 100,000 out of 180,000 surviving Hungarian Jews fled to the West or to Palestine after the war.[43] Polish Jews (many of whom had survived the war in the Soviet Union) endured even more abuse upon returning home. Survivors recalled being greeted with sentiments such as "What, you're still alive?" The Polish government quickly sealed its borders to prevent the departure of Polish Catholics, while tolerating or even encouraging the emigration of Polish Jews. Some Poles actually posed as Jews or Germans in order to leave.

THE POLITICAL STAKES of east–west migration escalated with the Cold War itself. Partisans on both sides of the Iron Curtain depicted emigration as a journey between slavery and freedom in the 1950s and 1960s. While East Germans refugees arriving in transit centers in the West were welcomed with banners proclaiming "The Free World Greets You," the East German press denounced "the modern slave traders in Bonn and West Berlin," who stopped at nothing "to force people from our state into their clutches."[44]

In Czechoslovakia, an estimated 29,000 citizens fled their country after the 1948 coup.[45] According to Communist propaganda, these refugees wasted away in the desolate purgatory of Western refugee camps, where they shared the company of prostitutes, traitors, thieves, and (worst of all) Germans. Upon resettlement in the West, they were reportedly sentenced to permanent unemployment or hard labor in French mines or Canadian timber camps.[46] The socialist press marshaled (or fabricated) emigrant testimonies and letters to support these horror stories. "Mom, I curse the moment when the thought arose in my head to emigrate. I will be cursing that moment for the rest of my life," confessed

Dante Peklo, in a letter allegedly sent from the Valka refugee camp in Bavaria. "How I wish I could return home . . . but I can't, because I can't look all the people whom I betrayed in the eyes." In a second letter, he described the dispiriting physical and moral conditions of camp life: "Everything is full of dirt and stench, including the filthy children who wander the camp with no destination. It's the same among the adults, who have no goals, no work, and no money—fallen women, tough adolescents with the appearance of vagabonds . . . hustlers, criminals, and rabble galore. Yes, this is exile, glorious exile."[47]

Other emigrants sent letters that ended up in state security files rather than in newspapers. Otto Dänecke and Thadeus Krüger defected to West Germany from the East in October 1951. They sent word to their former co-workers a few weeks later. "Dear Karl Meier, say hello to all our co-workers. The manager and boss are big nobodies, and as for the money they still owe us, they can stick it up their asses. We arrived here and immediately got work that pays 1.30 DM per hour. The food is wonderful," they reported. "Every day 160 men arrive in Hanover from the East, the camp director said that everyone will be accepted, no one will be sent home, and they all immediately find work."[48]

Not everyone enjoyed such a smooth landing, however. East Germans were privileged, since the West German government did not generally deport emigrants from the Eastern zone—even as it distinguished between "real" political refugees (who enjoyed a privileged legal status) and illegal migrants.[49] Emigrants from other parts of the Eastern bloc, by contrast, had no guarantee of finding a new home or job quickly. Bohuslava Bradbrook, who fled Czechoslovakia in 1952, expected to be greeted with open arms upon arrival in the West. She had dismissed stories of hardship in Western refugee camps as propaganda and was counting on quickly resettling in Great Britain. "Surely, if one seeks asylum in the West, is it not obvious that one is coming as a friend and admirer? There cannot be so much difficulty for honest people who are ready to work," she presumed. But when she arrived in the British zone of Vienna, she was treated as a potential spy and interrogated for hours. It took Bradbrook over a year to gain a visa to Ireland, where she found work as a schoolteacher in August 1953. In the interim, she endured miserable conditions in the British, American, and French zones of Austria, working as a housecleaner and a cook. Only marriage to a British man ultimately secured her citizenship rights in the United Kingdom.[50]

Other refugees were disillusioned by material conditions in the West. They may not have expected a golden land, but they did expect electricity and running water. Horvath Savoy, who left Czechoslovakia at the age of fifteen in 1948, landed on a desolate farm in upstate New York, where he lived with an uncle. The first thing his uncle said to him, he recalled, was "'We got electricity six months ago.' Outside toilet, phone on the wall with a crank. My uncle, they looked at going to the movies as the devil's work. They wouldn't let me listen to popular music, I had to listen to gospel. . . . They were fanatical religious," he remembered. "I thought I lived much better in Czechoslovakia then he did in America."[51] Vera Dobrovolný's second thoughts about emigration began the moment that she landed in Chicago. "It wasn't the America we knew from movies and books. Those houses and everything—it was like, I was deeply, deeply disappointed. To me, America was behind."[52]

These stories did not sit well with Cold War mythology in America. In the 1950s and 1960s, "escapees" were heralded as living testimonials to the evils of totalitarianism. Sensational coverage of daredevil escapes from the Eastern bloc—like that of the "freedom train" in 1951—helped consolidate a new Western view of emigration as a fundamental human right. Escape stories crafted by Western journalists tended to pit clever escapees (embodying the capitalist values of individualism and resourcefulness) against a socialist system governed by buffoons and automatons.[53] Ludevit Ollarek exhibited the ideal qualities of the "escapee." In 1952, he managed to traverse the Iron Curtain in a "duck," an amphibian jeep acquired on the black market from the U.S. military. The *New York Times* reported that Ollarek, thirty-five, along with his wife, Katerina, his three children, and a colleague made their courageous "dash for freedom" across the icy waters of the Morava River in February of 1952. The day of their escape, they plied a Communist functionary with liquor and set out for the river. But the plan went awry when the jeep's motor stalled midstream, sputtering to a final stop only ten meters from the Austrian shore. The family members were forced to abandon all their possessions and swim for safety, barely evading the gunshots of Czechoslovak guards.[54]

Throughout the Cold War era, press conferences, memoirs, and radio and television broadcasts advertised the bravery of Eastern bloc defectors who voted with their feet. Émigrés themselves actively promoted these stories. "In order to carry on the persecution without eye witnesses, the Communists shut off Czechoslovakia from the free world. . . . Anyone attempting to flee the country did so at the risk of his life," declared Petr Zenkl, chairman of the exile Council of Free Czechoslovakia (and deputy prime minister of Czechoslovakia from 1946 to 1948). "The people answered by braving all obstacles and dangers to flee to the free world. . . . For many miles they crept at night in the bitter cold, carrying their children in their arms. They swam across rivers under gun-fire; they charged through the lines in a tractor; they hid in the coal of a freight car; they thought up amazing ways of escaping Communist slavery."[55]

Yet even as the Western press and anti-Communist groups lionized escapees and proclaimed a human right to exit, actual policies toward asylum seekers were much less generous. Initially, some policymakers hoped to encourage defection as a form of psychological warfare. In February 1948, George Kennan's Policy Planning Staff recommended that the United States promote defection in order to humiliate the Soviets and secure intelligence, and the National Security Council proposed a similar plan of action in 1951. But it was the height of the McCarthy era in the United States, and many Americans viewed East European refugees as closeted Communists and potential spies. In 1950, Senator Patrick McCarran, a Democrat from Nevada and a rabid anti-Communist, successfully sponsored the McCarran Internal Security Act. The act, passed over President Harry Truman's veto, banned any former or present member of a Communist organization from immigrating to the United States. That posed a serious obstacle for almost anyone who had grown up under communism. Even anti-Communist refugees from the Eastern bloc had often belonged to Communist youth organizations like the Young Pioneers, or had joined the Communist Party (whether voluntarily or under pressure) at some point in their lives.

Then, in 1952, Truman attempted to launch a U.S. escapee program, hoping to offer 300,000 new visas to refugees. Once again lawmakers, led by McCarran and Senator Francis Walter, Democrat of Pennsylvania, successfully blocked immigration from Eastern Europe. The McCarran-Walter Act, also known as the Immigration and Nationality Act of 1952, reaffirmed the quota system's discrimination against East Europeans. McCarren depicted immigrants from Eastern Europe as a threat to "Western civilization":

I believe that this nation is the last hope of Western civilization and if this oasis of the world shall be overrun, perverted, contaminated or destroyed, then the last flickering light of humanity will be extinguished. I take no issue with those who would praise the contributions which have been made to our society by people of many races, of varied creeds and colors. America is indeed a joining together of many streams which go to form a mighty river which we call the American way. However, we have in the United States today hard-core, indigestible blocs which have not become integrated into the American way of life, but which, on the contrary are its deadly enemies.[56]

Truman vetoed the McCarren-Walter Act, declaring, "We do not need to be protected against immigrants from these countries—on the contrary we want to stretch out a helping hand, to save those who have managed to flee into Western Europe, to succor those who are brave enough to escape from barbarism, to welcome and restore them against the day when their countries will, as we hope, be free again." His veto was overridden, however, by votes of 278–113 in the House and 57–26 in the Senate.

American red tape, reinforced by anti-Communist paranoia, turned out to be almost as impermeable as the Iron Curtain. In 1953, Dwight D. Eisenhower finally succeeded in getting a Refugee Relief Act through Congress, theoretically providing for 58,000 refugee admissions over two years. But the actual number of visas issued through the program was small because of attached restrictions (the quotas set by the McCarran-Walter Act remained in place). From June to December 1954, for example, the United States actually admitted only 50 refugees from Eastern Europe. In other words, even as U.S. press and propaganda celebrated the heroism of defectors, and defined Western freedom in terms of the right to exit, U.S. laws made it extremely difficult for East European refugees to enter the United States. Nor was freedom to travel absolute for American citizens during the McCarthy era. Most famously, the U.S. State Department revoked the passports of dissidents and fellow travelers such as Paul Robeson and W. E. B. Du Bois. [57]

MEANWHILE, Communist authorities were intent on luring defectors home. Only a few months after the Communist seizure of power, in June 1948, the Czechoslovak government began the first of many "amnesty" programs for repentant refugees, promising returnees that they would not be punished for illegally emigrating.[58] Beginning in 1955, in celebration of the tenth anniversary of the downfall of the Third Reich, highly publicized amnesty programs took effect across Eastern Europe. Ironically, these amnesties were justified by a purported distinction between political and nonpolitical emigrants—the same distinction used by international organizations and Western governments to distinguish between "bona fide" political refugees and economic migrants. The majority of emigrants, Communist officials insisted, were misguided adventurers, selfish materialists, or victims of Western propaganda. Such wayward—and presumably remorseful—migrants had not emigrated out of any real political hostility to socialism and could be rehabilitated if they returned home.

In 1956, for example, the East German State Planning Commission proposed a series of reforms designed to combat emigration and entice emigrants home. "The majority of citizens who leave the GDR [German Democratic Republic] don't do so because they disagree with the government of our people's democracy, or because they are fleeing the GDR, but above all owing to personal, economic, and other reasons," insisted one member of the commission. "They don't take flight, but rather emigrate. . . . They don't see or don't want to see that they damage the GDR and ultimately damage themselves with their personal decision, that consciously or unconsciously, they have committed treason against the GDR, the working class, and themselves."[59] In Czechoslovakia and Poland, emigration was numerically less significant, but officials also tended to cast migrants as immoral, insane, or deluded. In a 1962 meeting, Communist leaders in Czechoslovakia insisted that the vast majority of emigrants who fled the country after 1948 "went abroad out of political immaturity, lust for adventure, or to escape personal problems" rather than because of genuine political grievances.[60]

In this effort to lure emigrants home, both Czechoslovak and Polish authorities collected the addresses of exiled citizens and sent letters that many emigrants must have experienced as a form of harassment, if not terror. They also organized chain letter campaigns and meetings in refugee camps advertising their amnesty programs. The Czechoslovak government even distributed a bulletin called "The Voice of Home," replete with purported letters from children to their fathers, wives to husbands, and mothers to sons, begging their family members to come home.[61]

Some East European refugees responded to the call. These "re-defectors" were immediately pressed, bribed, or forced into the service of anti-Western propaganda campaigns. Ludwik Dziubek, a forty-year-old furrier, testified that he had made an impulsive decision to defect "under the influence of vodka" while navigating a Polish boat through Le Havre. He quickly recognized his folly. "I landed and reported to French authorities. They put me in prison for 15 days and I had to undergo questions and interrogations," he recalled. In subsequent days and weeks, he was recruited to spy against his country, and assigned a job that did not pay enough to cover his housing and food. "In despair, I began to drink." He later worked in a smelting factory, earning little money for hard work. "I was hungry. I was sleeping in the streets. Finally, I had enough. I turned to the Polish embassy." Upon return to Poland, he claimed to be more grateful than ever for the security and solidarity of socialist society. "I work, I earn a decent living, I am reunited with my wife and three children. Here, people are not treated like merchandise in the hands of blood traffickers."[62] In Poland, he could not travel, but he was free.

These amnesty programs were never a numerical success, however. Most émigrés cynically dismissed them. One Hungarian woman, interviewed in 1957, surmised that their purpose was to "lure the rich people home and take their dollars and jewels as soon as they reached the border."[63] The total number of individuals who chose to return to Czechoslovakia during the 1955 amnesty was 1,169, less than 5 percent of all those who had fled the country after 1948. Subsequent Czechoslovak amnesties produced still more meager returns. A 1960 amnesty reaped 355 returnees, and only 69 individuals seized the opportunity to return home in response to a 1965 amnesty.[64] In truth, the same issues that had handicapped repatriation efforts of the 1940s plagued the amnesty campaigns of the 1950s and beyond: the state could not make good on its promises.

The problem reflected a basic paradox. A social and economic system that denounced Western consumerism simultaneously sought to lure migrants home with material enticements. This problem was particularly acute in East Germany. Before the construction of the Berlin Wall, East German emigrants returned home in much greater numbers than Czechs or Poles, in part because it remained possible, if difficult, to move back and forth between the East and the West. In 1956, for example, the government of the GDR counted 73,931 returnees or new arrivals from the West, up from 72,928 the preceding year. The net loss of population was far larger, however. The number of emigrants to the West increased from 270,115 to 316,028 between 1956 and 1957.[65] As part of a concerted campaign to recruit West Germans to the GDR, the East German government began to promise so-called "refugees from the Federal Republic" plum jobs, vacations, and better apartments, crossing the line between guaranteeing social security and outright bribery. The hypocrisy was not lost on East Germans, who resented the privileges being doled out to re-migrants. A popular joke summed up the situation: "If it is a flat that you request, wander over to the West. Upon your re-embarkment, your reward is an apartment."[66]

The Polish government also resorted to bribery when propaganda failed. During the 1955 amnesty campaign, Polish returnees were offered free travel, food, and medical assistance, a cash bonus, and pension benefits for the years they had spent outside of Poland. Re-migrants who transferred foreign currency home through the Bank Polska Kasa Opieki enjoyed an inflated exchange rate of up to 111 złoty to the dollar instead of the actual rate of 4 złoty. A French diplomat calculated that a normal re-migrant with 1,000 złotys could purchase ten kilos of coffee upon return to Poland; taking advantage of the Bank Polska's offer, he or she could buy five cows or a nice German car. Nonetheless, as of November 1955, the Polish government reported that only one thousand citizens had taken advantage of the amnesty.[67]

Although the numbers were pathetically small, Western governments took these amnesties and re-defections seriously. Migrants *from* the West were embarrassing. They also seemed to represent a security threat in the context of Cold War paranoia about spying.[68] And they caused serious diplomatic conflicts. Any Pole who set foot on Polish soil was assumed to have reclaimed Polish citizenship—and was subject to Polish emigration and travel restrictions. The issue was particularly sensitive in cases of mixed marriage. French women married to Polish men, along with their children, were considered French by French law and Polish by Polish law, as were Polish women married to French men. If they returned to Poland for any reason, these women and their children could be held against their will by the Polish government.[69]

Trapped citizens regularly appeared in the offices of the French embassy in Poland, desperate for assistance, but there was little the French government could do for them. "Madame B., who is of modest means, has little political awareness, is ill-informed, and to be completely honest, rather naïve," lamented the French ambassador Pierre de Leusse in one case. Born between the wars in France to Polish parents (and therefore a French citizen by birth), she lived alone in Paris, where she ran a newspaper kiosk. She could not speak Polish, had no friends or family in Poland, and had never traveled to Poland. According to the ambassador, she was persuaded to "return" to Poland by articles in the French Communist newspaper *L'Humanité*. Upon arrival, Polish authorities promptly seized her French passport. She was assigned to live in an unheated barracks with no running water and deployed to a factory in the provinces. Miserable, unable to speak Polish, and reportedly shocked by the "standard of living that seemed incomparably worse than in France," she returned to Warsaw and appealed to the French embassy for assistance returning to France. French authorities could do nothing to help.[70]

In some cases, the Polish government deliberately used wives and children as hostages. Norbert Fialkiewicz, a French citizen of Polish origin, was married in France to Elisabeth-Marie, with whom he had two children, Georges-Norbert and Raphael-André. In July of 1950, his wife and children traveled to Poland on French passports, presumably to visit family members. Polish officials confiscated their French passports at the border and replaced them with Polish passports. Norbert personally appealed to the Ministry of Foreign Affairs, explaining that his wife had gone to Poland without his knowledge or consent. "I was convinced that my children were spending the vacation in the countryside. I should add that my wife is very anxious, and has suffered from neuro-psychiatric troubles and depression . . . and she left without warning me and without my consent."[71] Again, the French government could do nothing. In 1952, Ambassador Étienne Dennery even advised French consuls in Poland that the easiest way for French women married to Polish men to escape from Communist Poland was to get a divorce.[72]

A number of Czechoslovak women married to American men were also denied exit permits in the early 1950s. Jiři Thomas Kolaja, an American citizen who had been born in Czechoslovakia, went to visit family in Czechoslovakia in 1956 and married a Czech woman during his stay. A year later, his wife had not been granted permission to join her husband in the United States. Kolaja was a professor of sociology at a college for African American women in Talladega, Alabama, and his plight moved his students to appeal to the Czechoslovak embassy. A letter signed by ten students invoked both civil rights and human rights. "As Negroes, and as members of the minority group, we realize how it feels to be deprived of many of life's opportunities and pleasures. We feel that Dr. Kolaja is not only being discriminated upon, but as an individual he is being deprived of a right that you or anyone else should have; that is, the right to live with and love someone." Czechoslovak authorities, worried that the case "could be used as propaganda against the Czechoslovak Republic," decided to allow Mrs. Kolaja to join her husband in the United States a few months later.[73]

JOSEPH STALIN DIED in 1953, and in February of 1956 Premier Nikita Khrushchev delivered his secret speech denouncing Stalinist crimes. The so-called post-Stalin thaw that followed gradually melted borders between socialist states, and between Eastern and Western Europe. More and more East Europeans were permitted to cross the Iron Curtain to visit family and friends or simply to take a vacation. But the thaw also produced a change of rhetoric in the West about emigration. As long as only a few thousand souls per year managed to breach the Iron Curtain, it cost Western governments very little to proclaim a "human right" to emigrate. When travel and emigration assumed more of a mass character, however, the consensus around the "human right" to mobility tended to dissolve. Once East Europeans managed to travel to the West in greater numbers, it grew harder to gain recognition as a "bona fide" refugee.

As early as 1955, a memorandum from Pierre de Leusse, the French ambassador in Poland, alerted Parisian officials to the problems of adjustment faced by emigrants who had "chosen freedom" but ended up bitter and disillusioned in the West. Many of these so-called refugees, he insisted, were simply "young people, dazzled by the publicity given to certain sensational escapes and driven more by a spirit of adventure than by the absolute necessity to leave their country." They mistakenly imagined "that a single audacious act would suffice to create an enviable existence abroad." While "traversing the Baltic in a kayak" was certainly "an act of courage," the ambassador conceded, it was not sufficient to "guarantee its authors the job of their choice in a foreign factory."[74]

Two years later, another French ambassador, Éric de Carbonnel, expressed similar doubts about the political sincerity of defectors. That August, seventy Poles vacationing on a Polish cruise ship took advantage of a stopover in Copenhagen to defect. "In truth, it seems to me that it would be wrong to attribute political meaning to these defections," he reported. "Much more than a desire to flee the regime, it's the American mirage that incites people to try out this adventure."[75]

Officials in the East and the West ultimately colluded to keep the Iron Curtain sealed—continuing a pattern established in the late nineteenth century. In the East, dismissing emigrants as apolitical adventurers and miscreants allowed socialist regimes to depoliticize the ongoing exodus. In the West, the porous boundary between "genuine" political refugees and economic migrants helped square the circle between the supposed "human right" to emigrate and the persistence of severe limitations on immigration in the "free world."

The liberalization of travel laws certainly prompted an upswing of defections. In Czechoslovakia after 1963, citizens were able to travel to other socialist countries with relative ease, and to capitalist countries in growing numbers. The number of Czechs and Slovaks vacationing abroad expanded exponentially in a few short years. In 1967, over 2 million Czechs and Slovaks made 1,627,254 trips to socialist countries and 261,081 to capitalist countries. Not surprisingly, some travelers chose not to return home from their "vacations." In 1967 alone, 2,136 citizens took one-way trips to the West. Most were young and well educated.[76]

A popular means of escape from the 1960s onward was to travel to Yugoslavia and then cross the border to Austria or take a cruise ship to the West. This route was made possible by the fact that Yugoslavia's borders were already far more porous than those of other Eastern bloc countries. As of the late 1950s, growing numbers of Yugoslav citizens began to work in the West. Rather than suppress this emigration, the Yugoslav government decided to legalize and regulate it beginning in 1963–64, as part of a large-scale program of economic liberalization and reform. Between 1965 and 1970, the government signed bilateral migration treaties with France, Austria, Sweden, Germany, Australia, Holland, Luxembourg, and Belgium.[77]

Initially, West German authorities suspected Yugoslav migrants of spying and Communist agitation. These fears gradually subsided in the 1960s, as more West Germans ventured to the "red Adriatic" as tourists: 740,000 West Germans vacationed in Yugoslavia in 1967 alone. German employers, meanwhile, praised

Yugoslav workers for their skill and "assimilability," and appreciated that they were actually less likely to participate in labor protests than Spanish or Italian workers. In general, the presence of Yugoslav workers and tourists in the West—and of West European tourists in Yugoslavia—helped create an image of Yugoslavia as a kinder, gentler Communist state.[78]

By 1971, an estimated 775,000 Yugoslav citizens worked abroad, including 436,000 just in Germany. Western authorities and Yugoslav officials alike were deeply invested in the illusion that these emigrants were "guest workers," however, and that they would ultimately return home. In reality, between 65 and 80 percent of migrants from Yugoslavia made permanent homes abroad. Even when the Yugoslav government began to restrict emigration again (and when demand for workers contracted in the West on account of the global economic crisis) in the 1970s, Yugoslav citizens maintained the right to possess passports for travel abroad, and foreign travel stayed relatively unrestricted. With its less vigilantly guarded borders, Yugoslavia therefore remained a potential port of exit for other East European defectors.[79]

In spite of greater freedom to travel, legal opportunities to emigrate from Eastern Europe remained limited in the 1960s and 1970s, with few exceptions. Germans, for example, were allowed to emigrate from Poland in several waves starting in the late 1950s. A total of 500,000 Polish citizens emigrated permanently between 1960 and 1980, most claiming to be ethnic Germans and settling in West Germany under the rubric of "family reunification." Many were women joining family members in Germany. As a result, women were overrepresented among the Poles who emigrated permanently after 1960, and particularly among those emigrating to the West. For every 100 men who emigrated legally between 1962 and 1973, there were 127 female emigrants. Single women were also more likely to get permission to go abroad. In general, the emigration of women could be explained and justified (in the East and the West) as a "nonpolitical" exodus, a humanitarian policy of "family reunification" or a temporary diversion, rather than political "defection."[80]

This did not, however, prevent Polish officials from attempting to deter women from emigrating or traveling to the West. In the mid-1960s, for example, a growing number of Polish students, mostly young women, traveled to France to work as au pairs or maids. Polish and French authorities tended to agree that these young women were not driven by politics, or even by genuine educational, social, or cultural ambitions. Polish women, they insisted, were drawn to France by the allure of Parisian fashion. In 1964, Jan Gerhard, an official at the Polish embassy in France, published a lengthy missive describing the fate of Polish migrant women in the Polish periodical *Nowa Kultura*.[81] Jeanne P., a young Polish student from a "good family," was one of his informants. She moved to Paris to work as a nanny and maid. The job was anything but glamorous. "The children are unbearable, I have work up to my neck, they treat me like a dog, and what's more they pay me only 200 francs a month," she complained. When Jeanne told her boss she was quitting, the woman tried to hit her and threatened to turn her in to the French police. In spite of this abuse, Jeanne refused to return to Warsaw. "How can I return in a state like this?" she exclaimed. "From Paris? Look how I am dressed. I haven't even been able to buy a single miserable skirt. I'd like to buy myself something, save a little money. I think you can understand that?" This young woman carried her pursuit of Western fashion beyond all reason, Gerhard lamented. "Her mission to conquer . . . a dress, a bag, shoes and gloves from Monoprix continues. It is more important than all of the humiliations."

Girls like Jeanne, he held, were addicted to a self-destructive illusion. "They are like roulette players who can't leave the table.

They would like to return 'well-dressed' but they don't have the money. They would like to return with knowledge of the French language . . . but they don't have the time to learn it. They would like to have a diploma to show off, but they haven't studied anything. How can they return?" Eventually, he claimed, the girls would return to their families. And in spite of their stories of marvelous nights spent walking along the Seine and trips to the Louvre, he asserted, one could easily observe "the eagerness with which they devour the food that they can finally consume until they are full, and the relief with which they return to their normal bedrooms, rather than to the beds that their employers put in the kitchen or cage-like rooms in the attic." Gerhard's article was typical of socialist propaganda denouncing emigration to the West, with its strident warnings about the empty promises of Western consumerism and the harsh conditions of capitalist labor. Its pedagogical message to Polish women was clear: they were better off staying home.

WHETHER DRIVEN BY POLITICS or by a desire to shop, the increase in travel between East and West contributed to further political reform, and to the dramatic upheavals of the 1960s and beyond in the Eastern bloc. In the context of the so-called Prague Spring, Czechoslovakia's borders seemed to open overnight. At least 1,720,620 Czechoslovak citizens traveled abroad in 1968, including 690,622 who visited destinations in the West. New passport laws were in the works that would have allowed unrestricted travel as of 1969.[82]

For a brief period, censorship was even lifted in Czechoslovakia, and the press began to call for the amnesty of all postwar emigrants. In a May 1968 article in *Svobodné slovo*, editors maintained that "among those who illegally fled the Republic, whether out of fear of persecution, dissatisfaction with limited personal freedoms, a desire for adventure or a desire for free enterprise, were many accomplished people, political leaders, athletes, scientists, who did not have the intention of damaging our republic. . . . [O]ur compatriots abroad must be rehabilitated."[83]

Oliver Gunovský was a typical beneficiary of the Prague Spring reforms. When he was four years old, in 1948, his father fled Czechoslovakia under threat of arrest for his involvement in black-market activities. Oliver and his mother stayed behind. Throughout his entire youth, Oliver paid for the political "sins" of his father. His educational opportunities were limited, and although he had no contact with his father and did not even know where he was living, his applications to travel abroad were always flatly refused. He was a champion cross-country skier, but he was never allowed to compete outside the country.

In 1965, Oliver discovered that his father was in England. By this time, some Czechoslovak citizens were being granted passports to travel to the West. "I tried to go for vacation to England to visit with my father. When I went to the passport office, the man told me, he looked at the black book again and said 'Ah, you're not going anywhere, just don't even bother.'" But he did not give up, until one day the answer changed.

> Every time I tried again, he told me "Get out of here, I told you, you're not going anywhere," until the spring of 1968, when the same man says "Please come in and sit down. I'll be with you in a minute." So I thought, "Uh oh, something changed, something is brewing." So then I got a visa and I was just married for a few months at that time, but I was so afraid that the system was going to change again, that they were going to take the travel permission away from me, that I didn't even wait until my wife had papers

ready. I just wanted to get out and go to England before somebody said "No, no that was wrong, you're not going anywhere."

Gunovský was in England on August 20, 1968, when Soviet tanks rolled into Prague and crushed the reform movement. He never returned home. His wife managed to join him that fall. The couple eventually resettled in Ontario, Canada, where Oliver opened a restaurant specializing in Central European cuisine.[84]

Out of 100,000 Czechs and Slovaks who happened to be on the other side of the Iron Curtain that day, 40,000 remained in the West, and another 15,000 fled in the wake of the invasion. This was a particularly worrisome exodus from the government's perspective. More than one-third of the emigrants were from the intelligentsia, including many valuable doctors and scientists. Most were young.[85] A post-1968 amnesty for emigrants brought the usual meager returns: a total of 3,723 individuals returned between 1969 and 1970. These were mostly less qualified workers who had difficulty finding employment in the West (particularly given the economic recession of the 1970s), and individuals who had left family members behind in Czechoslovakia and could not get them out.[86]

In Czechoslovakia, the period following the Prague Spring invasion, known as "normalization," brought a return to Stalinist restrictions on travel. A law passed in October 1969 tightly sealed Czechoslovak borders, rolling back the liberalizing reforms of the 1960s. Travel to the West was permitted only in order to visit very close relatives or with prohibitively expensive group tours. With few exceptions (such as elite athletes), Czechoslovak citizens could not travel to attend conferences or participate in foreign exchanges. The number of Czechs and Slovaks traveling to the West declined immediately and dramatically, from well over 600,000 in 1969 to under 50,000 in 1970.[87]

The emotional cost was high for many of these émigrés. In his novel *Ignorance*, the Czech novelist Milan Kundera describes the images that haunt Irena, a character who flees the Czech Republic after the invasion in 1968. At night, she is afflicted by terrifying nightmares in which she is on a plane that unexpectedly turns around and takes her back to Czechoslovakia; or in which she is pursued by the secret police. During the day, she is overcome with nostalgia, as landscapes and images from Prague assault her unexpectedly. "The same moviemaker of the subconscious who, by day, was sending her bits of the home landscape as images of happiness, by night would set up terrifying returns to that same land. The day was lit with the beauty of the land forsaken, the night by the horror of returning to it. The day would show her the paradise she had lost; the night, the hell she had fled."[88]

In 1968, the Soviet Union successfully asserted its control over its satellites. Press reports in Czechoslovakia once again denounced emigrants who were "seduced abroad by big cars or illusions about so-called freedoms," only to find themselves destitute and desperate in the West.[89] But after 1968, few people on either side of the Iron Curtain believed such rhetoric or the claim that socialist regimes were protecting the "freedom" of their citizens with barbed wire and machine guns.

CHAPTER SEVEN

Free to Stay or Go

In the semifinals of the 1975 U.S. Open, eighteen-year-old Martina Navratilova of Czechoslovakia lost to American powerhouse Chris Evert in two sets. Evert went on to win her fourth Grand Slam and her first U.S. Open title. But it was Navratilova who stole the headlines, when she went directly from Forest Hills to the office of the U.S. Immigration and Naturalization Service in New York City to declare her intention to defect.[1]

Asked to explain her decision, Navratilova responded simply, "I wanted my freedom." But what did freedom mean by 1975? The Western press celebrated the athlete's rapid transformation into a model American teenager and capitalist. "Once they were the tired and the poor waving at the Statue of Liberty as they arrived," reported the *New York Times.* "Martina Navratilova doesn't fit that image." She reportedly donned a Gucci shoulder bag and loafers to her first press conference. Three months later, the *International Herald Tribune* updated readers on Navratilova's rapid Americanization:

Martina Navratilova, a teen-age defector from Czechoslovakia, learned fast. She is now a 19-year old capitalist who drops trade names as comfortably as Jack Nicklaus or Arnold Palmer and who stands to earn more than half a million dollars next year. . . . As one of the world's four best women tennis players, the Czechoslovak born star has become a walking delegate for conspicuous consumption. She wears a raccoon coat over 30 dollar jeans and a floral blouse from Giorgio's, the Hollywood boutique. She wears four rings and assorted other jewelry, including a gold necklace with a diamond insert shaped in the figure 1. . . . The usual status-symbol shoes and purse round out the wardrobe. She owns a $20,000 Mercedes Benz 450SL sports coupe. She is fluent in American slang, which she learned on seven tennis trips to the United States beginning in February 1973.

Navratilova herself testified that she had defected because Czechoslovak authorities had warned that she was becoming "too Americanized" and were threatening to prevent her from playing tournaments in the West. She was happy to agree with them, lamenting only that she was gaining weight from eating too many "hamburgers and ice cream cones" on the pro tour.[2]

Back in Czechoslovakia, the Czechoslovak Tennis Federation announced that the tennis star had "suffered a defeat in the face of the Czechoslovak society." The regime also blamed her defection on her lust for Western celebrity and material goods. "She had all possibilities in Czechoslovakia to develop her talent, but she preferred a professional career and a fat bank account."[3] Ironically, journalists on both sides of the Iron Curtain seemed to agree by 1975 that American freedom was tantamount to freedom to consume.[4]

That same year, East European governments signed the Helsinki Accords, which were intended to relax tensions between East and West. At the time, this seemed like a victory for the USSR, since the accords included clauses that guaranteed the stability of national frontiers in Eastern Europe. Eastern bloc countries hoped that the agreement would attract economic investment and credit from the West. But the Helsinki Accords also included promises to liberalize travel regulations, promote tourism, and reunite families separated by the Iron Curtain. Inadvertently, they offered East European dissidents a very effective tool with which to demand reform and generate international publicity for their plight.[5]

The Helsinki Accords provided a powerful, universalist language for dissidents. Freedom of exit had already been anointed a "human right" back in 1948, in the United Nations Declaration on Human Rights. It was not until the 1970s, however, that human rights activists began to form a global movement.[6] Exiled dissidents in the West increasingly used the language of human rights to denounce socialist abuses of civil rights, including the right to exit. The Czechoslovak and Polish governments continued to use children as hostages in the 1970s, for example, refusing to release minors whose parents had emigrated. Now, though, the separation of families across national borders was widely condemned as a human rights abuse. Human rights organizations and Western governments began to lobby for the release of some seven hundred children still trapped in Czechoslovakia. The agitation was successful: the Czechoslovak government yielded to the pressure and gradually released most of the children—out of fear both of negative international publicity and of losing Western loans.[7]

Other changes were under way in the Cold War politics of emigration. The profile of migrants transformed in the 1970s, as dissident intellectuals and celebrity defectors began to take center stage. There had always been a place in the West for intellectual and cultural luminaries from Eastern Europe. The "ideal" East European emigrant throughout the early Cold War had not, however, been a scientist, doctor, or novelist. He or she was a farmer, a miner, a domestic servant, or a factory worker—someone willing to work hard for low wages and fuel booming postwar economies in the West. That image subtly shifted in the late 1960s and the 1970s. In part, the sociological profile of actual emigrants changed, as the refugees who fled Czechoslovakia and Poland in 1968, in particular, tended to have a higher education. Western economies were also transforming. The 1970s brought oil shocks, growing restrictions on immigration in Western Europe, and the rise of technology and service-based industries. The "ideal" refugee from Eastern Europe—the least threatening immigrant—was now an engineer, intellectual, or tennis star, not a factory worker who would compete for ever scarcer manufacturing jobs.

Then, in the 1970s and 1980s, several Eastern bloc governments introduced reforms that attempted to "normalize" relations with the West and with emigrants abroad. These initiatives did not reflect a change of heart regarding emigration in Eastern Europe. Rather, they represented efforts by desperate governments to raise foreign currency. Socialist regimes were searching for new ways to placate dissatisfied citizens in the 1970s and 1980s. Consumer goods—everything from televisions and washing machines to blue jeans and automobiles—were powerful currency in this quest for legitimacy. East European governments largely financed the shift to a consumer economy with loans from the West. Repaying these loans was possible only with a continuous influx of foreign currency, which flowed into the country along with tourists and visitors from the West, or in the form of remittances from migrants working abroad.

Many East Europeans enjoyed their first trips to the West in the 1970s and 1980s. In Hungary, those over the age of fifty-five were allowed more freedom to travel than younger (more employable) citizens, but all Hungarians could take one trip abroad per year, provided it was financed by outside sources. Out of around 500,000 Hungarians traveling to the West each year in the 1980s, 5,000 remained abroad.[8] Yugoslavia had already liberalized its travel policies in the 1960s. By 1971, 3.8 percent of Yugoslav citizens lived outside of Yugoslavia, making it the second-largest exporter of people in Europe (after Italy). Even once the West European demand for migrant labor contracted in the 1970s, the number of Yugoslavs living abroad only increased, thanks to family reunification programs, reaching 836,000 by 1981. There was no returning to closed borders there.[9]

Travel remained heavily restricted in the process of "normalization" in Czechoslovakia after 1968. In 1977, however, the Czechoslovak government began to allow emigrants to retroactively legalize their emigration to the West, by registering with the Czechoslovak consulate and paying hefty fees in foreign currency. The fees were justified as a form of repayment to the socialist state for the emigrants' education and welfare—the classic mercantilist justification for emigration taxes.[10]

The catch was that these "legal" emigrants were now required to sign a document pledging that they would not behave in an "unfriendly" way toward the regime. Those who complied were rewarded with permission to visit Czechoslovakia (bringing foreign currency with them, it was hoped). Individuals who refused to comply were punished with loss of citizenship and banned from visiting family. The clear intent of the law, beyond raising currency, was to isolate politically active emigrants and stir dissension within emigrant communities. The law succeeded on both counts, as many emigrants faced a gut-wrenching choice between signing the agreement in order to retain contact with family members and staying true to their political principles.[11]

As of 1972, Poles and East Germans could cross each other's borders without a visa. They did so en masse, leading to an immediate jump from 1 million to 10 million travelers abroad each year. After the Helsinki conference in 1975, it became easier for Poles to go west as well. In 1981, 1.2 million Poles ventured beyond the Iron Curtain. As always, there was a direct link between the rise of tourism and the number of defections. An estimated 500,000 Poles did not return home from their "vacations" abroad between 1960 and 1980.[12]

Emigration from East Germany diminished to a trickle after the Berlin Wall was erected. There too, though, the need for foreign currency helped loosen the regime's grip on its people. Beginning in the 1960s, it was possible for citizens with parents or children on the other side of the wall to apply for "compassionate leave" to attend family events in the West. Anyone seen as a flight risk was typically denied permission, however, including those with few family connections in the GDR or individuals seen as politically unreliable. As in Czechoslovakia, travel abroad became a reward for political compliance.[13]

East Germany also began to sell its citizens to raise foreign currency. Starting in the 1960s, around 293,000 East Germans, including a number of prominent dissidents, were allowed to leave permanently for the West in exchange for hefty ransoms paid by the West German government. Erich Mende, the West German deputy chancellor who helped create the program, called it "a traffic in human beings that is very close to a slave trade," echoing decades of rhetoric linking emigration to slavery.[14] Migrants were also exchanged for more favorable loan conditions, as Willy Brandt, the Social Democratic West German chancellor from 1969 to 1974, attempted to normalize relations between the two Germanies. Whereas socialist governments had once bitterly denounced the "human traffickers" who lured their citizens to the West, they now willingly brokered a trade in migrants for their own purposes.

Romania also ransomed Jews and Germans for profit. The exchange of Romanian Jews for money and agricultural products had begun covertly after the Second World War. A Jewish businessman in London named Henry Jacober served as the middleman between private individuals in the West and the Romanian secret service. Jacober traded briefcases full of cash, typically $4,000 to $6,000 per emigrant (depending on the individual's age and educational status), for exit permits to the West. When Israeli intelligence officials got wind of the deals, they decided to get in on the scheme, with the approval of Prime Minister David Ben-Gurion. At Khrushchev's insistence, the Romanians began to demand agricultural products instead of cash. Soon Romanian Jews were traded for everything from cattle and pigs to chicken farms and cornflake factories. The ransom of Jews continued under the rule of the Romanian dictator Nicolae Ceaușescu after 1969. The price of exit could go up to $50,000, depending on the migrant's age, education, profession, family status, and political importance. Israel refused to pay for young children and retirees.

Selling Jews was so profitable that the ransom scheme expanded to include ethnic Germans, who were sold to West Germany for suitcases stuffed with U.S. dollars. Germans, like Jews, were priced on the basis of their educational attainment and ransomed for rates ranging from $650 for an unskilled worker to $3,298 for an emigrant with a master's degree or equivalent. Romania also received interest-free loans from West Germany in exchange for releasing Germans. In the mid-1970s, Ceaușescu famously boasted, "Jews, Germans, and oil are our best export commodities." Around 235,000 Jews and 200,000 Germans escaped Romania through these deals. During Ceaușescu's regime alone, an estimated 40,577 Jews were ransomed to Israel for $112,498,800; West Germany made payments of at least $54 million in exchange for exit permits for German emigrants.[15]

Like Romania, Poland allowed (or encouraged) Germans and Jews to leave Poland in the name of "family reunification." A basic goal of emigration policy since 1918—expelling unwanted national minorities—thus continued well into the late socialist era, now under the banner of humanitarianism and human rights. Ethnic Germans (or those successfully classified as ethnic Germans, or *Volksdeutsche*) were released in several waves throughout the postwar era.[16] Many of the migrants were nationally indifferent Silesians, Masurians, or Pomeranians who "rediscovered" their German roots after the war. In December 1955, the German Red Cross provided the Polish government with a list of 180,000 individuals in Poland who had registered for emigration. Representatives of the Polish Red Cross replied that there were not even 180,000 Germans in Poland. The source of the dispute, of course, was that Polish and German authorities disagreed about how to define a Pole. They had long competed to claim nationally indifferent (and often bilingual) Silesians as "authentic" Poles or Germans. Neither side was right; most Silesians were loyal above all to their region and to the Catholic Church, rather than to the German or Polish nation.[17]

The second wave of emigration in 1971–72 produced further conflicts, both about how to define a Pole and how to define a family. The Polish government once again insisted that there were no "real" Germans remaining in Poland: those who registered to emigrate were simply economic opportunists. By this point, however, many West Germans agreed, pejoratively labeling new emigrants "Volkswagen Germans." Yet the German Red Cross reported that 275,000 individuals had already registered for emigration from Poland to the Federal Republic, and it speculated that up to 700,000 eligible Germans might be living in Poland.[18]

The 1971 agreement went beyond the official rubric of "family reunification" for the first time, including ethnic Germans even if they had no family in Germany. Issuing exit permits also enabled the Polish government to dump undesirable citizens. Internal Polish guidelines specified that individuals who "spread recidivist propaganda," along with those "who burden the country with respect to a poor work ethic, degeneration, criminals, alcoholics, chronically ill pensioners, etc.," should all be granted visas to West Germany.[19]

The vast majority of Poles who applied to emigrate were turned down, however. Out of 267,647 applications to emigrate to the Federal Republic between 1970 and 1975, 214,297, or 77.5 percent, were rejected.[20] Applying to emigrate was risky, moreover, since applicants often faced retaliation. An aging widow from the Second World War lost her farm because she filed an application to emigrate in 1964. Her application was denied eight times in six years. "Now I have no pension, no field, and no ability to emigrate. Should I simply make an end to my life? Should we Germans simply be ruined? They will never turns us into Poles," she protested.[21]

Polish propaganda countered that emigrants to West Germany were exploited and struggling to integrate into German society. By refusing to issue visas, the government insisted that it was actually protecting prospective emigrants and their children. In an article entitled "Humanitarian Action?" the Polish daily *Słowo Powszechne* thus lamented "the tragedy of these people, who had a secure position in Poland." Their children, meanwhile, "cry out in the Polish language that they want to return."[22] The struggle of children to adjust to German society was a favorite theme of anti-emigration propaganda, as journalists represented the (authentically "Polish") children of emigrants as victims of their opportunistic parents. Julian Bartosz, writing in *Prawo i Życie*, also questioned the authenticity of emigrants' family ties to Germany. "The general definition of the 'family unit' is ever more generously interpreted. The sister travels to her sister and drags her husband, three children, and mother-in-law with her. . . . The father is 'united' with the father of his aunt and brings his entire family along," Bartosz lamented. "For many of the underage emigrants, who are condemned to the fate of becoming detested 'Pollacks' by the whims of their parents, our big-hearted gesture is actually a great injustice."[23]

By early 1970, over 400,000 Polish citizens had decamped for West Germany, and over the next ten years, various laws and accords permitted another 250,000 to join them.[24] Each agreement between Poland and the Federal Republic was publicized as a "purely humanitarian" effort to reunite divided families, but Poland's need for foreign currency certainly greased the wheels. In the 1955 agreement, for example, the West German government agreed to purchase 300,000 tons of imported Polish goods.[25]

Predictably, even as Polish officials attempted to minimize the loss of population through "family reunification," they actively promoted the departure of Poland's remaining Jews. In 1968, in the context of the "anti-Zionist" campaign, 12,927 Jews left or were deported from Poland. The superficial pretext for the purges was the Arab-Israeli war that began in June 1967. In a speech that month, the Polish leader Władysław Gomułka depicted Polish Jews as a fifth column that supported Israeli imperialism. The "anti-Zionist" campaign quickly developed into a blunt anti-Semitic assault on Poland's remaining Jews.

The deeper context for this attack was a long-standing division between a faction of the Polish Communist Party that had spent the Second World War in Moscow (including many Jewish Communists) and one whose members had spent the war in Poland (including Gomułka himself). Student demonstrations in March of 1968 inflamed the campaign, as Communist officials sought to blame the social protests on a Jewish, alien element. The government's anti-Semitic offensive ultimately served as a useful outlet for the population's pent-up frustrations with the Communist system itself. Suddenly, people could vent their rage about Stalinist violence and terror, the corruption and unjustified privileges of the party elite, economic shortages and stagnation—as long as all of these "shortcomings" were blamed on Jews.[26]

The result was an open purge of Jews from universities, government, and factory jobs. Jews were encouraged to emigrate, but forced to choose Israel as their destination, in order to reaffirm the myth that they were Zionist conspirators (only 25 percent of the emigrants ultimately settled there). Significantly, the majority of the emigrants were educated elites. The largest number were engineers and doctors, but the group also included 500 university professors and scientists, 200 journalists, editors, and writers, 100 artists, actors, and musicians, and 520 former state officials.[27] Halina Zawadzka, who left Poland in 1968, recalled years later,

> Everything started collapsing then. I lost hope that a Jew would ever be able to live in Poland without the stigma of his or her origin. The feeling of pre-war humiliation returned. . . . Fear that had been suppressed from the time of the war now resurfaced. Embittered and disillusioned, I decided to emigrate from Poland. I was parting from all my nearest and dearest, I was leaving behind everything I had achieved. I was going to strangers in an unknown world. . . . [T]he past was being repeated.[28]

This final purge of Polish Jews did not end the upheaval in Poland, however. Riots and strikes erupted in 1970–71 and again in 1976 in response to planned increases in food prices. In a significant defeat for the government, the unrest forced Gomułka to resign in 1971, and the price increases were canceled. Then, in 1978, Karol Józef Wojtyła, a relatively young Pole, became Pope John Paul II. Enormously popular in Poland, he urged Polish Catholics not to compromise on their principles. After another wave of strikes in 1980, Lech Wałęsa, leader of the strikers in the Baltic ports (Gdansk and Gdynia) and cofounder of the Solidarity trade union, signed an agreement with the government that not only gave the workers wage increases and rolled back price increases but also established an unprecedented legal right to organize independent trade unions. In 1981, in an attempt to regain control of the situation, the Polish government appointed the military general Wojciech Jaruzelski head of state. Jaruzelski called for a truce of three months, during which he hoped to stabilize the economy and negotiate with the workers. No agreement was reached, however, and at the end of the year, Jaruzelski imposed martial law in an effort to crush the Solidarity movement.

The result was another rapid exodus from Poland. Around 150,000 of the Poles who were outside of Poland at the time decided not to return home, and tens of thousands more fled toward Austrian refugee camps. By January 1982, 50,000 Polish refugees were stranded in Austria, where they were being housed in army barracks and hostels for lack of space in camps.[29]

This put the United States in an awkward position. Before 1980, immigrants from Communist states had automatically been accorded the status of refugees in the United States. In 1980, however, Congress had passed the U.S. Refugee Act, which finally adopted the language of the 1951 United Nations Convention on the Status of Refugees. The Refugee Act now defined refugees as individuals with "a well-founded fear of persecution, based on race, religion, national origin, or membership in any social organization." According to this criterion, most Polish migrants were no longer considered refugees. In the opinion of Richard Day, general counsel of the U.S. Senate Subcommittee on Immigration, Refugees and International Law, the majority of migrants from Poland were coming to the United States for economic reasons.

"What we hear about are food shortages, fuel shortages, not polit-ical reasons." As a result, tens of thousands of Poles were forced to live underground in the United States as illegal immigrants. "Our people live like hunted game," contended one Polish immigrant in 1981. "You stay as close as possible to the family, don't social-ize much, don't talk at work, hide behind someone else's Social Security card, don't get a driver's license." The Reagan administra-tion did ban the expulsion of Polish immigrants from the United States, but it did not automatically extend asylum to Polish refu-gees. Global politics clearly played a role in the decision: the United States feared that if Poles received asylum, it might be obliged to admit refugees who were fleeing right-wing regimes allied with the United States. Senator Alan K. Simpson (Republican of Wyoming), chair of the Senate immigration committee, explained, "We have to be very cautious about any broadening of the definition of 'ref-ugee,' because, besides the Poles, thousands of Haitian and Salva-doran immigrants claim to have fled political persecution."[30]

Jerry W. was a typical victim of the new law. He arrived in the United States with his wife and child on a tourist visa in 1982. Jerry filed for asylum six weeks later, citing his activities as a Solidarity member and his fears of reprisal for having sponsored union meet-ings. Because he had not brought his Solidarity membership card with him (he claimed that he was afraid to travel with it), his appli-cation was rejected. He was given fifteen days to return to Poland or face deportation hearings.[31] The numbers fluctuated from year to year, but in 1985, 62 percent of Poles who applied for asylum in the United States were turned down. Although they were not actually deported, they lived in a state of limbo and fear.[32] Poles still enjoyed an advantage over refugees fleeing right-wing regimes allied with the United States, however. Only 3 percent of 8,537 applicants for asylum from El Salvador and 7 percent of Nicaraguan applicants were successful in 1984, for example.[33]

Then, in 1985, Mikhail Gorbachev came to power in the USSR and announced his new policies of perestroika (restructuring) and glasnost (openness). The flight from Eastern Europe accelerated rapidly over the next four years, as travel regulations liberalized. In March of 1989, the *Washington Post* reported that thousands of East Europeans had been "drawn by westward hopes" in the past year, constituting the largest movement from the East to the West since the beginning of the Cold War. "Drawn by the twin beacons of political liberty and economic prosperity, tens of thousands of Poles, Soviets, East Germans and other East Europeans are flooding into western countries, especially West Germany." Some were simply taking advantage of new travel policies to go shopping in the West or earn a bit of hard currency, but many planned to stay for good. More than 165,000 Poles arrived in West Germany in 1988, triple the number that had emigrated in 1987. The number of East Germans fleeing to West Germany doubled, to 59,000, in the same period. "I'm willing to spend a year there [in West Germany] sleeping under a bridge, because I know that later I'll be able to achieve something," one young steelworker declared.[34]

The Hungarian government, already one of the more liberal regimes in the Eastern bloc, lifted most of its restrictions on travel to the West in 1988–89. Then, on May 2, 1989, Hungarian border guards dismantled the electrified fence between Hungary and Austria. East Germans seized the opportunity to go "on vacation" in neighboring Hungary, where thousands sought refuge in the West German embassy. By September 1989, sixty thousand citizens of the GDR were camped out in embassies in Budapest, Prague, and Warsaw, waiting for an opportunity to escape to the West.

They got their chance on September 10, when the Hungarian foreign minister declared on television that his government would not prevent these Germans from simply walking across the border into Austria. In three days' time, 22,000 East Germans slipped

An East German man hangs on the fence of the West German embassy in Prague, while a Czech policeman attempts to pull him down, October 2, 1989. The man maintained his grip and was let into the embassy by a West German diplomat.

AP Photo/DE/stf/Diether Endlicher.

through the first holes in the Iron Curtain, deeply embarrassing the East German government. In an effort to control the damage, officials offered the refugees safe passage back to East Germany and on to West Germany in a sealed train, but the strategy backfired. When the train made a pit stop in Dresden, thousands of protestors scrambled to climb aboard. They were beaten back by the police, inciting a riot, which was captured by TV cameras and broadcast around the world, a major public relations fiasco for the regime.[35]

By the end of the 1980s, nothing symbolized the bankruptcy of socialist regimes more profoundly than the walls, watchtowers, and barbed wire fences that kept the citizens of the Eastern bloc captive. The Berlin Wall had become the quintessential symbol of Communist oppression, a television backdrop and platform for visiting dignitaries and Cold Warriors from the United States. "Tear down this wall!" demanded Ronald Reagan, in his 1987 speech from the Brandenburg Gate in Berlin. Eventually, the wall came down, in small part thanks to the fumbling of a mid-level bureaucrat named Günter Schabowski. Without authorization, Schabowski announced the immediate liberalization of travel restrictions on East German TV on November 9, 1989. Germans wasted no time hacking the wall to bits with garden tools and whatever other sharp objects they could find (there was a shortage of hammers), pushing past dazed border guards in a contagious euphoria. Almost overnight, a symbol of terror was transformed into a souvenir of communism's collapse.

BY 1989, the link between mobility and freedom seemed absolute, confirmed by the astonishing rapidity with which the first crack in the wall appeared to bring down the entire system. And yet there was nothing inevitable about the association of freedom, mobility, and capitalism in the twentieth century. The fundamental tensions between a proclaimed "human right" to exit and the principle of national sovereignty were never resolved; states continued to insist on the right to control their borders. Nor could anyone resolve contradictions between an image of East European emigrants as heroic "escapees" and "freedom fighters" and ongoing suspicions that migrants from the East might be undesirable citizens, spies, or opportunists.

The revolution of 1989 was therefore no fairy-tale ending to the saga of the Cold War. The dissolution of physical borders did not magically erase half a century of divisions between East and West. If anything, growing east–west mobility after 1989 initially seemed to widen the gulf. Even before the wall fell, as the number of migrants moving west increased, some West Germans began to complain about Poles and East Germans who allegedly lived off welfare and crowded the Western market for jobs and apartments. In August 1988, Theo Summer, editor in chief of *Die Zeit*, responded to the grumbling with a warning not to "erect a concrete wall in our heads against the liberated Germans from the East, who are able to come to us after so many years."[36]

His warning was prescient. After 1989, chants of "We Are One People!" echoed around the world as the ground was prepared for German reunification. At first, it seemed that fifty years of division had been overcome. But many Germans soon suffered from the shock of mutual nonrecognition, and caricatures and resentments proliferated on both sides. In the slang of the time, *Besser-Wessies* (West German know-it-alls) faced off against the *Jammer-Ossies* (whining Easterners).[37] *Der Spiegel* declared the "end of the honeymoon" only two months after the wall fell, citing an epidemic of shoplifting by "visitors from the Republic of Shortages [*Mangelrepublik*] beguiled by seductively displayed goods." *Wessies* resented everything from the 100-deutschmark welcome money and welfare benefits doled out to East Germans to their alleged lack of respect for West Berlin's parking regulations. These tensions did not disappear overnight. Sommer's "wall in the head" became popular shorthand for the persistence of social, cultural, and psychological divisions between Easterners and Westerners well into the 1990s and 2000s. While there was no turning back on reunification, some *Ossies* eventually began to express a sentimental longing for East German food brands, domestic interiors, and (imagined or real) social solidarity, which was labeled *Ostalgie*.[38]

The movement from the East to the West was massive, particularly when it became clear that no "economic miracle" was coming to East Germany anytime soon. Approximately 2.45 million people, around 14 percent of the East German population in 1989, migrated to West Germany between 1991 and 2006 (around 20 percent of these migrants eventually returned to the East), while 1 million moved from west to east, mostly entrepreneurs, managers, and civil servants. The young and educated were most likely to go to the West, and women were more likely to decamp than men. The result was a perceived demographic hollowing out of rural East Germany, and a proliferation of stereotypes of the East as backward, racist, and resentful.[39]

The only thing that provoked more tension and anxiety than the invasion of the *Ossies* was the opening of German frontiers to neighbors farther east. Between 1989 and 2004, when eight former socialist countries joined the European Union, an estimated 3.2 million people from Eastern Europe (not including the former Soviet Union) emigrated west.[40]

The collapse of communism also precipitated a wave of returns, as exiled East Europeans came home, often for the first time in decades. Some came to visit, others to stay for good. It is difficult to establish precise numbers, since many individuals continued to live between two homes, but an estimated 69,704 Poles returned to post-Communist Poland in the 1990s.[41] Even in the early euphoria of the transition era, these returns were often painful or uneasy. Re-migrants discovered that they no longer recognized the places and people they had left behind. Josef, a character in Milan Kundera's novel *Ignorance*, returns from Denmark to Czechoslovakia for the first time in twenty years. "Before leaving Denmark, he had considered the coming encounter with places he had known, with his past life, and had wondered: would he be moved? Cold? Delighted? Depressed? Nothing of the sort. During his absence, an invisible broom had swept across the landscape of his childhood, wiping away everything familiar; the encounter he had expected never took place." Even the Czech language had changed in his absence. Irena meanwhile returns to Prague from Paris, only to learn that she does not fit in with her former friends. "I could go back and live with them, but there'd be a condition: I'd have to lay my whole life with . . . the French, solemnly on the altar of the homeland and set fire of it. Twenty years of my life spent abroad would go up in smoke, in a sacrificial ceremony. . . . That's the price I'd have to pay to be pardoned. To be accepted. To become one of them again."[42]

ACROSS MOST OF EASTERN EUROPE, the revolution of 1989 and the migrations that followered were remarkably peaceful, but the breakup of Yugoslavia produced more bloodshed and more refugees than Europe had experienced since the end of the Second World War. The war began in June of 1991, when Slovenia and Croatia declared their independence from Yugoslavia. In response, the Yugoslav army, commanded by the Serbian nationalist leader Slobodan Milošević, shelled Slovenia for several weeks (before allowing it to secede) and occupied large parts of Croatia. The violence escalated when Croatian and Muslim Bosnians voted for independence in March 1992. In reply, Bosnian Serbs declared their own "Serbian Republic" within Bosnia and besieged Sarajevo. As the war escalated, both Serbian and Croatian forces engaged in ethnic cleansing, driving non-Croatian or non-Serbian civilians from their homes, businesses, and land in order to create ethnically homogeneous territories.[43]

The United Nations Refugee Convention had been designed after World War II precisely to protect victims from this kind of terror, but Western governments were reluctant to intervene. As of July 1992, more than 2 million people had been displaced in the former Yugoslavia, but only a minority resettled elsewhere. Germany had accepted 200,000 refugees; Austria and Hungary each took in 50,000, Sweden 45,000, and Switzerland 17,500. France and Britain had accepted only 1,200 refugees each.[44] Many Western diplomats feared that offering asylum to Yugoslav refugees would "reward" ethnic cleansing. They wanted refugees to stay close to home, so that they could return easily after the conflict ended. Most Yugoslav refugees were therefore sheltered in "safe havens" within the former Yugoslavia, which were poorly protected by UN peacekeeping forces. The cost of inaction was high. On July 11, 1995, the Serbian general Ratko Mladić entered one such "safe haven" in Srebrenica and slaughtered 7,400 men and boys, in the worst massacre on European soil since the Second World War.

The United States ultimately accepted 168,644 refugees from the former Yugoslavia.[45] Most spent long periods waiting in refugee camps in Europe before they received their visas, during which they were plagued by anxieties. "It took us a year and half to come to America. In that year we didn't know what to expect. We knew America only through movies, newspapers and music videos," recalled one Bosnian refugee. "We were afraid of poverty. . . . We thought we wouldn't be able to step out on street because of drugs, murders and similar things. We were afraid that there was no health insurance similar to what we had." They came to America anyway, since "everything looked better than going back to Bosnia with no future at all."[46]

Upon arrival, some found their worst fears confirmed. A Bosnian who arrived in the United States in 1996 with his wife recalled his initial disappointment. "JFK was a shock to us after the glossy airport in Frankfurt, Germany. Everything was so old and dirty. Everything looked like a big joke. This was America?!? . . . Where are the big buildings? Where are the people in suits and ties? Where are the limousines? This cannot be America!" The couple's first impressions did not improve when they arrived in Utica, New York, their new home. "Out on the street was loud. Some people were screaming. Glass was breaking somewhere. Three houses across the street were burned almost to the ground. Is there maybe a civil war in America that we didn't know about?"[47] Others felt they were better off in the United States, however. "We have never lived better than now," one refugee affirmed. "Before I worked from sunup to sundown and had nothing. Now I work less hours and we have enough." Another young woman who was initially homesick in the United States gradually adapted. "People are friendly in this country. . . . This is the place to be. Everything is free and open."[48]

A second massive exodus from the former Yugoslavia took place in 1999, when Milošević once again began to persecute Albanian Kosovars. In response to ongoing repression, the Kosovo Liberation Army (UCK), a resistance organization that used terrorist tactics, launched attacks on Serbian police and villages. In retaliation, Milošević unleashed a new campaign of deportations and massacres against the Albanian population. More than 950,000 Albanians fled their homes, mostly to neighboring Macedonia or Albania. The conflict finally ended when NATO forces occupied Kosovo and Milošević agreed to remove his troops in June 1999. Many Albanians returned to their homes, but many others found refuge in Western Europe or the United States.[49]

Once again, refugees often struggled to adapt to a culture that only vaguely matched their expectations. American humanitarian agencies deliberately scattered Albanian refugees in small communities throughout the United States, rather than concentrating them in large urban centers. The trauma of war and displacement was therefore heightened for many by a profound sense of isolation. "There you are, in Crystal City, Missouri," one woman recalled. "It is my first time being away, I am seventeen, and this place is very different from my expectations of America. I had expected bright lights, tall buildings. In Crystal City, there is a K-Mart, a Wal-Mart, one Main Street and one stoplight, and that's it. I was very homesick." Many Albanian Kosovars ultimately opted to return home, though younger refugees were more likely to stay. A Kosovar who arrived as a child explained, "You do feel nostalgic about home and you do miss it. But deep down, you realize, as you walk down a street that this is it, this is pretty much your place, this is the end of the train. For the parents, home will always be over there, but for you, this is it."[50]

Perhaps his decision to stay was aided by the fact that he had so much company. Even before the war, Albania had the highest emigration rate in East Central and Southeastern Europe, particularly among young people. Albania was the last stronghold of communism in Eastern Europe. Whereas most Eastern bloc countries had begun to relax travel restrictions in the 1970s and 1980s, Albania built thousands of concrete bunkers and barbed wire fences along its border, and declared defection punishable by up to ten years' imprisonment and internal exile for the defectors' family.[51]

The first major wave of emigration therefore began only in July 1990, when around 4,500 Albanians stormed Western embassies in Tirana. One group rammed through the gates of the Italian embassy in a truck; several thousand others catapulted themselves over the fence of the West German embassy. On July 13, 1990, 3,915 Albanian refugees arrived in Italy in the middle of the night on a cruise ship commandeered by the United Nations.[52] Another 45,000 migrated by boat to Italy in the spring and summer of 1991. At first they were welcomed, but by August 1991 Italy was turning refugees back to Albania, deporting an estimated 17,000 that month. Violent clashes erupted between Albanians and Italian police that August, as refugees attempted to break out of the soccer stadium in Bari where they were being forcibly detained (and from which they were being forcibly repatriated to Albania).

The episode became emblematic of the challenges faced by Italy after its rapid transition from a country of emigration to one of immigration. Clara Bisegna of the Italian Foreign Ministry explained, "We tried to understand. . . . We had all these many Italians going abroad when we were very poor." But public sympathy for the refugees eroded quickly amid suspicions that the Albanians were not "authentic" political refugees—that they were simply looking to enjoy higher wages and better living conditions in Italy.[53]

Albanian Communists were not completely ousted until March 1992. Throughout the 1990s, Albania remained the poorest country in Europe, and 20 percent of the working-age population left the country once the gates opened permanently. Albania's emigration rate was four to six times higher than that of other former Communist countries. By 2010, some 1,705,000 Albanians were living abroad, with 750,000 in Greece, 450,000 in Italy, and 400,000 in the United States.[54]

Beyond Albania, the expansion of the European Union in the first decade of the twenty-first century stimulated east–west migrations on a scale not seen for a hundred years. Not surprisingly, EU expansion also raised new anxieties about the costs and benefits of a Europe without internal borders. In 2005, in the lead-up to an infamous French vote against the EU constitution, the "Polish plumber" became a symbol of Western fears about a potential invasion of cheap East European workers. At the time, a grand total of 150 Polish plumbers were unclogging French pipes; only 5,537 Poles had taken advantage of their newfound freedom of movement to move to France in 2004. That did not stop French opponents of the

EU from raising the specter of hordes of East Europeans arriving by the busload (or flying in on low-cost airlines) to steal French jobs.[55] The Polish Ministry of Tourism cleverly replied to the insult with a tongue-in-cheek poster featuring a handsome and sexy young plumber. "I am staying in Poland. Come visit in great numbers," he beckoned.

Poles did emigrate en mass to Western Europe after 2004, but most of them chose the United Kingdom, Ireland, or Sweden as their destinations, where they faced fewer labor market restrictions. The number of Poles who spent more than two months abroad more than doubled, from around 1 million in 2004 to 2.3 million in 2007. The numbers were large enough to renew anxieties about emigration back home in Eastern Europe. The Polish Chamber of Commerce even started a campaign called "Wracaj do Polski" ("Return to Poland") in 2007.[56]

In the Czech Republic, which experienced a much smaller post-EU exodus, politicians also attempted to summon emigrants home. Their appeals echoed decades of rhetoric about the need to foster links between the imagined Czech diaspora and the homeland. "We should increase the interest of Czech society in Czechs who permanently or temporarily live abroad. We should appeal to them to return. Not only physically but also 'virtually.' That way these people can enrich Czech society with their experiences," declared the Czech senator Tomáš Grulich of the Conservative Civic Democratic Party (Občanská demokratická strana) in October 2013.[57] In Hungary, meanwhile, government officials, fearful of a brain drain, imposed new restrictions on the mobility of college graduates who receive scholarships from the state. Students are required to live and work in Hungary for up to ten years after graduation to repay their debt to the government. Students and parents have complained that the law violates the European Union's guarantee of freedom of movement.[58]

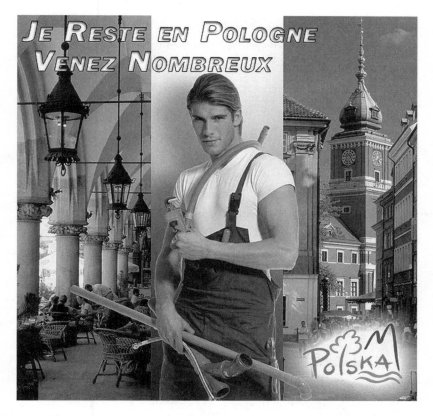

JE RESTE EN POLOGNE
VENEZ NOMBREUX

POLSKA

"I am staying in Poland. Come visit in great numbers."
Polish tourism poster challenging the negative
sterotype of the so-called Polish plumber.
Courtesy of the Polish Tourist Organization.

What the numbers and debates don't fully capture, however, is the new reality of East European mobility since 2004. Just as in the late nineteenth century, relatively open borders and labor markets within the EU have created new and more diverse patterns of short-term and long-term mobility. Some Poles, for example, work for a few years in the West, save up money to start a business or buy property, and then return home. There are also circular migrants who come and go; young people who spend a year or two abroad for the sake of getting an education or new work experiences; and, of course, individuals who emigrate permanently. In general, migrants tend to respond quickly to changing economic conditions in Europe. Thanks to relatively few barriers to mobility, return migration is more common among East Europeans who migrate within the EU than among those who come to the United States, where the difficulties of obtaining a visa make repeated round-trips more problematic.[59]

In September 2008, the Polish economy was doing well. The *New York Times* reported that a growing number of Polish immigrants were leaving Greenpoint, Brooklyn, to return to Poland. In Greenpoint, long a hub of Polish American life, Polish newspapers were struggling to stay afloat, Polish delis were closing up shop, and Lot Airlines was selling more one-way than round-trip tickets. Monika Just, aged twenty-six, had arrived in the United States in 2005 and overstayed her visa. Three years later, she decided to return to Poland. "I don't have a life here," she explained. "I just have a job. All I do is work." Poles like Just were drawn home by expanding economic opportunities in Poland as well as by new opportunities within the European Union, just a short flight from home. According to State Department statistics, Polish migration to the United States declined dramatically between 2008 and 2009, from 104,855 to 75,856 a year later, thanks to a combination of the U.S. financial crisis and increasing opportunities for employment in Europe.[60]

As of 2011, Poles were the second-largest immigrant group in the United Kingdom (after migrants from the Indian subcontinent). Polish was also the second-most-common language after English (beating out Welsh), with 546,000 individuals declaring Polish as their native tongue.[61] The increasing visibility of Polish communities in the United Kingdom has prompted diverse responses. On the one hand, there has been a predictable wave of nationalism and xenophobia. In 2008, a features writer for the *Daily Mail* tabloid even offered one hundred pounds for "anonymous horror stories of people who have employed East European staff, only for them to steal from them, disappear, or have lied about their resident status."[62]

Others have actively celebrated Polish contributions to the British economy and culture. Lech Mintowt-Czyz, whose great grandfather had been the minister of health in Poland when the Nazis invaded, defended immigrants by arguing that the UK had gotten the "best" of Polish society (a classic fear of opponents of emigration):

> The truth is that people who have the character to travel halfway round the world to start a new life are exactly the people we should want in Britain—not just Poles, but Kosovans, Romanians, Somalis, Syrians, Malians and Afghans too. . . . These countries aren't pushing their rubbish on to us—they are losing their best and brightest. Here's the truth. The Polish plumbers we all know and love aren't good just because there is some sort of Polish-plumbing-genius DNA—but because the Polish plumbers who make the journey are the most determined, go-getting, hard-working cream of the crop that the country has to offer. The teeth-sucking, it'll-cost-you, I-can-do-it-in-September sort of Polish plumber absolutely exists, but they are still in Poznan scratching their backsides.[63]

East Central European countries are no longer, however, among the world's top exporters of people, as they were in the early twentieth century. While the Russian Federation ranked second and Ukraine fifth in the number of emigrants in 2005, Poland came in sixteenth, with 2.3 million people living abroad that year.[64] In certain respects, the inclusion of former Eastern bloc countries into the European Union represents the realization of a dream formulated more than a hundred years earlier. East Europeans have finally secured the privileges of "white" Europeans. In contemporary debates about immigration in Europe, East Europeans are often praised as the "good" immigrants—in rhetorical opposition to migrants from outside Europe (especially nonwhite or non-Christian migrants), whose capacity to assimilate is continually questioned by opponents of immigration.[65] The former British Conservative Party chairman and MP Norman Tebbit thus declared in September 2013 that Brits should not fear migrants from Eastern Europe. "We don't have much of a problem with people like the Poles, the Czechs, the Slovaks. . . . [T]hey're not the problem," he insisted. "The bigger problem that is caused in our cities is caused by immigrants from the Third World who have got no intention of integrating here. . . . They are people who left their country, came here and are trying to recreate their country in our country."[66]

The long and troubled story of east–west migration is still not over, however. As freedom of mobility extends farther eastward and southward within the EU (and new countries vie for membership), right-wing nationalists and sensationalist media outlets stir up fresh waves of xenophobia. Roma and Sinti migrants from Eastern Europe are currently among the most visible scapegoats for European fears about open borders. Designated for extermination by the Nazi regime, Roma and Sinti have been targets of violence and persecution in both Western and Eastern Europe for centuries. Like the "wandering Jew," they have been stereotyped as quintessential nomads whose mobility threatens state sovereignty and social order. In 2010, the French government expelled more than a thousand Roma migrants to Romania following a clash between police officers and Roma in Grenoble and Saint-Aignan. The European Commission, Roma advocacy groups, and opponents of the government of President Nicolas Sarkozy of France all condemned the deportations.[67] The expulsions didn't stop, however, and more than ten thousand Roma were "repatriated" to Romania from France in 2010. Those who left voluntarily received a payment of three hundred Euros from the French government.[68] These "repatriations" continued even after Sarkozy left office. At least three thousand Roma were expelled from France in the first eight months of 2013.[69]

On January 1, 2014, Romanians and Bulgarians acquired the right to move and work freely in Europe (until 2014, they had been required to have an invitation from an employer or be "self-employed" in order to stay abroad longer than three months). Predictably, anticipation of swelling migration from Southeastern Europe generated a renewed outburst of anti-Roma agitation across Europe. The French interior minister, Manuel Valls, declared in September 2013 that aside from a "handful of families," Roma cannot be integrated into French society and that most should be deported. According to one opinion poll, 77 percent of the French population agrees with him.[70]

Meanwhile, in the United Kingdom, a tabloid headline provocatively warned British citizens, "The Pickpockets Are Coming," stoking fears of a mass invasion of criminals and child traffickers. The article described Roma gangs in France who

> will stop at nothing to intimidate and steal. . . . Brazenly targeting their victims in broad daylight at cashpoints, on crowded pavements and in parks and Metro stations, the increasingly aggressive gangs are causing chaos and misery in the French capital. . . . And, as Britain prepares to allow

thousands of immigrants from Romania and Bulgaria to seek work in the UK . . . there is every chance of similar Roma gangs coming to the United Kingdom.[71]

All eyes in Germany are also on Bulgaria and Romania, and on a feared invasion of Sinti and Roma migrants. According to one poll, as of March 2013, two-thirds of Germans wanted to limit freedom of mobility within the EU. Jacques Delfeld of the Association of German Sinti and Roma has protested, "Whenever we are discussed in connection with poverty, criminality, and prostitution, we are being seen as a unified group. . . . [T]he fact that most Sinti and Roma here are German citizens and not at all poor is ignored."[72] In reality, according to a recent report of the German Bundestag, the unemployment rate among Bulgarians and Romanians in Germany (9.6 percent) is lower than the national average for immigrants (16.4 percent).[73] And yet the populist right continues to incite fears of "poverty immigrants" (*Armutszuwanderer*), who will allegedly arrive en masse to feed off the German welfare state. Interior Minister Hans-Peter Friedrich, of the center-right CSU, declared in May 2013, "Whoever comes to Germany in order to collect welfare must be sent home."[74]

The shadow of human trafficking also continues to follow migrants from Eastern Europe. The fall of the Iron Curtain generated a booming transnational sex industry.[75] Some Westerners purchased sex from the prostitutes working the highway between Dresden and Prague, while others surfed the Internet for Polish and Ukrainian mail-order brides, or traveled to Prague to take advantage of new opportunities for gay sex tourism.[76] Most transactions were "voluntary," in that sex workers entered the trade knowingly (if out of desperation). "East European girls are desperate to work here," claimed a sex club owner in the Netherlands. "And they're very popular with the clients. They're cheaper and they'll do things Dutch girls won't—at least in the beginning." According to one Polish prostitute, many women working in Dutch brothels sent money back home without telling anyone how they were earning it.[77]

Press coverage tends to focus on the minority of women forcibly trafficked into prostitution. Sex trafficking is certainly a real phenomenon in contemporary Eastern Europe. A recent study estimated that about half of the seventeen thousand migrant women working as prostitutes in the United Kingdom are from Eastern Europe. Officials suspected that around four hundred of these East Europeans had been forcibly trafficked. Victims of trafficking are notoriously hard to detect, and the line between voluntary and forcible prostitution easily blurs when the victims are young, impoverished, dependent, and unable to speak the local language.[78]

Sensationalist tabloid reports about sex trafficking are not simply a humanitarian response to a violent crime, however. They also stir anti-migrant sentiment in contemporary Europe, by playing up the criminality of East European migrants. Headlines like "Tricked, Beaten and Sold as a Sex Slave—The Diary of Mia, Aged 14" and "Kidnap, Beating, Rape: My Story of Sex Slavery in UK" are intended to both shock and titillate, promising details of an East European underworld. "Fleeing poverty and unemployment, they are tricked or lured by 'dancers wanted' ads or direct approaches from 'friends of friends,' promising jobs in flower shops or as au pairs. Instead they end up in brothels, brutalized by pimps in Germany, Holland, Belgium, and even Britain, where demand for young, white, compliant, and above all cheap East European girls has become insatiable," wrote Katherine Butler for the *Independent* in 1997.[79]

This type of reporting has a long and lurid pedigree. W. T. Stead, the British editor of the *Pall Mall Gazette*, pioneered the genre. He famously sought to expose child prostitution in London in 1885 by personally arranging the purchase and sale of a thirteen-year-old girl for a brothel. Stead then proceeded to observe and describe her initiation into prostitution in pornographic detail. The paper sold so many copies that it ran out of paper to print on. Copies of the issue in which the story was published traded hands for twenty times their newsstand price. That article helped give rise to a moral panic and an international campaign against "white slavery" in Europe, which intersected with and fueled contemporary anti-emigration and anti-immigration campaigns.[80] As early as 1910, the socialist feminist Emma Goldman criticized this movement for obscuring the deeper social causes of prostitution, labor migration, and exploitation. "It is much more profitable to pretend an outraged morality than to get to the bottom of things," she observed.[81]

In 2013, as anxieties about the immigration of Romanian and Bulgarian Roma and Sinti intensified, sensational press reports continued to focus on gangs of traffickers allegedly "luring disabled Romanians to Britain and forcing them to beg on the high street," or kidnapping children for slavery or sex in the West.[82] As Goldman observed more than a hundred years ago, these stories obscure the much broader and more mundane conditions of social inequality and discrimination that drive the sex trade. The vast majority of homeless, unemployed, or otherwise exploited migrants in Europe—men, women, and children—are not victims of forcible sex trafficking. They are victims of racism, social exclusion, discrimination, poverty, and low wages, and they are often individuals seeking a better life.

In reality, moreover, even as the media sensationalize sex trafficking, the "traffic" of East European women to the West—as wives, nannies, and domestic servants, as well as prostitutes—has been central to the construction of the European Union. As

Anca Parvulescu argues, "On their way to market, East European women manufacture their backwardness; they present themselves as pre-feminist ideal wives in order to have a chance to attract attention." The traffic in women thus reinforces Eastern Europe's peripheral status within Europe at the same time that it symbolizes European integration.[83]

All of this suggests that the end of the Cold War did not end the long-standing debate about the relationship between freedom and mobility, or about the conditions under which mobility can be free. As long as the EU continues to expand, enabling greater numbers of people to move and work freely within its borders, such debates will continue. They are linked not only to the ongoing globalization of the labor market but also to pressing questions about where Europe's boundaries should lie (and who is really "European"). In the wake of the 2008 financial crisis, staggeringly high youth unemployment rates in parts of Europe have forced many young people to seek work abroad—mainly in Northern Europe and the United Kingdom. In 2012, Irish emigration reached heights not seen for twenty-five years. In Poland, emigration has again been on the upswing since 2011. Emigration is also the new reality for many young people in Southern Europe. As of September 2013, unemployment for workers under the age of twenty-four reached 56 percent in Spain, 57 percent in Greece, and 40 percent in Italy. Melissa Abadía, a twenty-seven-year-old from eastern Spain, moved to Amsterdam to find work in 2009. Trained as a nurse, she now works in the stockroom of a clothing store. She felt she had no choice but to leave home. "I hate the fact that I have to do this," she reflected. "Leaving your country should be a choice, not an obligation."[84]

Well beyond Europe, the global migration flows of the twenty-first century generate unresolved questions and concerns about the human and social costs of emigration. The Oxford economist Paul

Collier has recently argued that emigration hurts poor countries by drawing away their "fairy godmothers"—young, educated elites who are needed at home. "Migrant families do well for themselves by jumping into a chain of lifeboats headed for the developed world, but this can be at the expense of the vastly larger group of families left behind," he maintains. This was precisely the argument made by East European governments for over a century in order to justify restrictions on individual mobility. Collier even implies that Western countries should "help" nations suffering from excess emigration by further limiting immigration.[85]

EVEN IF COLLIER is correct in his assessment of emigration's costs, should the individual right to move be sacrificed for the sake of the national collective? Would Collier make the same trade-off if it concerned his own ability to relocate? On the other hand, we cannot deny that the "choice" to emigrate is often made under terrible conditions, inflicting severe psychic costs on individuals and families. Yoani Sánchez, a Cuban writer, left Cuba for Switzerland in 2002. She was tormented by guilt. "To sit in front of a plate of food, delicious and piled high, was one of the most painful moments of my days in exile. What would my mother be eating right now? Had she ever tasted a kiwi? Will she go to bed tonight with an empty stomach?" The material fruits of emigration were "at hand, succulent, tantalizing," she reflected. "So painful, however, was the transplanting of my roots that I could not enjoy the taste of what I'd achieved." When she returned home, she found herself on the other side of this terrible equation.

Each year she updates her address book and counts the growing number of family members and friends scattered around the world. "Those who depart should know that they leave behind a trail of mixed feelings. Yearning, worries, happiness, relief," she reflects. "A sea of people with their red dots on the map on the wall, their best clothes put away for the day their relative returns; people who, at the end of every year, have to redo their address books, and erase, erase, erase."[86]

It is tempting, in the wake of 1989, to celebrate postsocialist mobility in Europe and beyond as a pure expression of the "freedom" that was denied to East Europeans for so many decades. Sánchez's words caution against idealizing a liberal world of unfettered mobility. It matters a great deal whether the decision to live and work abroad is made out of desperation or ambition. The lesson of one hundred years of anti-emigration activism in Eastern Europe should not simply be that borders are repressive and that movement is emancipatory. We should take seriously the real concerns about the health and welfare of migrants and the integrity of families that drove and radicalized opponents of emigration in Eastern Europe for one hundred years. We should do our best to guarantee that migration is more "free," in every sense of the term: that individuals are not forced to seek work abroad because of unbearable poverty or discrimination at home; that the conditions in which migrants live and work are equal to those of native workers; that migrants applying for asylum are not detained in prisons for years on end; that children and parents are not separated by arbitrary deportations; and that migrants from both within and outside Europe are treated with dignity regardless of their social class, nationality, race, religion, gender, or sexuality.

As East Europeans become simply "Europeans," they increasingly enjoy the freedom to come or go, at least within the European Union. Formerly fortified borders between the East and the West are now tourist attractions, highway rest stops, or grassy fields. This freedom has been achieved at the cost of countless lives. But the privilege of mobility remains inherently exclusionary. While Poles and Czechs now fly through passport controls at European airports, the Mediterranean has become a graveyard for desperate asylum seekers from Africa: the International Organization for Migration estimated that at least fourteen thousand migrants died attempting to cross the Mediterranean between 1988 and 2014. Between January and April 2015 alone, fifteen hundred individuals drowned in the Mediterranean. The language of freedom and slavery continues to frame the debate about migration in contemporary Europe, moreover. In the aftermath of an April 2015 shipwreck off the Libyan coast that left at least eight hundred dead, Prime Minister Matteo Renzi of Italy blamed the smugglers who transported the migrants, calling them "the slave drivers of the 21st century." By blaming individuals who transport migrants for the tragedy, Renzi continued a trend born in the nineteenth century, when emigration agents were often charged with human trafficking. Of course, blaming smugglers also conveniently obscures the reasons why refugees are so desperate to leave home, and exculpates the governments of sending and receiving countries, whose laws drive migrants to take desperate measures.[87]

In contemporary Europe, mobility remains a privilege associated with freedom. The sentiments that animated a century of activism against emigration have not entirely disappeared, however. It is clear that for many Europeans, true freedom includes the freedom to stay home. A world in which individuals are compelled by poverty or persecution to seek work abroad is no more free than one in which state borders are closed and locked.

In 2008, Jerzy Sawka, editor of the *Gazeta Wyborcza* in Wrocław, reflected on the recent wave of emigration from Poland: "After the entrance of Poland to the European Union, there was an avalanche of departures to Great Britain. This was a painful experience. Plumbers, masons, taxi drivers, nurses, doctors disappeared from the market. The price of professional services skyrocketed. Politicians competed to find the scapegoats for this exodus," he recalled. "The mayor of Wrocław even appealed to emigrants to return to our city. Nobody responded, because emigration was too new, emigrants too proud and full of hope, and they were empowered by British pounds." In only a few short years things changed dramatically, however. "Today emigration is not a one-way ticket. It is possible to return at any time. . . . Today more people are returning than departing. They are returning richer in experiences, knowledge, skills. . . . They bring huge potential to our country. The transfer of ideas, knowledge, and culture greatly enriches us." Sawka speculated that these new migrants were determining for themselves how long to stay away, whether to remain in the West forever or to return home to Poland. He was not worried. "Both choices are good," he concluded. "We are free."[88]

Acknowledgments

*T*he Great Departure is a story of movement. As I followed my emigrants across Europe and the Atlantic, I was fortunate to discover many new places, and to see my own city of Chicago and the United States through the fresh eyes of the millions of East European migrants who landed here. I was also guided and motivated by countless conversations with colleagues and friends. I am extraordinarily grateful for the many communities, in Europe and the United States, who made the research and writing of this book possible (and less lonely).

My research was facilitated by the generous support of several institutions, including the American Council of Learned Societies, the National Endowment for the Humanities, the Botstiber Institute for Austrian-American Studies, and the Social Sciences Division at the University of Chicago. Several individuals pushed me to sharpen my writing. I am especially grateful to my editor, Alane Salierno Mason, whose editorial guidance helped bring the emigrants to life, and to my agent, Don Fehr, for his sage advice and support throughout the process. I was also fortunate to have several outstanding research assistants. In Warsaw, Michal Wilczewski tracked down valuable archival sources. In Chicago, Eric Phillips and Preston Thomas heroically assisted with permissions and the final preparation of the manuscript.

I am also grateful to several colleagues and friends whose generous and insightful feedback nudged me in productive directions. Kenneth Moss and Lisa Moses Leff pushed me to integrate Jewish experiences of emigration into my broader narrative. In Chicago, Deborah Cohen, Julie Cooper, Edin Hajpardasic, Emily Osborn, and Alice Weinreb provided moral, social, and intellectual support. I could not have written this book without the steadfast friendship of Leora Auslander, who has inspired me to think creatively about transnational history, migration, gender, and race since I arrived at Chicago.

I completed most of the writing of this book during a blissful sabbatical in 2013–14. I am grateful to the entire staff of the American Academy in Berlin, which provided me with a beautiful home in Berlin and constant culinary and intellectual stimulation. I thank Carol Scherer and Pamela Rosenberg in particular, for so generously taking care of me when I broke my foot. The entire class of fall 2013 should be remembered for its camaraderie, but I owe special thanks to Jim Brophy and Kiran Desai for their exceptional kindness and companionship.

I was equally lucky to spend four months at the European University Institute in the extraordinary company of Charles Devlin, Regina Grafe, Dirk Moses, Pavel Kolar, Lucy Riall, and Natasha Wheatley. It is hard to imagine a more intellectually and socially stimulating community. Laura Downs has inspired me since graduate school, and it has been a pleasure to continue our long-standing conversations on Florentine terrazzas. Finally, Pieter Judson continues to make me love history. It has been a special joy to be a part of his new community in Florence. This book has been greatly enriched by his advice, wit, and friendship, all of which I cherish.

I thank my family, especially my parents, Marc and Debbie Zahra, and my grandmother Marjorie Shane, for their lifelong encouragement of my intellectual pursuits, and for an extraordinary adventure in Italy in March 2014.

Finally, I dedicate this book to William Irvine, who burst unexpectedly into my life just as I was writing the final chapter. I am grateful to him for making it so much harder to leave home, and for making me happier than I ever imagined I could be.

Notes

Introduction

1   Letter from Faustina Wiśniewska, February 13, 1891, and letter from Faustina Wiśniewska to her parents, undated, in Witold Kula, Nina Assorodobraj-Kula, and Marcin Kula, *Writing Home: Immigrants in Brazil and the United States, 1890–1891*, ed. and trans. Josephine Wtulich (Boulder, CO, 1986), 443–46.

2   Around 2,145,266 subjects of the Dual Monarchy landed on American shores between 1901 and 1910. Italy was close behind, with 2,135,877 immigrants to the United States in the same period. Adam McKeown, "Global Migration, 1846–1940," *Journal of World History* 15 (June 2004): 156–60, 167; Annemarie Steidl, Wladimir Fischer-Nebmaier, and James W. Oberly, "The Transatlantic Migration Experience: From Austria-Hungary to the United States, 1870–1950" (unpublished manuscript), 137; Samuel L. Baily, *Immigrants in the Lands of Promise: Italians in Buenos Aires and New York City, 1870–1914* (Ithaca, 1999), 54. Statistics on emigration vary. Austro-Hungarian authorities recorded a total of 3,547,000 emigrants to all overseas destinations from Austria-Hungary between 1876 and 1910, and 2,953,587 to the United States. Heinz Fassmann, "Die Bevölker-

ungsentwicklungen," in *Die Habsburgermonarchie 1848–1918*, vol. 9, pt. 1 (Vienna, 2010), 173–75.

3   McKeown, "Global Migration, 1846–1940," 156–60, 167. For a global perspective on migration, see also Donna R. Gabaccia and Dirk Hoerder, eds., *Connecting Seas and Connected Ocean Rims: Indian, Atlantic, and Pacific Oceans and China Seas Migrations from the 1830s to the 1930s* (Leiden, 2011).

4   *Protokoll der im k.k. Handelsministerium durchgeführten Vernehmung von Auskunftspersonen über die Auswanderung aus Österreich* (Vienna, 1912), 190.

5   Michael Just, *Ost und südosteuropäische Amerikawanderung, 1881–1914* (Stuttgart, 1988), 45. For steamship fares, see Mark Wyman, *Round-Trip to America: The Immigrants Return to Europe, 1880–1930* (Ithaca, 1996), 24.

6   Cited in Frederick Whelan, "Citizenship and the Right to Leave," *American Political Science Review* 75 (1981): 650.

7   On relationships between slavery, abolitionism, "freedom," and "free labor" in slave societies, see Eric Foner, *Free Soil, Free Labor, Free Men: The Ideology of the Republican Party before the Civil War* (New York, 1995); Edmund Morgan, *American Slavery, American Freedom* (New York, 2003); Thomas Holt, *The Problem of Freedom: Race, Labor, and Politics in Jamaica and Britain, 1832–1938* (Baltimore, 1991); Julie Saville, *The Work of Reconstruction: From Slave to Wage Laborer in South Carolina, 1860–1870* (New York, 1994); Amy Dru Stanley, *From Bondage to Contract: Wage Labor, Marriage, and the Market in the Age of Slave Emancipation* (New York, 1998); Marjorie Wood, "Emancipating the Child Laborer: Children, Freedom, and the Moral Boundaries of the Market in the United States, 1853–1938" (PhD diss., University of Chicago, 2011).

8   On the domestic slave trade, see esp. Walter Johnson, *Soul by Soul: Life inside the Antebellum Slave Market* (Cambridge, MA, 1999).

9   Upton Sinclair, *The Jungle: The Lost First Edition* (Memphis, TN, 1988), 94.

10   Adam M. McKeown, *Melancholy Order: Asian Migration and the Globalization of Borders* (New York, 2011), 10.

11 Frederick Jackson Turner, *The Frontier in American History* (New York, 1920), 19, 24. For a more recent examination of the link between westward expansion and ideas of freedom, see, e.g., Gunther Peck, *Reinventing Free Labor: Padrones and Immigrant Workers in the North American West, 1880–1930* (Cambridge, UK, 2000).

12 Joseph Roth, *The Wandering Jews*, trans. Michael Hofmann (New York, 2001), 93, 95.

13 Louis Adamic, "This Crisis Is an Opportunity," *Common Ground* 1, no. 1 (Autumn 1940): 62–63.

14 See Larry Wolff, *Inventing Eastern Europe: The Map of Civilization on the Mind of the Enlightenment* (Stanford, 1994). On the political consequences of anxieties about backwardness within Eastern Europe, see Larry Wolff, *The Idea of Galicia: History and Fantasy in Habsburg Political Culture* (Stanford, 2010); Maria Todorova, "The Trap of Backwardness: Modernity, Temporality, and the Study of Eastern European Nationalism," *Slavic Review* 64 (2005): 140–65.

15 On the transnational consolidation of an imagined "white" community, see Marilyn Lake and Henry Reynolds, *Drawing the Global Colour Line: White Men's Countries and the International Challenge of Racial Equality* (Cambridge, UK, 2008). On whiteness and immigration in the United States, see Matthew Frye Jacobson, *Whiteness of a Different Color: European Immigrants and the Alchemy of Race* (Cambridge, MA, 1998); David R. Roediger, *Working toward Whiteness: How America's Immigrants Became White: The Strange Journey from Ellis Island to the Suburbs* (New York, 2005); Karen Brodkin, *How Jews Became White Folks and What That Says about Race in America* (New Brunswick, NJ, 1998); Thomas A. Guglielmo, *White on Arrival: Italians, Race, Color, and Power in Chicago, 1890–1945* (Oxford, 2004).

16 Roth, *The Wandering Jews*, 102.

17 Roger P. Bartlett, *The Settlement of Foreigners in Russia, 1762–1804* (Cambridge, UK, 1979), 23–30.

18 Aristide Zolberg, "The Exit Revolution," in *Citizenship and Those Who Leave: The Politics of Emigration and Expatriation*, ed. Nancy Green and François Weil (Urbana, IL, 2007), 33–60.

19   Nancy L. Green, "The Politics of Exit: Reversing the Immigration
     Paradigm," *Journal of Modern History* 77 (June 2005): 282. For this
     narrative, see also John Torpey, *The Invention of the Passport: Sur-
     veillance, Citizenship, and the State* (Cambridge, UK, 2000); Jane
     Caplan and John Torpey, eds., *Documenting Individual Identity:
     The Development of State Practices in the Modern World* (Princeton,
     2001); Zolberg, "The Exit Revolution"; Gérard Noiriel, *La tyrannie
     du national: Le droit d'asile en Europe, 1793–1993* (Paris, 1991); Saskia
     Sassen, *Guests and Aliens* (New York, 2000); Michael Marrus, *The
     Unwanted: Refugees from the First World War through the Cold War*
     (Philadelphia, 2002); Claudena Skran, *Refugees in Interwar Europe:
     The Invention of a Regime* (Oxford, 1995). Recently several historians
     have challenged this framework by focusing on policies of expulsion
     and control in Western Europe in the nineteenth century. See Ger-
     ald L. Neuman, *Strangers to the Constitution: Immigrants, Borders,
     and Fundamental Law* (Princeton, 1996); David Feldman, "Was the
     Nineteenth Century a Golden Age for Immigrants? The Changing
     Articulation of National, Local and Voluntary Controls," in *Migra-
     tion Control in the North Atlantic World: The Evolution of State
     Practices in Europe and the United States from the French Revolution
     to the Inter-war Period*, ed. Andreas Fahrmeir, Olivier Faron, and
     Patrick Weil (New York, 2003), 167–77; Andreas Fahrmeir, *Citizens
     and Aliens: Foreigners and the Law in Britain and the German States,
     1789–1870* (New York, 2000); Paul-André Rosental, "Protéger et
     expulser les étrangers en Europe du XIXe siècle à nos jours," *Annales.
     Histoire, Sciences Sociales* 66 (April–June 2011): 335–73.

20   On British emigration policies and empire in the nineteenth century,
     see Marjory Harper and Stephen Constantine, *Migration and Empire*
     (Oxford, 2012); David Feldman and M. Page Baldwin, "Emigration
     and the British State, 1815–1925," in *Citizenship and Those Who Leave*,
     135–55. On penal colonies, see, e.g., Stephen A. Toth, *Beyond Papil-
     lon: The French Overseas Penal Colonies, 1854–1952* (Lincoln, NE,
     2006); Cassandra Pybus, *Epic Journeys of Freedom: Runaway Slaves
     of the American Revolution and Their Global Quest for Liberty* (Bos-
     ton, 2007). On British child emigration schemes, see Geoffrey Sher-

ington, "Fairbridge Child Migrants," in *Child Welfare and Social Action in the Nineteenth and Twentieth Centuries*, ed. Jon Lawrence and Pat Starkey (Liverpool, 2001), 53–80; Ellen Boucher, *Empire's Children: Child Emigration, Welfare, and the Decline of the British World, 1869–1967* (Cambridge, UK, 2014). On "surplus women," see Kathrin Levitan, *A Cultural History of the British Census: Envisioning the Multitude in the Nineteenth Century* (New York, 2011), 134–38.

21 Michael Whitaker Dean, "'What the Heart Unites, the Sea Shall Not Divide': Claiming Overseas Czechs for the Nation" (PhD diss., University of California, Berkeley, 2014), 13–14.

22 Ibid., 19–30, quotations from Tyl play 29–30.

23 Louis Adamic, *Laughing in the Jungle: The Autobiography of an Immigrant in America* (New York, 1932), 3, 5.

24 Ibid., 8–9.

25 Clair W. Perry, Adam Laboda—Pittsfield #1, 1938, Folklore Project, Life Histories, 1936–39, U.S. Work Projects Administration, Federal Writers' Project, Library of Congress, 7.

26 When the U.S. immigration bureau began to keep track of return migration in 1908, it estimated that 39.5 percent of migrants returned to Austria and 37.9 percent returned to Hungary. At least 400,000 emigrants returned to Austria-Hungary from the United States between 1900 and 1910. For numbers, see Heinz Fassmann and Rainer Münz, eds., *Einwanderungsland Österreich? Historische Migrationsmuster, aktuelle Trends und politische Massnahmen* (Vienna, 1995), 25; Steidl, Fischer-Nebmaier, and Oberly, *The Transatlantic Migration Experience*, 70. The quotation is from Adamic, *Laughing in the Jungle*, 104.

27 Letter from Joseph Cybulski to Sophie Cybulska, February 16, 1891, in *Writing Home*, 222–24.

28 Jonathan D. Sarna, ed. and trans., *People Walk on Their Heads: Moses Weinberger's Jews and Judaism in New York* (New York, 1982), 58–60.

29 Letter from anonymous Jewish Polish male, 1912, in Isaac Metzger, comp. and ed., *A Bintel Brief*, vol. 1, *Sixty Years of Letters from the Lower East Side to the Jewish Daily Forward* (Garden City, NY, 1971), 214.

30   Adamic, *Laughing in the Jungle*, 103.

31   On Russian emigration policies and "filtration," see Eric Lohr, *Russian Citizenship: From Empire to Soviet Union* (Cambridge, MA, 2012), 83–114, 195. On Polish nationalist concerns about emigration, see Benjamin Murdzek, *Emigration in Polish Social-Political Thought, 1870–1914* (Boulder, CO, 1977). On Hungarian emigration policies, see Julianna Puskás, *Ties That Bind, Ties That Divide: 100 Years of Hungarian Experience in the United States*, trans. Zora Ludwig (New York, 2000).

32   Susan L. Carruthers, *Cold War Captives: Imprisonment, Escape, and Brainwashing* (Berkeley, 2009).

33   https://www.youtube.com/watch?v=fK1MwhEDjHg, accessed March 29, 2015.

34   Pertti Ahonen, *Death at the Berlin Wall* (New York, 2011), 3.

Chapter 1

1   *Der galizische Menschenhandel vor Gericht*, zusammengestellt aus den Berichten des "Deutschen Volksblattes" über den wadowicer Proceß (Vienna, 1890), 195.

2   Ibid., 205. For the text of the closing statement, see also "Matactwa emigracyne," *Czas*, February 19, 1890, pp. 2–3.

3   Henryk Sienkiewicz, *After Bread: A Story of Polish Emigrant Life to America*, trans. Vatslaf A. Hlasko and Thomas H. Bullick (New York, 1897), 16–17, 58, 162, 165.

4   For statistics, see Senator William P. Dillingham, *Emigration Conditions in Europe*, Reports of the Immigration Commission, 61st Cong. (Washington, DC, 1911), 351. On emigration from Hungary, see Julianna Puskás, *Ties That Bind, Ties That Divide: 100 Years of Hungarian Experience in the United States*, trans. Zora Ludwig (New York, 2000).

5   Heinz Fassmann, "Die Bevölkerungsentwicklungen," in *Die Habsburgermonarchie 1848–1918*, vol. 9, pt. 1 (Vienna, 2010), 173–75.

6   Leopold Caro, *Auswanderung und Auswanderungspolitik in Österreich* (Leipzig, 1909), 8. For statistics, see also Michael John, "Push and Pull Factors for Overseas Migrants from Austria-Hungary in the 19th

and 20th Centuries," in *Austrian Immigration to Canada: Selected Essays*, ed. Franz A. J. Szabo (Carleton, CA, 1996), 59–60; Annemarie Steidl, Wladimir Fischer-Nebmaier, and James W. Oberly, "The Transatlantic Migration Experience: From Austria-Hungary to the United States, 1870–1950" (unpublished manuscript), 70, 137; *Protokoll der im k.k. Handelsministerium durchgeführten Vernehmung von Auskunftspersonen über die Auswanderung aus Österreich* (Vienna, 1912), 190.

7   Baron Louis De Levay, "The Hungarian Emigration Law," *North American Review* 182, no. 590 (January 1906): 119; Ausweis über den Stand der Auswanderungssachen, October 7, 1914, Carton 3327, sig. 6 VZ 18, Justiz Ministerium (JM), Allgemeine Strafsachen (AS), Allgemeine Verwaltungsarchiv (AVA), Österreichisches Staatsarchiv (OeStA).

8   De Levay, "The Hungarian Emigration Law," 111. On British attempts to regulate emigration agents, see Marjory Harper and Stephen Constantine, *Migration and Empire* (Oxford, 2012), 277–305.

9   Adam M. McKeown, *Melancholy Order: Asian Migration and the Globalization of Borders* (New York, 2011), 67–85, interview cited on p. 85.

10 Ibid., 115.

11 Ibid., 84–85.

12 Abschrift, Kriegsministerium, Auswanderung aus Galizien und Bukowina, Agentumtriebe, June 25, 1913, Carton 3325, Sig 6 VZ 18, JM, AS, AVA, OeStA.

13 On economic and social conditions in Galicia, see esp. Alison Frank, *Oil Empire: Visions of Prosperity in Austrian Galicia* (Cambridge, MA, 2005).

14 On nationalism in Austria-Hungary, see esp. Pieter M. Judson, *Guardians of the Nation: Activists on the Language Frontiers of Rural Austria* (Cambridge, MA, 2007).

15 Puskás, *Ties That Bind*, 90; Leopold Caro, "Das Los unserer Auswanderer, Vortrag gehalten in der 157. Plenarversammlung der Gesellschaft österreichischer Volkswirte vom 15 Jänner 1907," *Volkswirtschaftliche Wochenschrift* (Vienna), 1907, 6; Monika Glettler, *Pittsburgh-Wien-Budapest: Programm und Praxis der National-*

itätenpolitik bei Auswanderung der Slowaken um 1900 (Vienna, 1980), 401–6.

16 Eric Lohr, *Russian Citizenship: From Empire to Soviet Union* (Cambridge, MA, 2012), 94–107.

17 Caro, "Das Los unserer Auswanderer," 6.

18 Cited in Benjamin P. Murdzek, *Emigration in Polish Social-Political Thought, 1870–1914* (Boulder, CO, 1977), 174.

19 *Der galizische Menschenhandel vor Gericht*, 187.

20 (Charles) Semsley-(Roman) Dobler Report, July 1906–January 1907, Casefile 51411/52, Report to Frank P. Sargent, Commissioner General of Immigration, January 16, 1907, 8, Reel 1, pt. 4, Series A, Subject correspondence files, Records of the Immigration and Naturalization Service, [microform].

21 M. Celmer to Francis Nowacki, in Witold Kula, Nina Assorodobraj-Kula, and Marcin Kula, *Writing Home: Immigrants in Brazil and the United States, 1890–1891*, ed. and trans. Josephine Wtulich (Boulder, CO, 1986), 206.

22 Joseph Roth, *The Wandering Jews*, trans. Michael Hofmann (New York, 2001), 7. Roth is referring here to camps for refugees in Austria-Hungary during World War I.

23 Cited in Puskás, *Ties That Bind*, 85–86.

24 Letter from Simon Sosieński, January 15, 1891, in *Writing Home*, 413–14.

25 Interview of Anna Kupinsky by Janet Levine, March 4, 1993, in Ellis Island Oral History Project, Series EI, no. 260 (Alexandria, VA, 2003), 7.

26 Jack Wertheimer, *Unwelcome Strangers: East European Jews in Imperial Germany* (New York, 1987), 14.

27 On emigration from imperial Russia, see esp. Lohr, *Russian Citizenship*, 83–114, for numbers 195; Alison K. Smith, "The Freedom to Choose a Way of Life: Fugitives, Borders, and Imperial Amnesties in Russia," *Journal of Modern History* 83, no. 2 (June 2011): 243–71; Murdzek, *Emigration*, 35–78.

28 Philip Cowen Report, December 1906, Casefile 51411/56, Folder 1, Immigration from Russia, December 31, 1906, Reel 1, pt. 4, Series A,

Subject correspondence files, Records of the Immigration and Naturalization Service [microform].

29 Paul Weindling, *Epidemics and Genocides in Eastern Europe, 1890–1945* (Oxford, 2000).

30 On the origins of the 1892 cholera outbreak in Hamburg, see Richard J. Evans, *Death in Hamburg: Society and Politics in the Cholera Years* (New York, 2005), 281–85. Evans argues that the epidemic probably did come from Russia.

31 Aristide R. Zolberg, "The Archaeology of Remote Control," in *Migration Control in the North Atlantic World: The Evolution of State Practices in Europe and the United States from the French Revolution to the Inter-war Period*, ed. Andreas Fahrmeir, Olivier Faron, and Patrick Weil (New York, 2003), 195–222.

32 On the role of nongovernmental organizations in regulating immigration and public health, see Tobias Brinkmann, "Points of Passage: Reexamining Jewish Migrations from Eastern Europe after 1880," in *Points of Passage: Jewish Transmigrants from Eastern Europe in Scandinavia, Germany, and Britain, 1880–1914* (New York, 2013), 9–17; Katja Wüstenbecker, "Hamburg and the Transit of East European Immigrants," in *Migration Control in the North Atlantic World*, 229, 233.

33 Samuel A. Eppler Report, December 21, 1906, 29, Casefile 51411/54, Folder 1, August–December 1906, Reel 1, pt. 4, Series A, Subject correspondence files, Records of the Immigration and Naturalization Service [microform].

34 Mary Antin, *From Plotzk to Boston: A Young Girl's Journey from Russia to the Promised Land* (Princeton, 1985), 42.

35 Andrea Komlosy, *Grenze und ungleiche regionale Entwicklung: Binnenmarkt und Migration in der Habsburgermonarchie* (Vienna, 2003); Waltraud Heindl and Edith Saurer, eds., *Grenze und Staat: Passwesen, Staatsbürgerschaft, Heimatrecht und Fremdengesetzgebung in der österreichischen Monarchie, 1750–1867* (Vienna, 2000).

36 Staatsgrundgesetz vom 21. Dezember 1867 (R.G.Bl. 142/1867), über die allgemeinen Rechte der Staatsbürger für die im Reichsrate vertretenen Königreiche und Länder, Artikel 4.

37 *Memorandum! Nähere Ausführungen zu der bei dem hohen k.k. obersten Gerichtshofe und der hohen k.k. Generalprokuratur eingebrachten Richtigkeitsbeschwerde der in dem wadowicer Emigrationsprocesse verurtheilten Julius Löwenberg u. Simon Herz* (Wadowice, 1890), 34–35.

38 Instruktion für die Funktionäre der Canadian Pacific Railway in Galizien, May 1913, Carton 3325, sig. 6 VZ 18, JM, AS, AVA, OeStA.

39 "Aus dem Gerichtssaale: Wadowice," *Neue Freie Presse*, February 25, 1890, p. 6.

40 Nicole Phelps, *U.S.-Habsburg Relations from 1815 to the Paris Peace Conference: Sovereignty Transformed* (Cambridge, UK, 2013), 186–89.

41 De Levay, "The Hungarian Emigration Law," 117–18.

42 "Ungarischer Gesetzartikel II vom Jahre 1909 über die Auswanderung, Sanktioniert 18. February 1909," in Franz Ritter von Srbik, *Die Auswanderungsgesetzgebung: Die wichtigsten europäischen Auswanderungsgesetze und ihre wichtigste Vollzugsvorschriften* (Vienna, 1911), 30, Carton 3238, Ministerium für Landesverteidigung, Kriegsarchiv, OeStA.

43 *Memorandum!*, 34–35.

44 Überseeische Auswanderung via Hamburg, January 25, 1914, Carton 28, Fach 15, Administrativ Registratur (AR), Ministerium des Aussern (MdA), Haus-, Hof- und Staatsarchiv (HHstA).

45 Powderly Report, European Investigation 1906–07, 40, Casefile 51411/51, Folder 1, Reel 1, pt. 4, Series A, Subject correspondence files, Records of the Immigration and Naturalization Service [microform], 25–26, 73.

46 Martha Gardner, *The Qualities of a Citizen: Women, Immigration, and Citizenship, 1870–1965* (Princeton, 2005). On the rejection rate at Ellis Island, see Dorothee Schneider, "The United States Government and the Investigation of European Emigration during the Open Door Era," in *Citizenship and Those Who Leave*, 198. On the "poor physique" clause, see Vincent J. Cannato, *American Passage: The History of Ellis Island* (New York, 2009), 206–15.

47 Interview of Louise Nagy by Dana Gumb, September 16, 1985, in Ellis

Island Oral History Project, Series AKRF, no. 33 (Alexandria, VA, 2003), 15, 20.

48 Roth, *The Wandering Jews*, 102–3.

49 J.Z., "Proces przeciw ajentom emigracynym," *Kurjer Lwowski*, November 16, 1889, p. 5.

50 "Aus dem Gerichtssaale: Ein Monstre-Proceß," *Bukowinaer Rundschau*, December 17, 1889, p. 4.

51 "Aus dem Gerichtssaale: Wadowice," *Neue Freie Presse*, November 24, 1889, pp. 6–7; J.Z., "Proces przeciw ajentom emigracynym," *Kurjer Lwowski*, November 21, 1889, p. 4.

52 Previous histories of the trial have generally assumed that the accusations against the agents were true. See Mark Wyman, *Round-Trip to America: The Immigrants Return to Europe, 1880–1930* (Ithaca, 1993), 30–31; Pamela S. Nadell, "From Shtetl to Border: East European Jewish Emigrants and the 'Agents' System, 1868–1914," in *Studies in the American Jewish Experience*, ed. Jacob P. Marcus and Abraham J. Peck, vol. 2 (Boston, 1984), 49–78; Martin Pollack, *Kaiser von Amerika: Die grosse Flucht aus Galizien* (Vienna, 2010). Very helpful is Grzegorz Maria Kowalski, *Przestępstwa emigracyjne w Galicji, 1897–1918* (Cracow, 2003), which contains an extensive bibliography, but no specific citation of Wadowice court records.

53 I was able to access the complete coverage of the Viennese liberal *Neue Freie Presse*; the anti-Semitic Viennese *Deutsche Volksblatt*; the Polish conservative *Czas*, published in Cracow; and the *Kurjer Lwowski*, published in Lwow/Lemberg/Lviv.

54 "Aus dem Gerichtssaale: Wadowice," *Neue Freie Presse*, January 29, 1890, p. 7.

55 *Der galizische Menschenhandel vor Gericht*, 10, 7.

56 Harris to Department, December 8, 1899, in Zoltán Kramár, *From the Danube to the Hudson: U.S. Ministerial and Consular Dispatches on Immigration from the Habsburg Monarchy, 1850–1900* (Atlanta, 1978), 42–43.

57 Stern to Department, May 19, 1880, in *From the Danube to the Hudson*, 48–49.

58 Caro, *Auswanderung und Auswanderungspolitik*, 69.

59 Dillingham, *Emigration Conditions in Europe*, 11.

60 Caro, *Auswanderung und Auswanderungspolitik*, 53, 65–67; Murdzek, *Emigration*, 137–38.

61 *Der galizische Menschenhandel vor Gericht*, 15, 31.

62 Ibid., 35.

63 Ibid., 37–41.

64 "Sprawy Sądowe. Matactwa emigracyne," *Czas*, December 19, 1889, p. 3; *Der galizische Menschenhandel vor Gericht*, 141–49.

65 "Aus dem Gerichtssaale: Ein Monstre-Proceß," *Bukowinaer Rundschau*, December 17, 1889, p. 4.

66 See also "Wadowice, Paraguay, und Karlowitz," *Österreichische Wochenschrift*, November 22, 1889, p. 825; "Aus dem Gerichtssaale: Ein Monstre-Proceß," 4; "Aus dem Gerichtssaale: Wadowice," *Neue Freie Presse*, November 27, 1889, p. 5.

67 For a collection of the *Deutsche Volksblatt*'s coverage of the trial, see *Der galizische Menschenhandel vor Gericht*.

68 On Brody as a center of the emigration trade and of Jewish life, see Börries Kuzmany, "Center and Periphery at the Austrian-Russian Border: The Galician Border Town of Brody in the Long Nineteenth Century," *Austrian History Yearbook* 42 (2011): 67–88.

69 *Der galizische Menschenhandel vor Gericht*, 131. See also "Sprawy Sądowe: Matactwa emigracyne," *Czas*, December 14, 1889, p. 3.

70 *Der galizische Menschenhandel vor Gericht*, 131.

71 Verzeichnis der behördlichen bekannten Agenten der Austro-Americana, 1914 (probably spring), Carton 3326, Sig 6 VZ 18, JM, AS, AVA, OeStA.

72 See case files in Carton 3325, Sig 6 VZ 18, JM, AS, AVA, OeStA.

73 On blood libel trials, see esp. Helmut Walser Smith, *The Butcher's Tale: Murder and Anti-Semitism in a German Town* (New York, 2003).

74 For examples of anti-Semitic coverage of the Wadowice trial, see esp. *Der galizische Menschenhandel vor Gericht*; *Proces Wadowicki w portretach i scenach* (Cracow, 1889); "Jüdischer Menschenhandel: Ein trauriges Culturbild aus Halbasien," *Deutsche Volksblatt*, June 15, 1889.

75 Keely Stauter-Halsted, "'A Generation of Monsters': Jews, Pros-
    titution, and Racial Purity in the 1892 Lviv White Slavery Trial,"
    Austrian History Yearbook 38 (2007): 25–35; Nancy M. Wingfield,
    "Destination: Alexandria, Buenos Aires, Constantinople: 'White
    Slavers' in Late Imperial Austria," *Journal of the History of Sexuality*
    20 (2011): 291–311.

76 Bertha Pappenheim and Sara Rabinowitsch, *Zur Lage der jüdischen
    Bevölkerung in Galizien*, in Bertha Pappenheim, *Sisyphus: Gegen
    den Mädchenhändel—Galizien*, ed. Helga Heubach (Freiburg, 1992),
    88–89.

77 Malte Fuhrmann, "'Western Perversions' at the Threshold of Felicity:
    The European Prostitutes of Galata-Pera (1870–1915)," *History and
    Anthropology* 21, no. 2 (June 2010): 159–72.

78 *Memorandum!*, 5.

79 "Aus dem Gerichtssaale," *Neue Freie Presse*, February 23, 1890, p. 7.

80 Quoted in Murdzek, *Emigration*, 167. See also Puskás, *Ties That Bind*,
    80.

81 On mercantilism and emigration policies in Europe in the first half
    of the nineteenth century, see Zolberg, "The Exit Revolution," 33–60.

82 Friedrich Hey, *Unser Auswanderungswesen und seine Schäden*
    (Vienna, 1912), 5.

83 Ibid., 7.

84 Emigration, Jussen to Department, February 11, 1886, in *From the
    Danube to the Hudson*, 30.

85 Adamic, *Laughing in the Jungle*, 26–27.

86 Hey, *Unser Auswanderungswesen*, 9.

87 Murdzek, *Emigration*, 99–100, 146–57, quotation 99. For a recent
    study, see Jeffrey Williamson and Timothy Hatton, *The Age of Mass
    Migrations: Causes and Economic Impact* (Oxford, 1998).

88 *Stenographisches Protokoll der Sitzungen des Subkomitees des Budget
    Ausschusses für Schifffahrt Angelegenheiten* (Vienna, 1913), 85.

89 *Der Galizische Menschenhandel vor Gericht*, 205.

90 Ibid., 187–95. For Ogniewski's closing statement, see also "Aus dem
    Gerichtssaale: Wadowice," *Neue Freie Presse*, February 18, 1890, p. 7;
    ibid., February 23, 1890, p. 7; "Matactwa emigracyne," *Czas*, Febru-

ary 19, 1890, pp. 2–3; J.Z., "Proces przeciw ajentom emigracynym," *Kurjer Lwowski,* February 19, 1890, p. 2.

91 J.Z., "Proces przeciw ajentom emigracynym," *Kurjer Lwowski,* March 13, 1890, p. 5; "Aus dem Gerichtssaale: Wadowice," *Neue Freie Presse,* March 13, 1890, p. 6.

92 Dillingham, *Emigration Conditions in Europe,* 351.

93 (Charles) Semsley-(Roman) Dobler Report, July 1906–January 1907, Casefile 51411/52, Report to Frank P. Sargent, Commissioner General of Immigration, January 16, 1907, 8, Reel 1, pt. 4, Series A, Subject correspondence files, Records of the Immigration and Naturalization Service [microform].

94 *Stenographisches Protokoll der Sitzungen des Subkomitees des Budget Ausschusses für Schifffahrtsangelegenheiten* (Vienna, 1913), 21, Carton 3329, Sig 6 VZ 18, JM, AS, AVA, OeStA.

95 "Die Auswandererhyänen: Der Inhaber des Kolumbus," *Reichspost,* September 10, 1913; "Das Anwesen der Menschenfrächter," *Reichspost,* August 30, 1913; "Ist das Direktion am Platz?," *Deutsche Volksblatt,* September 25, 1913.

96 Hohes k.k. Kriegsministerium in Wien, Abschrift, July 17, 1913, Carton 3325, Sig 6 VZ 18, JM, AS, AVA, OeStA.

97 Abschrift zu JMZ 32637/13, October 25, 1913, Sig 6 VZ 18, JM, AS, AVA, OeStA.

98 Entweichung Wehrpflichtiger aus Nordungarn, December 11, 1912; Wychodźtwo obowiązanych do służby wojskowej, December 12, 1913; Emigracya austryackich podannych za rosyjskami paszportami, December 20, 1913, sig. 124, C.K. Dyrekcja Policji w Krakowie (DPKr) 1852–1918, Archiwum Państowe w Krakowie (APKr).

99 Zentralstelle zur Überwachung der Auswanderungsbewegung, March 5, 1914; Wychodźtwo z galicyi i Węgier pod pretekstem pątnictwa i odwiedzania targów, June 20, 1914, sig. 125, DPKr 1852–1918, APKr.

100 An die k.k. Oberstaatsanwaltschaft, November 5, 1913; An die k.k. Oberstaatsanwaltschaft in Krakau, Carton 3325, Sig 6 VZ 18, JM, AS, AVA, OeStA; Auswanderungsbewegung—Einrichtung des Kontrolldienstes, February 19, 1914, sig. 180; Mitwirkung der Eisenbahn

an der Bekämpfung der unbefugten Auswanderung, March 5, 1914; Auswandererkontrolldienst, Mitwirkung der Finanzorgane, April 25, 1914, sig. 125, DPKr 1852–1918, APKr.

101 Aussagen des Verdächtigen Josef Krochmal, December 1913, Carton 3325, Sig 6 VZ 18, JM, AS, AVA, OeStA.

102 Canadian-Pacific Railway and Austrian Emigration, October 20, 1913, Records of the U.S. Department of State, Austria-Hungary and Austria 1910–24, Reel 56.

103 "Die Entvölkerung Österreichs," *Danzer's Armee Zeitung*, June 5, 1913, pp. 3–4.

104 "Verhaftungen," *Reichspost*, Vienna, October 17, 1913, p. 1.

105 Report by Samuel Altman, no date (ca. February 12, 1915), Reel 56, Austria-Hungary and Austria 1910–24, Records of the U.S. Department of State.

106 Polizeidirektion in Wien, Grünhut, Artur, Personaldaten, August 9, 1913, Carton 21, Fach 15, AR, MdA, HHstA.

107 In 1912–13, out of 2,072 instances in which men liable for the draft had been criminally transported overseas, only 111 (5.3 percent) could be pinned on the CPR by the Trade Ministry. Handelsministerium, Auswanderung nach Nordamerika, November 20, 1913, Carton 21, Fach 15, AR, MdA, HHstA; John, "Push and Pull Factors," 77.

108 Sam Altman, Haftentschädigung Anspruch, January 16, 1929; Bericht der Generalstaatsanwaltschaft, betreffend Samuel Altmanns, Haftlingsentschädigung, September 27, 1920, Carton 3329, Sig 6 VZ 18, JM, AS, AVA, OeStA.

109 Hans Chmelar, *Höhepunkt der österreichischen Auswanderung: Die Auswanderung aus den im Reichsrat vertretenen Königreichen und Ländern in den Jahren 1905–1914* (Vienna, 1974), 154.

110 Anfrage Dr. Ignacy Wróbel, Session 203, Sitzung am 12 März 1914, Stenographische Protokoll des Abgeordnetenhauses des Reichsrates, 1861–1918, 9723.

111 Bericht des Legationssekretärs Baron Sommaruga, May 31, 1917, Die Rückwanderung aus Amerika nach der Monarchie, Carton 56, Fach 15, AR, MdA, HHstA.

112 Consul Prochnik in St. Paul, September 17, 1915, Carton 56, Fach 15, AR, MdA, HHstA.

113 Note des kgl. ung. Ministers des Innern v. Sandor, November 9, 1916, Carton 56, Fach 15, AR, MdA, HHstA.

114 Abschrift einer Note des Herrn k.k. Ministers des Innern, March 15, 1916, Carton 56, Fach 15, AR, MdA, HHstA.

115 Note an das k.k. Generalkommisariat wegen wirtschaftlicher Massnahmen gegen eine Auswanderung nach dem Krieg, August 20, 1917, Carton 56, Fach 15, AR, MdA, HHstA.

116 "Aus dem Gerichtssaale: Wadowice," *Neue Freie Presse*, February 25, 1890, p. 6; ibid., December 7, 1889, p. 7.

117 Caro, *Auswanderung und Auswanderungspolitik*, 66–67.

118 Dillingham, *Emigration Conditions in Europe*, 388.

119 Stern to Department, July 15, 1886, in Kramár, *From the Danube to the Hudson*, 67.

120 Jussen to Department, September 10, 1888, in Kramár, *From the Danube to the Hudson*, 73.

121 Cited in Puskás, *Ties That Bind*, 56–57.

Chapter 2

1 Booker T. Washington, *The Man Farthest Down: A Record of Observation and Study in Europe* (New York, 1912), 4. For more on Washington, Park, and their projects in both Germany and Africa, see Andrew Zimmerman, *Alabama in Africa: Booker T. Washington, the German Empire, and the Globalization of the New South* (Princeton, 2010).

2 Washington, *The Man Farthest Down*, 4–5, 13.

3 Ibid.,12.

4 Ibid., 7.

5 Ibid., 77–78.

6 Ibid., 62–63.

7 Ibid., 84–85.

8 Ibid., 4.

9 General Consul Baron Hoening, Bericht über seine Bereisung der Südstaaten, April 12, 1908, Carton 53, Fach 15, Administrativ Reg-

istratur (AR), Ministerium des Aeussern (MdA), Haus-, Hof- und Staatsarchiv (HHstA).

10 Auswanderung nach den Südstaaten der Vereinigten Staaten von Amerika, April 23, 1908, sig. 126, c.k. Starostwo powiatowe w Chrzanowie, 1869–1918, Archiwum Państwe w Krakowie (APKr). See also Nicole Phelps, *U.S.-Habsburg Relations from 1815 to the Paris Peace Conference* (Cambridge, UK, 2013), 170–72.

11 "Austrian Immigration Temporarily Halted Here," *Daily Picayune*, December 2, 1908.

12 Whiteness studies have generally focused on how the perceived "whiteness" of particular migrant groups has shaped immigration policies and ethnic relations. Scholars have not, however, typically examined the effects of such racial anxieties on emigration politics. See, among others, Marilyn Lake and Henry Reynolds, *Drawing the Global Colour Line: White Men's Countries and the International Challenge of Racial Equality* (Cambridge, UK, 2008); Matthew Frye Jacobson, *Whiteness of a Different Color: European Immigrants and the Alchemy of Race* (Cambridge, MA, 1998); David R. Roediger, *Working toward Whiteness: How America's Immigrants Became White: The Strange Journey from Ellis Island to the Suburbs* (New York, 2005).

13 See, e.g., David Blackbourn, "Das Kaiserreich Transnational: Eine Skizze," in *Das Kaiserreich Transnational: Deutschland in der Welt, 1871–1914,* ed. Jürgen Osterhammel and Sebastian Conrad (Göttingen, 2004); Mark Mazower, *Hitler's Empire: How the Nazis Ruled Europe* (New York, 2009); Vejas Liulevicius, *The German Myth of the East: 1800 to the Present* (Oxford, 2009).

14 On Mexico, see Jorge Durand, "Migration Policy and the Asymmetry of Power: The Mexican Case, 1800–1900," in *Citizenship and Those Who Leave: The Politics of Emigration and Expatriation,* ed. Nancy Green and François Weil (Urbana, IL, 2007), 224–45. On China, see Carine Pina-Guerassimoff and Eric Guerassimoff, "The 'Overseas Chinese': The State and Emigration from the 1890s through the 1990s," ibid., 245–64. One country that has adopted a consistently negative stance toward emigration (similar to Eastern

Europe) has been Israel. See Ori Yehudai, "Out from Zion: Jewish Emigration from Palestine/Israel, 1945–1967" (PhD diss., University of Chicago, 2012).

15 On German emigration and nation building, see Sebastian Conrad, *Globalization and the Nation in Imperial Germany*, trans. Sorcha O'Hagan (Cambridge, UK, 2010); Krista O'Donnell, Renate Bridenthal, and Nancy Reagin, eds., *The* Heimat *Abroad: The Boundaries of Germanness* (Ann Arbor, 2005); Donna R. Gabaccia, Dirk Hoerder, and Adam Walaszek, "Emigration and Nation Building during the Mass Migrations from Europe," in *Citizenship and Those Who Leave*, 63–90; Andreas Fahrmeir, "From Economics to Ethnicity and Back: Reflections on Emigration Control in Germany, 1800–2000," ibid., 176–94.

16 Caroline Douki, "The Liberal Italian State and Mass Emigration, 1860–1914," in *Citizenship and Those Who Leave*, 91–113; Samuel L. Baily, *Immigrants in the Lands of Promise: Italians in Buenos Aires and New York City, 1870–1914* (Ithaca, 1999), 195–98; Mark Choate, *Emigrant Nation: The Making of Italy Abroad* (Cambridge, MA, 2008).

17 On emigration and its relationship to colonialism in Italy, see esp. Choate, *Emigrant Nation*; Douki, "The Liberal Italian State"; Philip V. Cannistraro and Gianfausto Rosoli, "Fascist Emigration Policy in the 1920s: An Interpretive Framework," *International Migration Review* 13, no. 4 (Winter 1979): 673–92; Carl Ipsen, *Dictating Demography: The Problem of Population in Fascist Italy* (Cambridge, UK, 1996), 51–65.

18 Cited in Benjamin Murdzek, *Emigration in Polish Social-Political Thought, 1870–1914* (Boulder, CO, 1977), 170.

19 Friedrich Hey, *Unser Auswanderungswesen und seine Schäden* (Vienna, 1912), 13–17.

20 Ibid. On the relationship between emigration and colonialism in Austria-Hungary, see Benno Gammerl, *Staatsbürger, Untertanen und Andere: Der Umgang mit ethnischer Heterogenität im britischen Weltreich und im Habsburgerreich, 1867–1918* (Vienna, 2010); Simon Loidl, "Kolonialpropaganda und Aktivitäten in Österreich-Ungarn,

1885–1918" (PhD diss., University of Vienna, 2012). On Czech colonialism and its relationship to emigration, see Michael Whitaker Dean, "'What the Heart Unites, the Sea Shall Not Divide': Claiming Overseas Czechs for the Nation" (PhD diss., University of California, Berkeley, 2014).

21 For accounts of the origins of Zionism in turn-of-the-century Europe, see Michael Brenner, *Zionism: A Brief History*, trans. Shelley L. Frisch (Princeton, 2003); David Engel, *Zionism* (Edinburgh, 2009); Ezra Mendelsohn, *Zionism in Poland: The Formative Years, 1915–1926* (New Haven, 1981).

22 For a comparative discussion of settler colonialisms in the twentieth century, see Caroline Elkins and Susan Pedersen, "Settler Colonialism: A Concept and Its Uses," in *Settler Colonialism in the Twentieth Century: Projects, Practices, Legacies*, ed. Caroline Elkins and Susan Pedersen (New York, 2005), 1–20.

23 Cited in Yosef Gorny, *Zionism and the Arabs* (Oxford, 1987), 35.

24 Murdzek, *Emigration*, 61–69; Gammerl, *Staatsbürger, Untertanen und Andere*, 56.

25 Manoel Ferreira-Correia and Cerro Azul, *Opis stanu Parana w Brazylii wraz z informacyami dla wychodzow*, trans. Jozef Siemiradzki (Lwow, 1896), 56–58, 80.

26 On the JCA, see Theodore Norman, *An Outstretched Arm: A History of the Jewish Colonization Association* (London, 1984), 70 (numbers).

27 "Aus Südamerika," *Die Welt*, March 4, 1898, p. 7.

28 Josef Zipfer, "Rückkehr jüdischer Colonisten aus Argentinien," *Die Welt*, May 27, 1898, p. 8; "Die Colonisten aus Argentinien," ibid., June 17, 1898, p. 12.

29 S. Werner, "Die argentinischen Greuel," *Die Welt*, July 15, 1898, pp. 7–8.

30 On the Jewish territorial movement, see Laura Almagor, "Saving a Jewish Europe in the World" (PhD diss., European University Institute, in progress); David Glover, "Imperial Zion: Israel Zangwill and the Origins of the Jewish Territorial Movement," in *The Jew in Late-Victorian and Edwardian Culture: Between the East End and East Africa*, ed. Eitan Bar-Yosef and Nadia Valman (New York, 2009), 131–44.

31 Gur Alroey, *An Unpromising Land: Jewish Migration to Palestine in the Early Twentieth Century* (Stanford, 2014).

32 "Kleiderconfection in den Colonien," *Die Welt*, June 11, 1897, p. 9.

33 Sigismund Gargas, Das polnische Auswanderungsproblem, Berlin 1919, sig. 3, f. 1162, Panstowy Urząd Emigracyny, Archiwum akt nowych (AAN), Warsaw.

34 Yfaat Weiss, "Central European Ethnonationalism and Zionist Binationalism," *Jewish Social Studies* 11 (September 2004): 106–7. On conversion rates in Vienna, see Marsha Rozenblit, *The Jews of Vienna, 1867–1914: Assimilation and Identity* (Albany, NY, 1983), chap. 6.

35 David Trietsch, "Die jüdische Emigrationsfrage," *Die Welt*, January 2, 1903, pp. 10–12.

36 See, among others, Todd Samuel Presner, *Muscular Judaism: The Jewish Body and the Politics of Regeneration* (New York, 2007); Arieh Saposnik, *Becoming Hebrew: The Creation of a Jewish National Culture in Ottoman Palestine* (Oxford, 2008).

37 Martin Buber, "From an Open Letter to Mahatma Gandhi" (1939), in *The Zionist Idea: A Historical Analysis and Reader*, ed. Arthur Hertzberg (New York, 1959), 465.

38 Elkins and Pedersen, "Settler Colonialism," 10–11.

39 Upton Sinclair, *The Jungle: The Lost First Edition* (Memphis, TN, 1988).

40 On the impact of *The Polish Peasant*, see Eli Zaretsky, "Editor's Introduction," in William I. Thomas and Florian Znaniecki, *The Polish Peasant in Europe and America* (Chicago, 1984), 10; Kathleen Neils Conzen, "Thomas and Znaniecki and the Historiography of American Immigration," *Journal of American Ethnic History* 16, no. 1 (Fall 1996): 16–25. For more on Znaniecki and Thomas, see also Zimmerman, *Alabama in Africa*, 225–30.

41 Martin Bulmer, *The Chicago School of Sociology: Institutionalization, Diversity, and the Rise of Sociological Research* (Chicago, 1984), 48.

42 On exile nationalism in the United States, see Phelps, *U.S.-Habsburg Relations*, 219–58.

43 William I. Thomas and Florian Znaniecki, *The Polish Peasant in Europe and America*. 2 vols. (New York, 1958), 1:75.

44 Ibid., 84–85.

45 Zaretsky, "Editor's Introduction," 5.

46 Thomas and Znaniecki, *The Polish Peasant*, 2:1826.

47 Ibid., 1:103.

48 Ibid., 814–17.

49 Ibid., 711.

50 Ibid., 745.

51 Ibid., 748–49.

52 Interview with unidentified Polish female by Henry Coles, October 1, 1937, WPA Box 85, 187:5, cited in Bruce M. Stave and John F. Sutherland, *From the Old Country: An Oral History of European Migration to America* (New York, 1994), 41, 102–4.

53 Thomas and Znaniecki, *The Polish Peasant*, 1:48–49.

54 Ibid., 2:1749–51.

55 *Protokoll der im k.k. Handelsministerium durchgeführten Vernehmung von Auskunftspersonen über die Auswanderung aus Österreich* (Vienna, 1912), 174.

56 Ibid., 111.

57 "Hirtenbrief der illyrischen Bischöfe über die Auswanderung," *Der Auswanderer* 5, no. 1 (January 1914): 10–11.

58 Thomas and Znaniecki, *The Polish Peasant*, 1:827–28.

59 Ibid., 842. On emigration's effect on gender roles in southern Italy and China, respectively, see Linda Reeder, *Widows in White: Migration and the Transformation of Rural Italian Women, Sicily, 1880–1920* (Toronto, 2003); Shelly Chan, "Rethinking the 'Left Behind' in Chinese Migrations: A Case of Liberating Wives in 1950s South China," in *Proletarian and Gendered Mass Migrations: A Global Perspective on Continuities and Discontinuities from the Nineteenth to the Twenty-first Centuries*, ed. Dirk Hoerder and Amarjit Kaur (Leiden, 2013), 451–66.

60 Ladislaus Schneider, *Die ungarische Auswanderung: Studie über die Ursachen und den Umfang der ungarischen Auswanderung* (Pozsony, 1915), 129.

61 Thomas and Znaniecki, *The Polish Peasant*, 1:803–6.

62 Helen and Karol Słoński to Frances Murawska, December 5, 1890,

in Witold Kula, Nina Assorodobraj-Kula, and Marcin Kula, *Writing Home: Immigrants in Brazil and the United States, 1890-1891*, ed. and trans. Josephine Wtulich (Boulder, CO, 1986), 411.

63 Louis Adamic, *The Native's Return: An American Immigrant Visits Yugoslavia and Discovers His Old Country* (New York, 1934), 39.

64 Interview of Pauline Parnes Reimer by Janet Levine, August 1, 1994, in Ellis Island Oral History Project, Series EI, no. 512 (Alexandria, VA, 2004), 41.

65 KUS-102, Box 5, Oral History Archives of Chicago Polonia, Chicago History Museum.

66 "Pamiętnik nr. 126. Służąca z New Castle, Pennsylwania," in Janina Dziembowska, ed., *Pamiętniki Emigrantów. Stany Zjednoczone*, vol. 1 (Warsaw, 1977), 573-74.

67 Walter Borkowski, Pittsburgh to Marianne Borkowska, January 21, 1891, in *Writing Home*, 196.

68 Thomas and Znaniecki, *The Polish Peasant*, 1:862-70.

69 Ibid., 890.

70 Powderly Report, European Investigation 1906-07, 50-51, Reel 1, pt. 4, Series A, Subject correspondence files, Records of the Immigration and Naturalization Service, [microform].

71 Washington, *The Man Farthest Down*, 20, 62, 70.

72 Louis Adamic, *Laughing in the Jungle: The Autobiography of an Immigrant in America* (New York, 1932), 321-22.

73 Abschrift, Kriegsministerium, Auswanderung aus Galizien und Bukowina, Agentumtriebe, June 25, 1913, Carton 3325, Sig 6 VZ 18, Allgemeine Strafsachen, Justiz, Allgemeines Verwaltungsarchiv, Österreichisches Staatsarchiv.

74 William Jenks, *Austria under the Iron Ring, 1879-1893* (Charlottesville, VA, 1965), 179-95, 196-220.

75 Theda Skocpol, *Protecting Soldiers and Mothers: The Political Origins of Social Policy in the United States* (Cambridge, MA, 1995), 8.

76 *Protokoll der im k.k. Handelsministerium durchgeführten Vernehmung*, 192-93.

77 Henryk Sienkiewicz, *After Bread: A Story of Polish Emigrant Life to*

America, trans. Vatslaf A. Hlasko and Thomas H. Bullick (New York, 1897), 60–61.

78 Interview with Morris Kavitsky by Morton Tonken, January 31, 1939, WPA, cited in *From the Old Country*, 49–50.

79 *Protokoll der im k.k. Handelsministerium durchgeführten Vernehmung*, 196–98.

80 For more on the contribution of migration to the emergence of social protection for workers on the national and international scale, see Paul-André Rosental, "Migrations, souveraineté, droits sociaux: Protéger et expulser les étrangers en Europe du XIXe siècle à nos jours," *Annales. Histoire, Sciences Sociales* 66 (April–June 2011): 335–73; Caroline Douki, "Protection sociale et mobilité transatlantique: Les migrants italiens au début du XXe siècle," ibid., 375–410.

81 Regierungsvorlage, Gesetz betreffend die Auswanderung, 1913, Carton 31, Fach 15, AR, MdA, HHstA.

82 M. Baumfeld, "Das österreichische Einwandererheim in New York," *Neues Wiener Tagblatt*, March 24, 1911, 11, Carton 27, Fach 15, AR, MdA, HHstA.

83 Adamic, *Laughing in the Jungle*, 107.

84 Duckiet, Walter, fl. 1941, "Polish Boarding Houses, 1890," in *America, the Dream of My Life: Selections from the Federal Writers' Project's New Jersey Ethnic Survey* ed. David Steven Cohen (New Brunswick, NJ, 1990), 295.

85 Julianna Puskás, *Ties That Bind, Ties That Divide: 100 Years of Hungarian Experience in the United States*, trans. Zora Ludwig (New York, 2000), 128.

86 Consul von Ploennies, Bericht über die Einwanderungheime in New York, July 1, 1911, Carton 27, Fach 15, AR, MdA, HHstA.

87 Interpellationsbeantwortung, June 17, 1910, Carton 29, Fach 15, AR, MdA, HHstA.

88 Extract from Health Department Report on Premises at nrs. 14 and 16 Greenwich Street, Reel 2, pt. 4, Series A, Subject correspondence files, Records of the Immigration and Naturalization Service.

89 Commissioner General of Immigration, September 1, 1909, Reel 3,

pt. 4, Series A, Subject correspondence files, Records of the Immigration and Naturalization Service.

90 Frage der weiteren Subventionierung der "Österreichischen Gesellschaft von New York," January 24, 1911, Carton 29, Fach 15, AR, MdA, HHstA.

91 Consul von Ploennies, Bericht über die Einwanderungheime in New York, July 1, 1911, Carton 27, Fach 15, AR, MdA, HHstA.

92 See Choate, *Emigrant Nation*, among others.

93 Phelps, *U.S.-Habsburg Relations*, 150.

94 Consul von Ploennies, Bericht über die Einwanderungheime; Österr. Heim und das Leohäus in New York, April 19, 1911, Carton 29, Fach 15, AR, MdA, HHstA.

95 Österreichisches Einwandererheim in New York, November 16, 1915, Carton 30, Fach 15, AR, MdA, HHstA.

Chapter 3

1 Karel Čapek, *Hordubal*, trans. M. and R. Weatherall (London, 1934), 14–15, 63.

2 Odpověd předsedy ministerské rady na interpelaci poslance Josefa Vrabce, January 21, 1921, Carton 244, Ministerstvo vnitra—Stára registratura (MV-SR), Národní archiv (NA).

3 Ladislas Buday, ed., *Émigration et retour des émigrés des pays de la sainte couronne hongroise de 1899 à 1913* (Budapest, 1918), 1.

4 On migration and sovereignty, see, among others, Wendy Brown, *Walled States, Waning Sovereignty* (Cambridge, MA, 2010); Annemarie Sammartino, *The Impossible Border: Germany and the East, 1914–1922* (Ithaca, 2010).

5 Leopold Caro, *Ku nowej Polsce* (Lwow, 1923), 13.

6 Mezinárodní ženský kongres ve Washingtoně, vystěhovalecká otázka, January 7, 1925, Carton 3798, Ministerstvo sociální péče (MSP), NA; *L'émigration polonaise, son importance et son organisation* (Warsaw, 1922), 10.

7 Protokol Estera Reisfeld, October 20, 1926; Letter to Hugh S. Cumming, Surgeon General, August 6, 1927; Robert F. Kelley, Division of East European Affairs, to Jan Stalinski, Second Secretary of

the Polish Legation, November 13, 1928, B26126, sig. 9716, Ministerstwo Spraw Zagranicznych (MSZ), Archiwum akt nowych (AAN), Warsaw.

8 Jan Žilka, "Americky hlas o otázce rasové a přistěhovalecké," *Československé emigrace* 3, nos. 7-8 (July-August 1928): 6-7.

9 For numbers, Janine Ponty, *Polonais méconnus: Histoire des travailleurs immigrés en France dans l'entre-deux-guerres* (Paris, 1988), 316. On immigration in interwar France, see Mary Dewhurst Lewis, *The Boundaries of the Republic: Migrant Rights and the Limits of Universalism in France, 1918–1940* (Stanford, 2007); Clifford Rosenberg, *Policing Paris: The Origins of Modern Immigration Control between the Wars* (Ithaca, 2006); Elisa Camiscioli, *Reproducing the French Race: Immigration, Intimacy, and Embodiment in the Early Twentieth Century* (Durham, NC, 2009).

10 Delegates from France, Great Britain, Italy, Greece, Germany, China, Japan, India, Brazil, Switzerland, Spain, Greece, South Africa, and Canada also attended. International Emigration Commission, *Report of the Commission* (Geneva, 1921).

11 International Labor Office, *Emigration and Immigration: Legislation and Treaties* (Geneva, 1922), xiv.

12 Jan Žilka, "Několik myšlenik o naší vystěhovalecké politice," *Československé emigrace* 3, no. 6 (June 1928): 1.

13 On the links between forced population transfers, humanitarianism, and colonialism between the wars, see Eric D. Weitz, "From the Vienna to the Paris System: International Politics and the Entangled Histories of Human Rights, Forced Deportations, and Civilizing Missions," *American Historical Review* 113 (December 2008): 1313-43; Dirk Moses, "Partitions, Forced Population 'Transfers' and the Question of Human Rights in the 1930s and 1940s" (unpublished paper).

14 Keith Watenpaugh, "Between Communal Survival and National Aspiration: Armenian Genocide Refugees, the League of Nations and the Practices of Interwar Humanitarianism," http://humanrightsinitiative.ucdavis.edu/files/2012/10/Watenpaugh-Between-Communal-Survival-and-National-Aspiration.pdf, accessed Jan-

uary 13, 2014; Weitz, "From the Vienna to the Paris System," 1335–38.

15 Tara Zahra, "The Minority Problem: National Classification in the French and Czechoslovak Borderlands," *Contemporary European History* 17 (May 2008): 137–65.

16 Henryk Satmajer, Referat w sprawie reemigracji Polakow z Ameryki do Polski, March 3, 1920, sig. 9943, B26353, MSZ, AAN; Zásady pro repatriaci československých příslušníků, July 15, 1920, Carton 2825, Předsednictva ministerské rady (PMR); Memorandum o otázkách vystěhovaleckých, přistěhovaleckách a osadních, December 3, 1924, Carton 245, MV-SR, NA.

17 Aleksander R. Miletic, *Journey under Surveillance: The Overseas Emigration Policy of the Kingdom of Serbs, Croats, and Slovenes in Global Context, 1918–1928* (Berlin, 2012), 92–96.

18 Wydanie paszportów zagranicznych do Ameryki obywatelstom polskim wyznanie mojzeszowego, May 19, 1920; Opis Ministerstwo spraw wewnętrznych, June 28, 1920, W sprawie wydawania paszportów do Ameryki, sig. 411, Starostwo Grodskie Krakowie, Archiwum państowe w krakowie (APKr).

19 Quoted in Anna Reczyńska, *For Bread and a Better Future: Emigration from Poland to Canada, 1918–1939* (Toronto, 1996), 131.

20 Czechoslovak Zionism was not, however, primarily oriented toward emigration to Palestine. On Zionism and the interwar Czechoslovak census, see Tatjana Lichtenstein, *Making Jews at Home: Zionism in Czechoslovakia, 1918–1938* (Bloomington, IN, forthcoming). On Zionism in interwar Poland, see Ezra Mendelsohn, *Zionism in Poland: The Formative Years, 1915–1926* (New Haven, 1981), quotation 112.

21 Organisace návratu Čechoslováků z Ameriky, 1920, Carton 244, MV-SR, NA.

22 Vladimir Mlynek, b. 1926, http://www.ncsml.org/Oral-History/Cleveland/20100629/48/Mlynek-Vladimir.aspx, accessed November 29, 2011.

23 Protokol z dnia 3 marca 1920 z posiedzenia w sprawie reemigracji Polaków z Ameryki, sig. 9943, B26353, Ministerstwo Spraw Zagranic-

znych, AAN; Mieczysław Szawleski, *Kwestja emigracji w Polsce* (Warsaw, 1927), 81; Adam Walaszek, *Reemigracja ze Stanów Zjednoczonych do Polski po I wojnie światowej (1919–1924)* (Cracow, 1983), 58–64.

24 Émigration et Reémigration, October 4, 1921, sig. 128, Pologne, Z-Europe, Archives des affaires étrangères, Paris (MAE).

25 Sigismund Gargas, Das polnische Auswanderungsproblem, Berlin 1919, sig. 3, Panstowy Urząd Emigracyny, AAN.

26 *L'émigration polonaise*, 7.

27 Pečlivost o československých repatriantov a emigrantov, May 13, 1921, Carton 531, II. Sekce- 2, bězná spisovna, Archiv ministerstvo zahraničních věcí (MZV).

28 Jacob Horak, "Effects of the War upon Emigration from Czechoslovakia," *Social Service Bulletin* 2 (March 1928): 78.

29 *Wychodźstwo Polskie w poszczególnych krajach* (Warsaw, 1926), 127.

30 Péče o přislušniky čs. Republiky, July 22, 1919, Carton 2825, Předsednictva Ministerské Rady, NA.

31 Mieczysław Szawlewski, *Wychodźstwo Polskie w stanach Zjednoczonych Ameryki* (Warsaw, 1924), 352.

32 Vracející Slováci z Ameriky, April 20, 1920, Carton 2825, Předsednictva Ministerské Rady, NA.

33 Český ústav zahraniční, *Vystěhovalecká príručka pre úřady sociálných pracovníkov a vystěhovalcov* (Prague, 1929), 102, Carton 29, Českslovenský ústav zahraniční-I (ČÚZ-I), NA.

34 *Informator dla Reemigrantów. Poradnik dla tych, którzy myśla o powrocie do Polski* (Warsaw, 1933), 18, 49–50.

35 Ibid., 49–59.

36 Aleksandar R. Miletic, "(Extra-)Institutional Practices, Restrictions, and Corruption. Emigration Policy in the Kingdom of Serbs, Croats and Slovenes (1918–1928)," in *Transnational Societies, Transterritorial Politics: Migrations in the (Post) Yugoslav Region, 19th–21st Century*, ed. Ulf Brunnbauer (Munich, 2009), 100.

37 International Emigration Commission, *Report of the Commission*, 75.

38 Notatka o działności urzędu emigracynego przy ministerstwie pracy i opieki społecnej, sig. 9958, Ministerstwo Spraw Zagranicznych;

Rozporządzenie Prezydenta Rzeczypospolitej z dnia 11 października 1927 o emigracji, sig. 9725, B26135, AAN.

39 Dariusz Stola, *Kraj bez wyjścia? Migracje z Polski 1949–1989* (Warsaw, 2010), 32.

40 Commission Internationale de l'Émigration, *Rapport de la Commission* (Geneva, 1921), 75. On Italy, see Philip V. Cannistraro and Gianfausto Rosoli, "Fascist Emigration Policy in the 1920s: An Interpretive Framework," *International Migration Review* 13, no. 4 (Winter 1979): 673–92; Carl Ipsen, *Dictating Demography: The Problem of Population in Fascist Italy* (Cambridge, UK, 1996), 51–65.

41 Morgane Labbé, "'Reproduction' as a New Demographic Issue in Interwar Poland," in *A World of Populations: The Production, Transfer, and Application of Demographic Knowledge in the Twentieth Century in Transnational Perspective*, ed. H. Hartmann and C. Unger (New York, 2014), 36–57; Adam Walaszek, "Wychodžcy, Emigrants or Poles? Fears and Hopes about Emigration in Poland, 1870–1939" (2002), available at http://www.utvandrersenteret.no/doc/adam%20walaszek.pdf, 10, accessed September 30, 2013.

42 "Vystěhovalci a jich zákonna ochrana," *Národní listy*, April 28, 1921.

43 Ján Žilka, ed., Zákon ze dne 15. února 1922 o vystěhovalectví, č. 71, *Sbírka zákonů a nařizení státu československého* (Prague, 1922), 219.

44 "Dávky za úřední úkony," in František Vyhnanovský, ed., *Cestovní pasy a vystěhovalectví* (Prague, 1939), 296.

45 Ochrana československého sklářství, July 3, 1936, Carton 2920, MSP, NA.

46 Vystěhovalecká agitace v Podkarpatské Rusi, October 10, 1922, Carton 3862, MSP, NA.

47 Omezení vstupu čsl. zemědelského dělnictiva do Francie, March 17, 1926, Carton 545, Ministerstvo zemědelství IV, Spisy 1918–34, NA.

48 Rozporządzenie Prezydenta Rzeczypospolitej z dnia 11 października 1927 o emigracji, B26135, sig. 9725, MSZ, AAN; Warunki uzyskania paszportow emigracynych do poszczelgonych krajow, 1925, sig. 57, Konsulat RP w Londynie, AAN; Stěhování žen a dívek do Argentiny, May 12, 1934; Stěhování žen a dívek do Argentiny, April 21, 1934, Carton 477, V. Sekce- 6, bězná spisovna, MZV.

49 Vystěhovalecká agitace v Podkarpatské Rusi, October 10, 1922, Carton 3862, MSP, NA.

50 Stižnost na pasový úřad, January 29, 1926, Carton 3685, MSP, NA.

51 Stížnost proti služnovskému úřadu v Mijavě, April 27, 1923, Carton 3863, MSP, NA.

52 Vystahovalecká agitacia na Slovensku, June 5, 1923, Carton 3863, MSP, NA.

53 Vystěhovalcká agitace, February 10, 1923, Carton 3863, MSP, NA.

54 Podloudné vystěhovalectví- Obranní opatření, April 10, 1924, Carton 517, V. Sekce- 6, běžná spisovna, MZV.

55 Protokol sepsaný z vyslavnectví Republiky Československé v Riu de Janeiro, July 26, 1922, Carton 3862, MSP, NA.

56 Protokol sepsaný dne 11 května 1923 u ministerstva sociální péče s vystěhovalcem Michalem Mičákem, February 11, 1923, Carton 3963, MSP, NA.

57 Vystěhovalectví, December 14, 1923, Carton 4048, MSP, NA.

58 Ladislav Černocký, "Podloudné vystěhovalectví," in *Československé vystěhovalectví. Jeho přičiny, důsledky a vyhlídky*, ed. Lev Zavřel (Prague, 1928), 50.

59 č. 265361, October 12, 1922, Carton 3864, MSP, NA.

60 Ludwik Lalikur do powiatowy Komendy w Żywcu, June 4, 1930; Michal Kuprcak, Jan Jafernik do powiatowy Komendy w Żywcu, November 4, 1930, sig. 269, Starostwo powiatowe w Żywcu, 1918–39, APKr.

61 Vyhlídky vystěhovalectví a novelisace zákon č. 71, 1922, December 7, 1935, Carton 4025, MSP, NA. For the final draft of the law, see Vládní nařižení ze dne 12 června 1936, č. 164, *Sbírka zákonů a nařizení státu československého* (Prague, 1936), 619–20.

62 Labbé, "Reproduction as a New Demographic Issue in Interwar Poland."

63 Memo from Jan Sykáček, September 20, 1924, Carton 3797, MSP, NA.

64 Francousko-česká komise, najímaní čsl. Zemědělského dělnictva a dílcích kolonů na Korsiku, March 16, 1928, Carton 486, V. Sekce- 6, bězná spisovna, MZV.

65 Informace o vyhlídkách pro vystěhovalce na Tahiti, 1928, MZV, V. Sekce- 6, bězná spisovna, Carton 486, MZV.

66 Okolnik nr. 183 w sprawie działności towarzystwa kolonizacynego w Warszawie, 16 grudnia 1926, sig. 58, Konsulat Generalny RP w Londynie, AAN.

67 "Musimy żądać," *Polska na Morzu* 5, no. 3 (March 1938): 2; "Emigracja polska," ibid., 6, no. 5 (May 1939): 6.

68 Marek Arpad Kowalski, *Dyskurs kolonialny w Drugiej Rzeczypospolitej* (Warsaw, 2010), 72.

69 Memorandum sur la question de l'extension aux territoires coloniaux d'Afrique des principes des mandats, May 23, 1939, sig. 9737, B26147, MSZ, AAN.

70 Ivo Sasek, *Les migrations de la population intéressant le territoire de la Tchécoslovaquie actuelle (depuis le XVIIe siècle à nos jours)* (Geneva, 1935), 142–43.

71 International Labor Organization, *Emigration and Immigration*, xiv, 56.

72 Zemská zpráva politická v Praze, January 21, 1921, Židoští vystěhovalci zdravotní závady v židoské radnici v Praze, Carton 531, II. Sekce- 2, bězna spisovna, MZV; Novostavba vystěhovalecké stanice v Libni, April 12, 1928, Carton 516, V. Sekce- 6, bězná spisovna, MZV.

73 On Czechoslovak institutions, see Jaroslav Vaculík, *Nástin českých a slovenských přeshraničních migrací v meziválečném období* (Brno, 2010). On Polish institutions, see Reczyńska, *For Bread and a Better Future*, 111–37.

74 *Našim krajancům a vystěhovalcům* (Prague, 1929), Carton 29, ČUZ-I, NA.

75 Zápis o poradě o organisaci místního poradnictví vystěhovaleckého, March 3, 1930, Carton 30, ČUZ- I, NA.

76 Jan Matušinský, stolař, August 11, 1929, Carton 29, ČUZ- I, NA.

77 Francis Albert, Senator, Rapport nr. 232, Sénat, 1922, sig. 271, Pologne, Z-Europe, MAE.

78 Francja, Rozmiary ruchu emigracyjnego i reemigracynego, 1938, sig. 2, Panstowy Urząd Emigracyny.

79 On the Polish embargo and the creation of the Committee, see Ponty, *Polonais méconnus*, 238–39, 265–66; Čsl. dělnice ve Francii-utvoření ochraného komitétu cizích pracovnic ve Francii, June 6, 1929, Carton 545, Ministerstvo zemědelství IV, Spisy 1918–34, NA.

80 Sasek, *Les migrations*, 70.

81 Paul-André Rosental, "Protéger et expulser les étrangers en Europe du XIXe siècle à nos jours," *Annales. Histoire, Sciences Sociales* 66 (April–June 2011) 357–58.

82 Ibid., 362; Sasek, *Les migrations*, 74.

83 Réclamation—Dingsheim, October 14, 1936, Carton 4054, MSP, NA.

84 Réclamation—Dingsheim, January 7, 1937, Carton 4054, MSP, NA.

85 Vystěhovalecká zpráva za rok 1930; Vystěhovalecká zpráva za rok 1931; Carton 3977, MSP, NA.

86 Ondrej Rabara, stižnost, November 8, 1939, Carton 4054, MSP, NA.

87 Ministerstvo sociální péče, *Informace pro vystěhovalce o Francii* (Prague, 1931), 20–21.

88 Zemědelské dělnictvo ve Francii—stížnosti, July 29, 1938, Carton 4054, MSP, NA.

89 Ignác Brázdovič, stížnost, October 29, 1938, Carton 4054, MSP, NA.

90 Julie Šalmiková, 1938, Carton 4054, MSP, NA.

91 Roland Hubscher, *L'immigration dans les campagnes françaises* (Paris, 1996), 227.

92 Elżbieta Łątka, "Les ouvrières polonaises en France dans l'entre deux-guerres: Quelques fragments d'histoires de ces inconnues," *Synergies Pologne*, special issue (2011): 59.

93 Anonymous Polish Immigrant, fl. 1908, "A Peaceful Law-Abiding Citizen," in *America, the Dream of My Life: Selections from the Federal Writers' Project's New Jersey Ethnic Survey*, ed. David Steven Cohen (New Brunswick, NJ, 1990), 83–84.

94 Anonymous Ukrainian Man, fl. 1939, "One Round of Hell after Another," in *America, the Dream of My Life*, 295.

95 Societé des Nations, *Le problème des migrations*, Report of the ILO to the Assembly of the SDN, September 9, 1937, 4, Carton 517, V. Sekce-6, bězná spisovna, MZV.

96 Joseph (Jozef) Kmet, 1930, http://www.ncsml.org/Oral-History/

Chicago/20110120/86/Kmet-Joseph.aspx#depression, accessed November 29, 2011.

97 International Labor Organization, *Exposé de la législation et de la pratique concernant le recrutement et le placement des travailleurs migrants* (Geneva, 1934), 242QO/2343, MAE. For Polish statistics concerning emigration to and re-migration from France between the wars, Francja, Rozmiary ruchu emigracyjnego i reemigracynego, 1938, sig. 2, Panstowy Urząd Emigracyny, AAN.

98 Raport emigracyny Konsulatu Generalnego R.P. w Nowym Yorku za lata 1930 i 1931, sig. 128, Konsulat Generalny RP w Nowym Yorku, AAN.

99 To U.S. from H.Q. (Suzanne Ferrière), April 19, 1932, Folder 28, SW109, Social Welfare Archive, University of Minnesota.

100 George Warren, "The Widening Horizon in Our Service to Foreign-Born Families," National Conference of Social Work, June 15, 1931, Folder 28, SW109, Social Welfare Archive, University of Minnesota.

101 J.K., "Les emigrés rentrent de France," *Robotnik*, December 31, 1931, sig. 433, Pologne, Z-Europe, MAE.

102 Navrh na úpravu evidence vystěhovalecké, June 20, 1924, Carton 4048, MSP, NA.

103 "On vous mettre dehors quand vous aurez fait votre devoir," translated from *Kuryer Codzienny*, January 22, 1932, December 9, 1931, sig. 433, Pologne, Z-Europe, MAE.

104 Émigration polonaise en France, August 24, 1934, sig. 433, Pologne, Z-Europe, MAE.

105 Le Ministre du Travail à Monsieur le Ministre des Affaires Étrangers, April 28, 1934, sig. 433, Pologne, Z-Europe, MAE.

106 Sdružení čsl. krajanských spolků v severní Francii, October 6, 1935, Carton 456, Sekce- 6, bězná spisovna, MZV.

107 Francja, Rozmiary ruchu emigracyjnego i reemigracynego, 1938, sig. 2, Panstowy Urząd Emigracyny, AAN; Aide-Mémoire, Polish Embassy in Paris, August 28, 1934, sig. 434, Pologne, Z-Europe, MAE.

108 "Faim et misère des ouvriers polonais en France," trans. from *Kurjer Codzienny*, May 31, 1934, sig. 433, Pologne, Z-Europe, MAE.

109 A/s Main d'oeuvre tchécoslovaque en France, December 4, 1934, 207QO/173, MAE.

Chapter 4

1 Interest of Poland in Participation in the Work of the Intergovernmental Committee, November 3, 1938, Folder Poland, Records of the Intergovernmental Committee on Refugees, 1938–47 (IGCR). Accessed through Intergovernmental Committee on Refugees: The West's Response to Jewish Emigration (Farmington Hills, MI, 2010).

2 Telegram from Warsaw to U.S. Secretary of State, August 30, 1938, Folder Poland, IGCR.

3 Quoted in Neil Smith, *American Empire: Roosevelt's Geographer and the Prelude to Globalization* (Berkeley, 2003), 298.

4 For numbers, see Richard Breitman and Alan M. Kraut, *American Refugee Policy and European Jewry, 1933–1945* (Bloomington, IN, 1987), 56; Deborah Dwork and Robert Jan van Pelt, *Flight from the Reich: Refugee Jews, 1933–1946* (New York, 2012).

5 Peter Becker and Peter Heumos, eds., *Drehscheibe Prag: Zur deutschen Emigration in der Tschechoslowakei, 1933–1939* (Munich, 1992).

6 Ing. Otto Eisler, žádost o povolení vjezdů do ČSR, June 17, 1938, Carton 483, V. Sekce- 6, běžná spisovna, Archiv ministerstvo zahraničních věcí (MZV).

7 Uprchlíci v obvodu policejního ředitelství v Mor. Ostravě, December 12, 1938, Carton 46, MPSP-R, NA.

8 Telegram from Carr, Prague, to U.S. Secretary of State, October 12, 1938, Folder: Czechoslovakia, IGCR.

9 Memorandum of the Position of the Jews in and from the Sudeten German Areas, November 1, 1938, Item: 468330, Folder: Czechoslovakia: Subject Matter, Refugees, 1933–44 New York Collection, Archive of the Joint Distribution Committee (JDC).

10 Transportování židů z obsazených území, November 14, 1938, Min-

isterstvo práce a sociální péče—repatriace (MPSP-R), Carton 161, Národni archiv (NA). For a complete account of Czechoslovak refugee policies during the Third Reich, see Kateřina Čapková and Michal Frankl, *Nejisté útočistě: Československo a uprchlíci před nacismem, 1933–1938* (Prague, 2008); Jan Benda, *Útěky a vyhánění z pohraničí českých zemí 1938–1939* (Prague, 2013).

11 Nežadoucé cizinci a emigranti, December 31, 1938, Carton 16, MPSP-R, NA.

12 Morris Troper, Report on Visit to Zbanszyn, November 13–14, 1938, Item: 509810, Folder Poland: Subject Matter, Refugees, 1933–44 New York Collection, JDC; Yehuda Bauer, *My Brother's Keeper: A History of the American Joint Distribution Committee, 1929–1939* (Philadelphia, 1974), 243–44.

13 "Hungary Expelling Foreign Jews from Ceded Czech Areas," *Jewish Telegraph Agency*, March 7, 1939; Report by Mrs. Marie Schmolka, November 27, 1938, Reel 498, 996, RG 11.001M94, Records of the Hebrew Immigrant Assistance Society (HIAS), Paris, USHMMA. HICEM, an organization designed to assist Jewish emigration, resulted from a merger of the Hebrew Immigrant Aid and Sheltering Society, the Jewish Colonization Association, and EMIGDIRECT, a German-Jewish emigration association.

14 Die Lage der Burgenländer Juden auf dem Schleppdampfer auf der Donau bei Rojka in Ungarn, 1104, Reel 498, RG 11.001M94, HIAS—Paris, USHMMA. On the *St. Louis*, see Sarah Ogilvie and Scott Miller, *Refuge Denied: The* St. Louis *Passengers and the Holocaust* (Madison, WI, 2006).

15 On Czechoslovakia, see Tatjana Lichtenstein, *Making Jews at Home: Zionism in Czechoslovakia, 1918–1938* (Bloomington, IN, forthcoming). On Habsburg Galicia, see Joshua Shanes, *Diaspora Nationalism and Jewish Identity in Habsburg Galicia* (Cambridge, UK, 2012), quotation 2. On the relationship between autonomism and Zionism in the United States, see James Loeffler, "Between Zionism and Liberalism: Oscar Janowsky and Diaspora Nationalism in America," *Association for Jewish Studies Review* 34, no. 2 (November 2010): 289–308.

On Zionism in interwar Poland, see Ezra Mendelsohn, *Zionism in Poland. The Formative Years, 1915–1926* (New Haven, 1981); Kenneth B. Moss, *Unchosen People: the Polish Jewish Condition and the Jewish Political Imagination, 1928–1939* (forthcoming).

16 Kenneth B. Moss, "Thinking with Restriction: Immigration Restriction and Polish Jewish Accounts of the Post-liberal State, Empire, Race, and Political Reason, 1926–39," *East European Jewish Affairs* 44, nos. 2–3 (2014): 206.

17 Interview of Herman Barrett, Rubin Barrett, and Ruth Barrett Teperman by Paul E. Sigrist, Jr., July 24, 1991, in Ellis Island Oral History Project, Series EI, no. 57 (Alexandria, VA, 2003), 63.

18 On British refugee policies, see Louise London, *Whitehall and the Jews, 1933–1948: British Immigration Policy, Jewish Refugees, and the Holocaust* (Cambridge, UK, 2003). On France, see Vicki Caron, *Uneasy Asylum: France and the Jewish Refugee Crisis, 1933–1942* (Stanford, 1999). On the United States, see David S. Wyman, *Paper Walls: America and the Refugee Crisis* (Amherst, MA, 1968); Breitman and Kraut, *American Refugee Policy.*

19 Breitman and Kraut, *American Refugee Policy,* 27.

20 Ibid., 9, 49, 64; Wyman, *Paper Walls,* 210.

21 Caron, *Uneasy Asylum,* 2–12.

22 London, *Whitehall and the Jews,* 11. On emigration to Palestine, see Francis R. Nicosia, *Zionism and Anti-Semitism in Nazi Germany* (New York, 2008), 283.

23 Cited in Meri-Jane Rochelson, "Zionism, Territorialism, Race, and Nation in the Thought of Israel Zangwill," in *The Jew in Late-Victorian and Edwardian Culture: Between the East End and East Africa,* ed. Eitan Bar-Yosef and Nadia Valman (New York, 2009), 150.

24 On the Jewish territorialist movement and the intersections of colonialism and Zionism, see Laura Almagor, "Saving a Jewish Europe in the World" (PhD diss., European University Institute, in progress); David Glover, "Imperial Zion: Israel Zangwill and the Origins of the Jewish Territorial Movement," in *The Jew in Late-Victorian and Edwardian Culture,* 131–44.

25 Moss, "Thinking with Restriction," 207.

26 For an assessment of Roosevelt's refugee politics, see Richard Breit-man and Alan M. Kraut, *FDR and the Jews* (Cambridge, MA, 2013); Smith, *American Empire*, 293–316.

27 Wyman, *Paper Walls*, 53–55. See also Yehuda Bauer, *Jews for Sale? Nazi-Jewish Negotiations, 1933–1945* (New Haven, 1994), 30–44.

28 Memorandum of Visit to Paris and Berlin, April 3rd–17th, 1939, Folder Wohlthat-Berlin, IGCR; "Jewish Congress Bars Ransom Plan," *New York Times*, January 17, 1939.

29 Dwork and van Pelt, *Flight from the Reich*, 98.

30 Bauer, *My Brother's Keeper*, 183–85.

31 Joel Cang, "The Opposition Parties in Poland and Their Attitude towards the Jews and the Jewish Problem," *Jewish Social Studies* 1, no. 2 (April 1939): 241–56.

32 Jan Ziemiński, *Problem emigracji żydowskiej* (Warsaw, 1937), 44; "Emigration of Jews from Poland Urged," *New York Times*, February 22, 1936; "Poles Seek Outlet for Big Population," ibid., August 2, 1936; L'antisemitisme en Pologne et l'attitude du clergé catholique, Folder 359, Reel 109, Fond 1190, WJC-Paris, RG-11.001M.36, USHMMA.

33 Problem emigracji żydowskiej, December 20, 1938, Sygnatura: 2/322/0/9909 - B 26319, Archiwum akt nowych, Warsaw.

34 "A propos d'un projet d'établissement d'israelites dans les colo-nies françaises," *Le petit parisien*, January 16, 1937, cited in Caron, *Uneasy Asylum*, 146.

35 Membre de l'exécutif du congres juif mondial s'est entretenu avec le ministre des colonies, January 22, 1937; The Limited Prospects of Jewish Settlement in French Colonies, Jewish Telegraph Agency, Paris, March 19, 1937, Folder 275, Reel 106, Fond 1190, RG-11.001M.36, USHMMA.

36 Caron, *Uneasy Asylum*, 146–54, quotations 153–54. See also Eric T. Jennings, "Writing Madagascar Back into the Madagascar Plan," *Holocaust and Genocide Studies* 21, no. 2 (Fall 2007): 187–217; Eric T. Jennings, "Last Exit from Vichy France: The Martinique Escape Route and the Ambiguities of Emigration," *Journal of Modern History* 74 (June 2002): 289–324.

37 Memorandum on the position of the Jews in Poland, London, 1938, Folder 317, Reel 107, WJC-Paris, Fond 1190, RG-11.001M.36, USHMMA.

38 On Jewish responses to "emigrationism," see Emmanuel Melzer, *No Way Out: The Politics of Polish Jewry, 1935–1939* (Cincinnati, 1997), 134–53, Erlich quotation 145–46; Moss, "Thinking with Restriction," 213–14.

39 Michael Głazer, *The Jewish Problem and the United States* (Warsaw, January 18, 1939), 40, 44, 51.

40 Michal Głazer, *Project for Financing of Jewish Emigration from Poland* (Warsaw, May 1938), 6.

41 Memorandum of Conversation, November 18, 1938, G. S. Messersmith, Folder Poland, IGCR.

42 Rapport sur l'état actuel du problème de l'émigration juive de Pologne, November 23, 1937, Reel 487, 1967; Memo from Leon Alter, November 19, 1937, Reel 485; RG 11.001M94, HIAS—Paris, USHMMA. On JEAS, see Moss, "Thinking with Restriction," 218–19.

43 See Andrea Orzoff, *The Battle for the Castle: The Myth of Czechoslovakia in Europe, 1914–1948* (Oxford, 2009).

44 See Jan Láníček, *Czechs, Slovaks and Jews, 1938–1948* (New York, 2013).

45 Jan Kabelík, "Potřebujeme nutně emigrační prostor," *Národní osvobození*, October 21, 1938, Carton 156, MPSP-R, NA.

46 Milena Roth, *Lifesaving Letters: A Child's Flight from the Holocaust* (Seattle, 2004), 55.

47 Ezra Mendelsohn, *The Jews of East Central Europe between the World Wars* (Bloomington, IN, 1987), 202–9. See also Rapport sur la situation actuelle des juifs en Roumanie, 1186-1193, Reel 462, RG-110001M, USHMMA.

48 Memo no. 720, The Situation of Jews in Rumania, January 25, 1939, Folder Rumania, IGCR.

49 Conversation between the US Under-secretary and a Romanian Minister, March 27, 1939, Folder Rumania, IGCR.

50 Memorandum from Theodore C. Achilles, December 9, 1938, Folder British Guiana, IGCR.

51 Telegram from Cordell Hull to Myron Taylor, January 14, 1939, Folder Portugal and Angola, IGCR.

52 Smith, *American Empire*, 293–305, quotation 295.

53 Ibid., 308–10.

54 On tropical medicine and race, see Deborah Neill, *Networks in Tropical Medicine: Internationalism, Colonialism, and the Rise of a Medical Specialty, 1880–1930* (Stanford, 2012); Warwick Anderson, *The Cultivation of Whiteness: Science, Health, and Racial Destiny in Australia* (Durham, NC, 2006).

55 On debates about Jewish "whiteness," see, among others, Jeffrey Lesser, *Welcoming the Undesirables: Brazil and the Jewish Question* (Berkeley, 1995); Eric. L. Goldstein, *The Price of Whiteness: Jews, Race, and American Identity* (Princeton, 2007); Matthew Frye Jacobson, *Whiteness of a Different Color: European Immigrants and the Alchemy of Race* (Cambridge, MA, 1999).

56 London, *Whitehall and the Jews*, 140; Statement of His Majesty's Government's views regarding the British Guiana Refugee Commission's Report, May 13, 1939, Folder Refugees, Settlement, British Guiana, IGCR.

57 Julius Savit, Guiana as a Refuge, Folder British Guiana, IGCR.

58 "Experts Hold Hope for Guiana Refuge," *New York Times*, June 3, 1939.

59 Memorandum from Theodore C. Achilles, December 17, 1938, Folder British Guiana, IGCR.

60 Dr. Ernst to Dr. Cumming, February 18, 1939, Folder British Guiana, IGCR.

61 Ibid.

62 From Robert T. Pell to Secretary of State, July 13, 1939, Folder Portugal and Angola, IGCR; "Plans Are Being Laid for Refugee Parley," *New York Times*, July 26, 1939.

63 US Dept. of State, Attitude of the Portuguese Authorities to Jewish Immigration in Angola, September 20, 1940, Folder Portugal and Angola, IGCR.

64 For the full story of the Dominican colony in Sosúa, see Marion A. Kaplan, *Dominican Haven: The Jewish Refugee Settlement in Sosúa,*

1940–1945 (New York, 2008); Allen Wells, *Tropical Zion: General Trujillo, FDR, and the Jews of Sosúa* (Durham, NC, 2009).

65 Refugee Settlement in the Dominican Republic, A Meeting at the Town Hall Club, New York, February 15, 1940, Box 2, Emigration Files Collection, Leo Baeck Institute.

66 Wells, *Tropical Zion*, xx.

67 R. Henry Norweb, Dominican Offer of Accepting Political Refugees from Europe, August 20, 1938, Folder Dominican Republic, vol. 1, IGCR.

68 "From Address of Generalissimo Trujillo after Signing of Agreement," Item ID 582542, Folder Agreements with the Dominican Republic, 1939–40, Records of the Dominican Republic Settlement Association (DORSA), 1939–77, JDC.

69 Wells, *Tropical Zion*, 79.

70 Kaplan, *Dominican Haven*, 90–97. On fears of "fifth columnists" and its impact on U.S. refugee policy, see Wyman, *Paper Walls*, 172–76.

71 Joseph A. Rosen, "New Neighbors in Sosúa," Survey Graphic, September 1941, Item 585752, Folder Publicity, 1936; 1939–41, DORSA, JDC.

72 James N. Rosenberg, "The Story of Sosúa," *American Hebrew*, November 1, 1940, Item 585777, DORSA, JDC.

73 Pat Frank, "Life in Sosúa," *Aufbau*, New York, February 7, 1941, Item 585757, Folder Publicity, 1936; 1939–41, DORSA, JDC.

74 N. Chanin, "A Visit to the Dominican Republic, the new home of Jewish Refugees," Translation from "Jewish Daily Forward," May 4, 1941, Item 585756, JDC.

75 Charles A. Thompson, "Dictatorship in the Dominican Republic," *Foreign Policy Reports* 12, no. 3, April 15, 1936, Item 585836, Folder Publicity, 1936; 1939–41, DORSA, JDC.

76 Rosenberg Diary, Item 582191, DORSA, JDC.

77 Cited in Kaplan, *Dominican Haven*, 27.

78 Moss, "Thinking with Restriction," 215–16.

79 On the discourse of "empty space" as a justification for colonialism, see Alison Bashford, "Nation, Empire, Globe: The Spaces of Popula-

tion Debate in the Interwar Years," *Comparative Studies in Society and History* 49 (January 2007): 193–94.

80 Cited in Almagor, "Saving a Jewish Europe in the World."

81 Louise London suggests that the British used the IGCR to deflect other proposals made to act on refugees' behalf. London, *Whitehall and the Jews*, 91.

82 Potvrzení, January 11, 1939, Carton 156, MPSP-R, NA.

83 Kamil Šlabák, Zpráva o činnosti t.zv. stopfordovy akce, Carton 158, MPSP-R, NA.

84 Financial Assistance to Czechoslovakia, January 27, 1939, Carton 158, MPSP-R, NA.

85 Ružena Pelantová, "Illegalní činnost za okupace," in Československí přestěhovalci v letech 1938–*1945*, ed. Jaroslav Šima (Prague, 1945), 281–84.

86 Otázka vystěhovalecká, January 28, 1939, Carton 155, MPSP-R, NA.

87 Auswanderungsaktionen von jüdischen Familien aus dem Gebiete des Protektorates, June 15, 1939, Carton 157, MPSP-R, NA.

88 Existenčí zajištení živnostníků- kteří se přistěhovali z území připojených k sousedním státům v souvislosti s převodem židoveského majetků, June 24, 1939, Carton 118, MPSP-R, NA.

89 Úřední záznam, August 3, 1939, Carton 118, MPSP-R.

90 Existenční zajištění živnostníků, July 20, 1939; Existenční zajištění živnostníků, 22 August 1939, Carton 118, MPSP-R.

91 Existenční zajištění živnostníků, June 26, 1939; Existenční zajištění uprchlíků, 28 July 1939, Carton 118, MPSP-R.

92 Existenční zajištění uprchlíků, July 7, 1939, Carton 118, MPSP-R.

93 Terezín- volné židovské byty pro přestěhovalce, March 31, 1942; Evakuace Terezína, March 25, 1942; Záznam o výsledku služební cesty do Terezína, Roudnice, ve věci stěhovací akce Terezín, April 13, 1942, Carton 199, MPSP-R, NA.

94 Interview of Seymore Zryb by Janet Levine, March 3, 2000, in Ellis Island Oral History Project, Series EI, no. 1133 (Alexandria, VA, 2004), 37.

95 See, e.g., Autobiography, Box 1, Folder 3, Alfred Werner Collec-

tion, Leo Baeck Institute, Center for Jewish History (CJH), New York.

96 Otto Braun, Neubydžow, Box 1, Folder 1; Folder Popper Family and Kraus Family, Box 2, Folder 7, Isidore Popper Collection, AR 25225, Leo Baeck Institute, CJH.

97 Joseph Roth, *The Wandering Jews*, trans. Michael Hofmann (New York, 2001), 126–27.

98 Dwork and van Pelt, *Flight from the Reich*, 388.

99 Removal of Household and Personal Effects by Emigrants, April 17, 1939; Memo to the American Ambassador, London, Folder Germany, IGCR.

100 Osnova vládního nařizení o dani z vystěhování, April 1939, Carton 4025, MSP, NA.

101 Cited in Wells, *Tropical Zion*, xi.

102 American Delegation, Draft Speech for the ILO Conference in Havana (1940?), Folder League of Nations, IGCR.

Chapter 5

1 Evacuation des déportés polonais du département de Meur-the-et-Moselle, April 18, 1945, Polonais en France (dossier général), Carton 84, Pologne 1944-49, Z-Europe, Archives des affaires étrangères (MAE), Paris.

2 Malcolm Proudfoot, *European Refugees, 1939–52: A Study in Forced Population Movement* (London, 1957), 159, 228, 259; Richard Bessel, *Germany 1945: From War to Peace* (New York, 2009), 256. On UNRRA's nationality statistics, see Andrew Janco, "The Soviet Refugee in Postwar Europe and the Cold War, 1945–61" (PhD diss., University of Chicago, 2011).

3 On Jews in postwar Poland and Germany, see esp. Jan T. Gross, *Fear: Anti-Semitism in Poland after Auschwitz* (Princeton, 2006); Atina Grossmann, *Jews, Germans, and Allies: Close Encounters in Occupied Germany* (Princeton, 2007).

4 R. M. Douglas, *Orderly and Humane: The Expulsion of the Germans after the Second World War* (New Haven, 2013).

5 Philipp Ther, "A Century of Forced Migration: The Origins and

Consequences of 'Ethnic Cleansing,'" in *Redrawing Nations: Ethnic Cleansing in East-Central Europe, 1944–1948*, ed. Philipp Ther and Ana Siljak (Lanham, MD, 2001), 54–57; Peter Gatrell, "World Wars and Population Displacement in Europe in the Twentieth Century," *Contemporary European History* 16 (November 2007): 415–26; Norman Naimark, *Fires of Hatred: Ethnic Cleansing in Twentieth-Century Europe* (Cambridge, MA, 2001); Agnes Tóth, *Migrationen in Ungarn, 1945–1948: Vertreibung der Ungarndeutschen, Binnenwanderungen und slowakisch-ungarischer Bevölkerungsaustausch* (Munich, 2001); Timothy Snyder, *The Reconstruction of Nations: Poland, Ukraine, Lithuania, Belarus, 1569–1999* (New Haven, 2003).

6 Howard Kershner, *Quaker Service in Modern War* (New York, 1950), 156.

7 Tony Judt, *Postwar: A History of Europe since 1945* (New York, 2005), 17–18.

8 There has been a wave of excellent scholarship on displaced persons in postwar Europe recently. See esp. Grossmann, *Jews, Germans, and Allies*; Gerard Daniel Cohen, *In War's Wake: Europe's Displaced Persons in the Postwar Order* (Oxford, 2012); Anna Holian, *Between National Socialism and Soviet Communism: Displaced Persons in Postwar Germany* (Ann Arbor, 2011); Adam R. Seipp, *Strangers in the Wild Place: Refugees, Americans, and a German Town, 1945–1952* (Bloomington, IN, 2013); Jessica Reinisch and Elizabeth White, eds., *The Disentanglement of Populations: Migration, Expulsion, and Displacement in Postwar Europe, 1944–49* (London, 2011); Avinoam Patt, *Finding Home and Homeland: Jewish Youth and Zionism in the Aftermath of the Holocaust* (Detroit, 2009); Peter Gatrell, *Free World? The Campaign to Save the World's Refugees, 1956–63* (Cambridge, UK, 2011); Tara Zahra, *The Lost Children: Reconstructing Europe's Families after World War II* (Cambridge, MA, 2011).

9 J. Donald Kingsley, *Migration from Europe: A Report of Experience* (Geneva, 1951), v, 2. On fears of overpopulation in Europe, see also Cohen, *In War's Wake*, 101–4.

10 État d'esprit des deux côtés du "rideau de fer," March 11, 1950, Pologne, 129, Europe, 1944–70, MAE. For more on the rhetoric of

"slavery" and "captivity" in the Cold War, see Gatrell, *Free World?*, 29–46; Susan Carruthers, *Cold War Captives: Imprisonment, Escape, and Brainwashing* (Berkeley, 2009).

11 On the perception and reality of DP criminality, see Seipp, *Strangers in the Wild Place*.

12 American Federation of International Institutes, Report to the Sixth Delegates Convention, Cleveland, June 10–12, 1949, Box 3, Folder 29, Immigrants Protective League of Chicago, University of Illinois, Chicago.

13 Behavior of displaced persons on board the ships during the voyage from Bremerhaven to the States or Canada, no date (after 1948), 43AJ/806, Archives nationales, Paris (AN).

14 See esp. Silvia Salvatici, "From Displaced Persons to Labourers: Allied Employment Policies in Postwar West Germany," in *The Disentanglement of Populations*, 210–28.

15 Salvatici, "From Displaced Persons to Labourers," 218; Cohen, *In War's Wake*, 103.

16 Avis aux personnes déplacées, September 17, 1948, 43AJ/798, AN.

17 Report on Psychological Problems of Displaced Persons, 1945, 37, JRU Co-operation with Other Relief Organisations: United Nations Relief and Rehabilitation Administration (UNRRA), Wiener Library, London.

18 Louise Holborn, *The International Refugee Organization: Its History and Work, 1946–1952* (New York, 1956), 272.

19 Conference of Employment and Vocational Training Officers, January 8–9, 1948, 43AJ/593, Archives nationales, Paris (AN).

20 Holborn, *The International Refugee Organization*, 285.

21 Progress Report of the Working Party on Special Needs of Women and Girls, 9F/3292, AN.

22 Dr. G. C. Kullman to L. M. Hacking, April 21, 1948, Provisional Order on Employment of Displaced Persons/Refugees; Employment of Displaced Persons/Refugees, Draft, April 12, 1948, 43AJ/593, AN.

23 *Report on the ORT Activities. August 1946–July 1947* (Paris, 1947), 42.

24 Samuel Gringauz, "The Only Bright Rays in the Gloomy Existence of the DPs," *ORT Bulletin* 2 (March 1948): 3, cited at http://dpcamps.ort .org, accessed February 9, 2012.

25 Cited in Sarah Kavanaugh, *ORT, the Second World War and the Rehabilitation of Holocaust Survivors* (Portland, OR, 2008), xiii.

26 Outline for Commission's Special Services Program, 1948, 43AJ/595, AN.

27 The IRO Educational Programme for Displaced Persons and Refugees, December 3, 1948, 43AJ/593, AN.

28 Holborn, *The International Refugee Organization*, 286.

29 Beatrice Behrman, Field Report, City and State, Baltimore MD, 4/17– 4/18/50, 3, Folder 917, Reel MKM 39, United Service for New Americans, CJH.

30 Letter from Ms. Lillian Taylor of Lapeer Michigan, no date (probably 1949), 43AJ/865, AN.

31 Proracki, Franciszek, April 29, 1948, 43AJ/472; Hmatyszyn, Wolodymyr, August 13, 1948, 43AJ/478, AN.

32 Recrutement de main d'œuvre étrangère pour la France, July 26, 1947, PDR/6/847, MAE; Roger Bloch, Enquête sur les Personnes déplacées en ZFO, June 26, 1948, PDR/FPA/1, MAE.

33 Note d'Information 39, March 31, 1948, PDR/6/804, MAE; Kingsley, *Migration from Europe*, 35.

34 Conférence de presse de M. Pierre Pflimlin, sous-sécretaire d'État à la Santé Publique et à la Population, April 5, 1946, 80AJ/75, AN.

35 Robert Debré and Alfred Sauvy, *Des français pour la France (le problème de la population)* (Paris, 1946), 125–26.

36 Martin Schain, *The Politics of Immigration in France, Britain, and the United States: A Comparative Study* (New York, 2008), 47; Leo Lucassen, *The Immigrant Threat: The Integration of Old and New Migrants in Western Europe since 1850* (Urbana, IL, 2005), 176.

37 Debré et Sauvy, *Des français pour la France*, 229. On the racialization of Islam, see Naomi Davidson, *Only Muslim: Embodying Islam in Twentieth-Century France* (Ithaca, 2012).

38 Louis Chevalier, *Le problème démographique nord-africain* (Paris, 1947), 209.

39 Étude sur l'immigration de la main d'oeuvre étrangère, November 3, 1966, F1a/5052, AN.

40 On Britain, see Kathleen Paul, *Whitewashing Britain: Race and Citizenship in the Postwar Era* (Ithaca, 1997); Diana Kay and Robert Miles, eds., *Refugees or Migrant Workers? European Volunteer Workers in Britain, 1946–51* (London, 1992).

41 Kathryn Hulme, *The Wild Place* (Boston, 1953), 237; Seipp, *Strangers in the Wild Place*, 149–50.

42 On racial exclusion in U.S. immigration law in this period, see Mae M. Ngai, *Impossible Subjects: Illegal Aliens and the Making of Modern America* (Princeton, 2004).

43 Frank Chelf, cited by Leonard Dinnerstein, *America and the Survivors of the Holocaust* (New York, 1982), 21.

44 Haim Genizi, *America's Fair Share: The Admission and Resettlement of Displaced Persons, 1945–1952* (Detroit, 1993), quotation 80, on anti-Semitism 66–111.

45 "Österreichische Nachkriegsgefangene: Volksdeutsche ausserhalb des Rechtes und der Demokratie," *Ost-West-Kurier*, February 2, 1951, p. 1.

46 Eduard Stanek, *Verfolgt, verjagt, vertrieben: Flüchtlinge in Österreich von 1945–1984* (Vienna, 1984), 17–18; United States High Commissioner for Austria, *Statistical Report of Displaced Persons and Refugees in Austria* (Vienna, June 30, 1952).

47 On the Moscow Declaration, see Jill Lewis, *Workers and Politics in Occupied Austria, 1945–55* (Manchester, 2007), 41–44.

48 See, e.g., Harry Ritter, "Austria and the Struggle for German Identity," *German Studies Review* 15 (Winter 1992): 111–29; Peter Utgaard, *Remembering and Forgetting Nazism: Education, National Identity, and the Victim Myth in Postwar Austria* (New York, 2003); Heidemarie Uhl, *Zwischen Versöhnung und Verstörung: Eine Kontroverse um Österreichs historische Identität fünfzig Jahre nach dem "Anschluss"* (Vienna, 1992).

49 Gesamtaufstellung der in Österreich befindlichen DPs und Flüchtlinge, July 16, 1949, Carton 9, 12u-34, Bundesministerium des Innern (BMI), Archiv der Republik (AdR), Österreichisches Staatsar-

chiv (OeStA). See also Umsiedlungsaktion—Durchführung in der englischen Zone, Vienna, September 18, 1946, Carton 35, Pol-II, Bundesministerium für auswärtige Angelegenheiten (BmfAA), AdR, OeStA.

50 Sigmund Gorski to Herr Bundespräsident, December 31, 1949, Carton 132, 12u- 34, BMI, AdR, OeStA.

51 Leo Maria Kundmann, "Volksdeutsche sind Altösterreicher!," *Wegwarte*, April 22, 1950, p. 1. *Wegwarte*, with an approximate circulation of 10,000, was a right-wing paper that supported the VdU (Verein der Unabhängigen) party.

52 "Die Volksdeutschen in Oberösterreich," *Die Presse*, February 26, 1949.

53 "Grundlagen des Bruderrechtes: Geschichte und Völkerrecht verpflichten Österreich zur Vertetung des Interessen der deutschsprachigen Heimatvertriebenen," *Wegwarte*, November 19, 1949, p. 1.

54 Tony Radspieler, *The Ethnic German Refugee in Austria, 1945 to 1954* (The Hague, 1955), 62.

55 On the development of "ethnicized economies" in postwar Europe through the importation of foreign labor, see Rita Chin and Heide Fehrenbach, "Introduction: What's Race Got to Do with It? Postwar History in Context," in Rita Chin, Heide Fehrenbach, Geoff Eley, and Atina Grossmann, *After the Nazi Racial State: Difference and Democracy in Germany and Europe* (Ann Arbor, 2009), 25.

56 DP Problem, Unterredung mit General Maclean, October 24, 1947, Carton 34, II-Pol 1947, BmfAA, AdR, OeStA.

57 "Österreichs rechtlose Vertriebene: Volksdeutsche ohne Staatsbürgerschaft in einem deutschen Staatswesen," *Der Fortschritt*, October 13, 1950, p. 10.

58 American Aid Societies for the Needy and Displaced Persons of Central and South-Eastern Europe, May 25, 1949, Carton 85, 12u-34, BMI, AdR, OeStA.

59 Radspieler, *The Ethnic German Refugee*, 32.

60 Auszug aus dem Lagebericht der Bundespolizeidirektion Innsbruck

für den Monat Februar 1949, March 2, 1949, Carton 12, 12u- 34, BMI, AdR, OeStA.

61 Memorandum of Agudas Israel, June 25, 1953, Carton 11, 12U-34, BMI, AdR, OeStA.

62 Radspieler, *The Ethnic German Refugee*, 45; Susanne Rolinek, *Jüdische Lebenswelten, 1945–1955: Flüchtlinge in der amerikanischen Zone Österreichs* (Innsbruck, 2007), 136.

63 Bevorzugte Einbürgerung jüdischer Flüchtlinge, October 5, 1953, Carton 11, 12u-34, BMI, AdR, OeStA, 3.

64 Radspieler, *The Ethnic German Refugee*, 80–81, 89.

65 Julius Raab, Bundeskanzleramt, Vorschlag der drei westlichen hochkommissäre zur Bildung eines Ständigen Komitees für Flüchtlingsfragen, March 25, 1954, Carton 304, II-Pol, BmfAA, AdR, OeStA; Radspieler, *The Ethnic German Refugee*, 61.

66 Fremdsprachige Flüchtlinge in Österreich, January 13, 1950, Carton 10, BMI, 12u-34, AdR, OeStA.

67 Cohen, *In War's Wake*, 50–57.

68 Ibid., 33–34. See also Holborn, *The International Refugee Organization*, 206–7.

69 Text of the 1951 convention can be found at http://www.unhcr.org/3b66c2aa10.html, accessed October 4, 2013. On the language of the convention, see Andrew Janco, "Unwilling: The One-Word Revolution in Refugee Status," *Contemporary European History*, forthcoming.

70 Cohen, *In War's Wake*, 38–49.

71 Holborn, *The International Refugee Organization*, 210. On the review board, see also Cohen, *In War's Wake*, 44–53; International Refugee Organization 1948–49, folder 69, Box 6, Archive of the Immigrants Protective League of Chicago, University of Illinois, Chicago.

72 International Refugee Organization, *Manual for Eligibility Officers* (Geneva, 1948), 22, 102, 43AJ/148, AN.

73 Ibid., 25.

74 Ibid., 9.

75 Holterman, Aurelia, no date (probably summer 1948), 43AJ/478, AN.

76 Beckers, Arthur, Case 19020, April 3, 1950, 43AJ/477, AN.

77   Anna Elisabeth Dybczak, Case 20.059, June 8, 1950, 43AJ/466, AN.

78   Lenke Fuszessery, Case 1.035.615, January 13, 1949, 43AJ/479, AN.

79   Maria-Marica Tomazic, Geneva 4541, July 7, 1949, 43AJ/475, AN.

80   Maria Mosonyj, Case 813-952, January 1950, 43AJ/477, AN.

81   Case no. 813,952, March 9, 1949, 43AJ/480, AN.

82   Edda Engelke, *Jeder Flüchtling ist eine Schwächung der Volks-demokratie: Die illegalen Überschreitungen am jugoslawisch-steirischen Grenzabschnitt in den fünfziger Jahren* (Vienna, 2011), 266, 272–73.

83   Anton Veverka, September 14, 1948, Case 992.966, 43AJ/479; Josef Bitto, April 28, 1950, Case 1.047.951, 43AJ/142, AN.

84   Drina Babic, October 15, 1948, Case 83.744, 43AJ/142, AN.

85   Garcarek, Stanislowa, July 5, 1948, Case 80.804, 43AJ/478, AN.

86   Cohen, *In War's Wake*, 54.

87   Slavka Boras, April 30, 1949, Case 83.745/3, 43AJ/142, AN.

88   Volker Ackermann, *Der "echte" Flüchtling: Deutsche Vertriebene und Flüchtlinge aus der DDR, 1945–61* (Osnabrück, 1995), esp. 115–17, 282–83.

89   "Das Jugoslawische Kommittee in Salzburg," *Fern der Heimat* 1, no. 5 (July 31, 1953): 1–2.

90   Engelke, *Jeder Flüchtling*, 63–66, quotation 66.

91   Brigitta Zierer, "Willkommene Ungarnflüchtlinge 1956?," in *Asylland wider Willen: Flüchtlinge in Österreich im europäischen Kontext seit 1914*, ed. Gernot Heiss and Oliver Rathkolb (Vienna, 1995), 157–71; Peter Haslinger, "Zur Frage der ungarischen Flüchtlinge in Österreich, 1956–57," in *Migration und ihre Auswirkungen: Das Beispiel Ungarn, 1918–55*, ed. Gerhard Seewann (Munich, 1997), 147–62.

92   Speech of Oskar Helmer before the UNREF Tagung Genf, January 29, 1957, Carton 433, Pol-II, BmfAA, AdR, OeStA.

93   "Nur 1000?," *Fern der Heimat* 3, no. 10 (October 31, 1957): 1–2.

94   Edda Engelke, *Jeder Flüchtling*, 92–93; *Fern der Heimat* 4, no. 4 (April–May 1958): 7.

Chapter 6

1   Information Bulletin Published by Council of Free Czechoslovakia,

Washington DC, no. 1, September 14, 1951, Europe, Tchécoslovaquie, 1944–70, 150, Archives des affaires étrangères (MAE), Paris.

2 "Úřední zpráva o únosu československých občanu v rychlikovém vlaku teroristickou bandou," *Rudé Právo*, September 16, 1951, p. 5.

3 "Escape from Homeland Welcomed as a Miracle," National Committee for a Free Europe, Inc. Czechoslovak Newsletter no. 14, October 3, 1951, 5, Box 545, Radio Free Europe Materials, Archive of Czechs and Slovaks Abroad, Regenstein Library, University of Chicago.

4 http://www.ncsml.org/Oral-History/Cleveland/20101007/63/Ruml-Karel.aspx#vlak, accessed July 17, 2012.

5 On the Cold War link between communism, captivity, and slavery, see Susan L. Carruthers, *Cold War Captives: Imprisonment, Escape, and Brainwashing* (Berkeley, 1999), 87.

6 Porada o omezení vystěhovalectví, December 14, 1945, Carton 176, Konsulární odbor- věcna spisovna, I, 1945–59, Archiv ministerstva zahraničních věcí (MZV).

7 Jan Rychlík, *Cestování do ciziny v habsburské monarchii a v Československu* (Prague, 2007), 26–36.

8 Dariusz Stola, *Kraj bez wyjścia? Migracje z Polski 1949–1989* (Warsaw, 2010), 41.

9 Othmar Nikola Haberl, *Die Abwanderung von Arbeitskräften aus Jugoslawien* (Munich, 1978); Krystyna Iglicka, *Poland's Post-War Dynamic of Migration* (Burlington, VT, 2001), 17, 19; Alan Dowty, *Closed Borders: The Contemporary Assault on Freedom of Movement* (New Haven, 1987), 115–19. On tourism within Eastern Europe, see Rachel Applebaum, "Friendship of the Peoples: Soviet-Czechoslovak Social and Cultural Contacts from the Battle for Prague to the Prague Spring, 1945–1969" (PhD diss., University of Chicago, 2012), chap. 5; Diane P. Koenker and Anne E. Gorsuch, *Turizm: Leisure, Travel, and Nation Building in Russia, Eastern Europe, and the USSR* (Ithaca, 2006).

10 Patrick Major, *Behind the Berlin Wall: East Germany and the Frontiers of Power* (New York, 2010), 25.

11 Dowty, *Closed Borders*, 69–71.

12 Memorandum concernant le problème des réfugiés et des personnes déplacées, March 5, 1948, 43AJ/798, Archives nationales, Paris (AN).

13 Figures from the inspection and filtration of repatriates, GARF, f. 9526, op. 3, d. 175, op. 4, d. 1, 1.62, 1.223. I thank Andrew Janco for providing me with these statistics. On forced repatriations, see Mark Elliot, "The United States and Forced Repatriation of Soviet Citizens, 1944–47," *Political Science Quarterly* 88, no. 2 (June 1973): 253–75.

14 Rainer Hofmann, *Die Ausreisefreiheit nach Völkerrecht und staatlichem Recht* (Berlin, 1988), 34–36.

15 Susan Carruthers makes this argument and explores this theme at length in *Cold War Captives*.

16 Poslanec Dr. Bedřich Steiner, Carton 85, Československý ústav zahraniční- II (ČÚZ-II), Národní archiv (NA).

17 Souhrnná zpráva ministerstva sociální péče o dosavadním průbehu, zbyvajicích úkolech a skončení reemigrační akce, October 6, 1948, Carton 268, MPSP-R.

18 Only 24,000 of these returnees came from nonsocialist bloc countries (approximately 12,915 from France and 11,117 from Austria). The rest of the re-migrants hailed primarily from the territory annexed by the USSR after the war (33,000), Romania (16,000), Poland (13,000) and Yugoslavia (6,000). Jaroslav Vaculík, *Poválecná repatriace československych tzv. přemístěných osob* (Brno, 2004), 26.

19 Malcolm Proudfoot, *European Refugees, 1939–52: A Study in Forced Population Movement* (London, 1957), 159.

20 On East European DPs in postwar Germany, see Anna Holian, *Between National Socialism and Soviet Communism: Displaced Persons in Postwar Germany* (Ann Arbor, 2011); Tara Zahra, *The Lost Children: Reconstructing Europe's Families after World War II* (Cambridge, MA, 2011); Andrew Janco, "Soviet Displaced Persons in Europe, 1941–1951" (PhD diss., University of Chicago, 2012).

21 M. Konopica, "Our Country Is Calling," "Repatriant" Series no. 1, Warsaw 1946, S-0401-3-3, United Nations Archive, New York.

22 Usnesení vlády ze dne 31 července 1945 o reemigraci, Carton 268, Ministerstvo práce a sociální péče—repatriace (MPSP-R), NA.

23 Zpráva o poměrech, ve kterých žijí v pohraničí naši čeští horníci, kteří sem byli přestěhovaní z Francie a Belgie, October 29, 1945, Carton 87, ČÚZ-II, NA.

24 Usnesení vlády ze dne 28. května 1946 o reemigraci; Usnesení vlády z 10. ledna 1947; Usnesení vlády ze dne 12. července 1948, Carton 268, MPSP-R; Směrnice pro poskytování sociálních výpomocí, sociálních a produktivních zájpůjček přistěhovalcům, 28 June 1947, Carton 1611, Uřad předsednictva vlády—bězná spisovná (ÚPV-bs), 1945–59, NA.

25 Returnees were similarly disruptive to state narratives in Mao's China. See Shelly Chan, "The Disobedient Diaspora: Overseas Chinese Students in Mao's China, 1958–66," *Journal of Chinese Overseas* 10, no. 2 (2014): 220–38.

26 Dopis, April 14, 1957 Jarmila Hassen, Carton 54, ČÚZ-II, NA.

27 Aide-mémoire sur la situation des Polonais en France, sig. 84; Les Polonais en France, May 1945, sig. 85, Pologne 1944–49, Z-Europe, Archives des affaires étrangères (MAE), Paris.

28 Main-d'oeuvre polonais en France et en Allemagne, May 27, 1945, sig. 84, Pologne 1944–49, Z-Europe, MAE.

29 Mineurs polonais, June 8, 1945; Note confidentiel, sig. 84, Pologne 1944–49, Z-Europe, MAE.

30 Accords franco-polonais de rapatriement, April 6, 1949, sig. 206, Pologne, Europe, 1944–70, MAE.

31 Guy Monge, vice consul à Wroclaw, May 22, 1947; Franchissements clandestins de la frontière et camps de travail, Consul de France à Katowice to French ambassador, May 28, 1951, sig. 209, Pologne, Europe, 1944–70, MAE.

32 Reemigrace z Rakouska, April 29, 1947, Carton 938, ÚPV-bs, NA.

33 František Strnad, Reemigrace z Rakouska, 1945–49, Carton 2; Žadosti reemigrantů o přidělení živností a zaměstnáni v ČSR, no date (1946), Carton 8, Anna Pabstová, Carton 9, č.f. 1263, Reemigrační kancelař rakouských Čechů a Slováků, NA.

34 Stižnost vídenských repatriantů, October 5, 1945, Carton 938, ÚPV-bs, 1945–59, NA.

35 Zápis o medziministerskej porade konanej na MZV dna 2 jula 1946 o

preverovani reeemigrantov z Rakouska, Carton 938, ÚPV-bs, 1945–
59, NA. On mixed marriage and the expulsions, see Benjamin Frommer, "Expulsion or Integration: Unmixing Interethnic Marriage in
Postwar Czechoslovakia," *East European Politics and Societies* 14, no.
2 (Spring 2000): 381–410.

36 Usídlení reemigrantů z Brém, Německo, August 27, 1946, Carton 87,
ČÚZ-II, NA. Skilled German workers could also be exempted from
expulsion. See David Gerlach, "For Nation and Gain: Economy, Ethnicity, and Politics in the Czech Borderlands, 1945–1948" (PhD diss.,
University of Pittsburgh, 2007).

37 Hugo Service, *Germans to Poles: Communism, Nationalism, and
Ethnic Cleansing after the Second World War* (Cambridge, UK, 2013).

38 Katerina Čapková, Michal Frankl, and Peter Brod, "Czechoslovakia," in *The YIVO Encyclopedia of Jews in Eastern Europe*, vol. 1 (New
Haven, 2005), 380–81.

39 Zápis o meziministerské poradě o vystěhovaleckých otázkách
v ministerstvu ochrany práce a sociální péče, April 15, 1946, Carton
176, Konsulární odbor- věcna spisovna, I, 1945–59, MZV.

40 On Jews in the 1930 census, see esp. Tatjana Lichtenstein, "Racial-
izing Jewishness: Zionist Responses to National Indifference in the
Interwar Period," *Austrian History Yearbook* 43 (April 2012): 75–97.

41 Transfer of People of Jewish Origin, May 29, 1945, 43/AJ/64, AN.

42 Document WR 178/3/48, February 5, 1946, 43/AJ/64, AN; Otázka
židovské národnosti, April 13, 1948, Carton 8245, Ministerstvo vni-
tra- nová registratura (MV-NR), NA. For more on the treatment of
Jews as "unwanted elements" in the postwar Czech borderlands, see
David Gerlach, "Beyond Expulsion: The Emergence of 'Unwanted
Elements' in the Postwar Czech Borderlands, 1945–50," *East European Politics and Societies* 24 (May 2010): 278–85.

43 On Poland, see Jan Gross, *Fear: Anti-Semitism in Poland after Auschwitz* (Princeton, 2006); Dariusz Stola, *Kraj bez wyjścia? Migracje z
Polski 1949–1989* (Warsaw, 2010), 32. On the return of Jews to postwar Hungary, see Alice Freifeld, "The Tremor of Cain: Return of the
Deported to Hungary," *Hungarian Studies* 18, no. 2 (2005): 243–50.

44 Cited in Major, *Behind the Berlin Wall*, 57, 108.

45 Usnesení schůze předsednictva ÚV ze dne 9. února 1965, svazek 94, a.j. 98/6, Kommunistická strana Československa—ústrední vybor (KSČ-ÚV)—Předsednictvo 1962-66, NA.

46 "The Emigres," *Mladá Fronta,* November 30, 1948 (translated and condensed), 86of.00/12-1548, Reel 4, Records of the U.S. Department of State Relating to the Internal Affairs of Czechoslovakia, 1945-49.

47 "Tábor Valka- koncentrák pro utečené," *Rudé Právo,* January 13, 1954, Carton 71, Petr Zenkl Papers, Archives of Czechs and Slovaks Abroad, Regenstein Library, University of Chicago.

48 Politische Erscheinungen im Kreis Wenzleben, October 26, 1951, DC1/394, Bundesarchiv Berlin.

49 Ackermann, *Der "echte" Flüchtling.*

50 Bohuslava Bradbrook, *The Liberating Beauty of Little Things* (Portland, OR, 2000), 19-20.

51 Savoy Horvath, b. 1933, Czech and Slovak Museum of America, Oral History Collection, http://www.ncsml.org/Oral-History/Chicago/20110712/120/Horvath-Savoy.aspx, accessed November 29, 2011.

52 Vera Dobrovolny, b. 1938, http://www.ncsml.org/Oral-History/Chicago/20110425/101/Dobrovolny-Vera.aspx, accessed July 30, 2012.

53 Carruthers, *Cold War Captives,* 59-63.

54 John MacCormac, "Slovak Family Braves Icy River, Flees to Austria in a Stalled 'Duck,'" *New York Times,* March 9, 1952.

55 Petr Zenkl, The Bait to Return Home to a Communist Paradise, 1955, Carton 72, Petr Zenkl Papers, Archives of Czechs and Slovaks Abroad, Regenstein Library, University of Chicago.

56 Senator Pat McCarran, *Congressional Record,* March 2, 1953, p. 1518.

57 Carruthers, *Cold War Captives,* 69-90. On U.S. policy toward Cold War refugees, see also Carl Bon Tempo, *Americans at the Gate: The United States and Refugees during the Cold War* (Princeton, 2008).

58 Záznam o poradě v ministertvu spravedlnosti dne 14.7.1948, Carton 58, Konsulární odbor- věcna spisovna, I, 1945-59, MZV.

59 Material für die Kommissionssitzung am 28 Februar 1957, DE1/6109, Bundesarchiv Berlin.

60 "The Emigres," *Mladá Fronta,* November 30, 1948 (translated and condensed), 860f.00/12-1548, Reel 4, Records of the U.S. Department of State Relating to the Internal Affairs of Czechoslovakia, 1945–49.

61 Zenkl, The Bait to Return Home.

62 Ludwik Dziubek, Souvenirs d'un ancien deserteur, no date (probably 1955), sig. 130, Pologne, Z-Europe, MAE.

63 CURPH Interview F-87 with a 1956 Hungarian Refugee: 38 Years Old, Female, housewife, 1957, HU OSA 414-0-2-4; Donald and Vera Blinken Collection on Hungarian Refugees of 1956: Transcripts of Refugee Interviews; Open Society Archives at Central European University, Budapest. Accessed online, http://www.osaarchivum .org/.

64 Návrh regulace výjezdu čs. Občanů do zahraničí, zejména do kapitalistických států a Jugoslávie, March 12, 1970, svazek 121, a.j. 195/14, KSČ-ÚV, Předsednictvo 1966–71, NA.

65 Material für die Kommissionssitzung am 28.2.1957, DE1/6109, Bundesarchiv Berlin.

66 On East German efforts to bribe emigrants back to the GDR, see Major, *Behind the Berlin Wall,* 56–88, quotation 84. For discussion of this issue among East German officials, see Material für die Kommissionssitzung am 28.2.1957, DE1/6109, Bundesarchiv Berlin.

67 Campagne de rapatriement, November 16, 1955, sig. 132, Pologne, Z-Europe, MAE.

68 Note du Ministère polonais des Affaires Étrangères sur l'OIR, April 22, 1952, sig. 130, Pologne, Z-Europe, MAE.

69 Nationalité de femmes françaises ayant épousé des étrangers, June 22, 1950; Protection des citoyens français en Pologne, November 27, 1950, sig. 212, Pologne, Z-Europe, MAE.

70 Confidences d'une rapatriée de France, December 31, 1955, sig. 132, Pologne, Z-Europe, MAE.

71 Norbert Fialkiewicz, September 2, 1950, sig. 212, Pologne, Z-Europe, MAE.

72 Instructions concernant les doubles nationaux, February 5, 1955, sig. 212, Pologne, Z-Europe, MAE.

73 Letter to International Union of Students, May 15, 1957, Carton 40, Teritorální odbory—obyčejné, 1945–59, MZV.

74 Nouvelle attitude de la Pologne à l'égard des émigrés, March 11, 1955, sig. 132, Pologne, Z-Europe, MAE.

75 A.s. des Polonais qui "choisissent la liberté," September 17, 1957, sig. 225, Pologne, Z-Europe, MAE.

76 Rychlík, *Cestování do ciziny*, 61, 73; Návrh regulace výjezdu čs. občanů, a.j. 195/14, svazek 121, KSČ-ÚV, Předsednictvo 1966–71, NA.

77 Ulf Brunnbauer, "Labour Emigration from the Yugoslav Region from the Late 19th Century until the End of Socialism: Continuities and Changes," in *Transnational Societies, Transterritorial Politics. Migrations in the (Post) Yugoslav Region, 19th–21st Century*, ed. Ulf Brunnbauer (Munich, 2009), 22–25; Karolina Novinscak, "The Recruiting and Sending of Yugoslav 'Gastarbeiter' to Germany: Between Socialist Demands and Economic Needs," ibid., 127–28.

78 Christopher A. Molnar, "Imagining Yugoslavs: Migration and the Cold War in Postwar West Germany," *Central European History* 47 (March 2014): 138–69.

79 Haberl, *Die Abwanderung von Arbeitskräften*, 69–79; Ivo Baučić, *The Effects of Emigration from Yugoslavia and the Problems of Returning Emigrant Workers* (The Hague, 1972).

80 Polish emigrants in this period settled primarily in West Germany (58 percent), the United States (14 percent), the GDR (8 percent), Israel (5 percent), and Canada (4 percent). Stola, *Kraj bez wyjścia?*, 177–79, 183–86.

81 Jan Gerhard, "D'une jeune fille, de Paris et du snobisme," *Nowa Kultura*, 6 January 1963 (translated from Polish), Pologne, 400, Europe 1944–70, MAE, Paris.

82 Richard Ivan Jobs, "Youth Movements: Travel, Protest, and Europe in 1968," *American Historical Review* 114, 3 (April 2009): 376–404; Rychlík, *Cestování do ciziny*, 80.

83 "Co s naší emigrací?" *Svobodné slovo*, May 8, 1968, Carton 1471, Ministerstvo zahraničních věcí—vystřižkový archiv, NA.

84 Oliver Gunovsky, b. 1944, National Czech and Slovak Museum Oral History Collection, http://www.ncsml.org/Oral-History/

Washington-DC/20110902/149/Gunovsky-Oliver.aspx, accessed July 30, 2012.

85 Návrh regulace výjezdu čs. občanů do zahraničí, March 12, 1970, a.j. 195/14, svazek 121, KSČ-ÚV, Předsednictvo 1966–71, NA. Thirty-six percent of individuals who traveled to capitalist countries in 1968–69 did not return, compared with 14 percent in 1967. For numbers, see Rychlík, *Cestování do ciziny*, 83.

86 Situace v čs. emigraci a naměty na opatření, a.j. 237/4, svazek 153, KSČ-ÚV- Předsednictvo 1966–71, NA; Rychlík, *Cestování do ciziny*, 86.

87 In 1969, 631,209 Czechs and Slovaks traveled to the West and another 112,529 traveled to Yugoslavia. In 1970, by contrast, only 49,720 made private trips to capitalist countries. Situace v čs. emigraci; Rychlík, *Cestování do ciziny*, 86.

88 Milan Kundera, *Ignorance*, trans. Linda Asher (New York, 2002), 17.

89 "Naděje a zklamání utečenců," *Práce*, June 21, 1972; "Klamný svět emigrace," *Svobodné slovo*, March 18, 1975; Jindřich Filipec, "O jednom smutném setkaní: Bída emigrace," *Rudé Právo*, June 28, 1975, Carton 6258, Ministerstvo zahraničních věcí—výstřižkový archiv, NA.

Chapter 7

1 "Miss Navratilova Asks U.S. Asylum: Czechoslovak Net Star Asks to Remain in U.S.," *New York Times*, September 7, 1975; "Urge to Freedom," ibid., September 10, 1975.

2 "Czech Star Cites Tennis as Reason for Defection from U.S.," *International Herald Tribune*, September 8, 1975, Carton 6258, Ministerstvo zahraničních věcí—výstřižkový archiv, Národní archiv (NA); Dave Anderson, "The Americanization of Martina," *New York Times*, September 8, 1975.

3 "Czech Defector Now a Capitalist," *International Herald Tribune*, December 11, 1975, Carton 6258, Ministerstvo zahraničních věcí—výstřižkový archiv, NA.

4 See Lizabeth Cohen, *A Consumers' Republic: The Politics of Mass Consumption in Postwar America* (New York, 2003).

5 Rainer Hofmann, *Die Ausreisefreiheit nach Völkerrecht und staat-*

lichem Recht (Berlin, 1988); Final Act of the Conference on Security and Cooperation in Europe, August 1, 1975, 14 I.L.M. 1292 (Helsinki Declaration). For a critical discussion of dissent, see Jonathan Bolton, *Worlds of Dissent: Charter 77, the Plastic People of the Universe, and Czech Culture under Communism* (Cambridge, MA, 2012).

6   See Samuel Moyn, *The Last Utopia: Human Rights in History* (Cambridge, MA, 2010).

7   "CSSR hält 700 Kinder zurück," *Die Welt*, February 23, 1976; "Ausreiseerlaubnis für Kinder von Exiltschechen," *Neue Zürcher Zeitung*, March 29, 1976; "Prag lässt 25 Kinder ausreisen," *Frankfurter Allgemeine Zeitung*, December 24, 1976, Carton 6258, Ministerstvo zahraničních věcí—výstřižkový archiv, NA.

8   Alan Dowty, *Closed Borders: The Contemporary Assault on Freedom of Movement* (New Haven, 1987), 121.

9   Ulf Brunnbauer, "Labour Emigration from the Yugoslav Region from the Late 19th Century until the End of Socialism: Continuities and Changes," in *Transnational Societies, Transterritorial Politics: Migrations in the (Post) Yugoslav Region, 19th–21st Century*, ed. Ulf Brunnbauer (Munich, 2009), 22.

10 Paulina Bren, "Tuzex and the Hustler: Living It Up in Czechoslovakia," in *Communism Unwrapped: Consumption in Cold War Eastern Europe*, ed. Paulina Bren and Mary Neuberger (New York, 2012), 31.

11 Vládní usnesení č. 58/1977; "Návrat do vlasti je možný kdykoli," *Rudé Právo*, June 1, 1977; "Prag will seine Beziehungen zu tschechoslowakischen Emigranten 'regeln,'" *Frankfurter Allgemeine Zeitung*, August 20, 1977.

12 Dariusz Stola, *Kraj bez wyjścia? Migracje z Polski 1949–1989* (Warsaw, 2010), 474–77.

13 Patrick Major, *Behind the Berlin Wall: East Germany and the Frontiers of Power* (Oxford, 2010), 198–200.

14 Dowty, *Closed Borders*, 125.

15 Radu Ioanid, *The Ransom of the Jews: The Story of the Extraordinary Secret Bargain between Romania and Israel* (Chicago, 2005), 83–148, quotation 125.

16 On "co-ethnic" immigration to West Germany after World War II,

see Jannis Panagiotidis, *Laws of Return: Co-ethnic Immigration to West Germany and Israel, 1948–1992* (Cambridge, UK, forthcoming).

17 On national ambiguity in Silesia, see esp. Brendan Karch, "Nationalism on the Margins: Silesians between Germany and Poland, 1848–1945" (PhD diss., Harvard University, 2010); James Bjork, *Neither German nor Pole: Catholicism and National Indifference in a Central European Borderland* (Ann Arbor, 2008); Stola, *Kraj bez wyjścia?*, 104–28; Hugo Service, *Germans to Poles: Communism, Nationalism, and Ethnic Cleansing after the Second World War* (Cambridge, UK, 2013).

18 Ursachen der Übersiedlungsbereitschaft, March 2, 1970; B85/765; Deutsch-polnische Verhandlungen, Deutsche Bevölkerung im heutigen polnischen Staates und Verwaltungsbereich, January 29, 1970, B85/766; Notizen aus den Warschauer Besprechungen mit den Polnischen Roten Kreuz vom 27 und 28 Januar 1971, B85/767, Archiv des Ministeriums für Auswärtige Angelegenheiten (MfAA), Berlin.

19 Notatka dotzcyąca zakończenia wyjazdów emigracyjnych do Niemieckiej Republiki Federalnej, January 1973, L1 / 302, Polska Zjednoczna Partia Robotnicza (PZPR), Komitet Centralny (KC), Wydział Administracyny, Archiwum akt nowych (AAN), Warsaw.

20 Notatka w sprawie wyjazdów emigracyjnych z Polskie w latach 1970–75, July 20, 1976, LI / 306, PZPR-KC, Wydział Administracyny, AAN.

21 Zur Situation vieler Deutschen in Polen, January 20, 1970, B85/765, MfAA, Berlin.

22 "Akcja humanitarna?," *Słowo Powszechne*, August 19, 1971, B85/876, MfAA.

23 Julian Bartosz, "Dzwoki Janczarow," *Prawo i Życie*, June 13, 1971, B85/876, MfAA.

24 Krystyna Iglicka, *Poland's Post-War Dynamic of Migration* (Burlington, VT, 2001), 20–23; Stola, *Kraj bez wyjścia?*, 473.

25 Besprechungen in Warschau, November 21, 1955; Memorandum, October 28, 1955, B85/729, MfAA.

26 Dariusz Stola, "The Hate Campaign of March 1968: How Did It Become Anti-Jewish?," *Polin* 21 (2009): 16–36.

27 Ibid.

28 Cited in Leszek W. Głuchowski and Antony Polonsky, "Introduction," *Polin* 21 (2009) 3.

29 David Shribman, "U.S. Cool to Giving More Poles Visas," *New York Times*, January 24, 1982.

30 Samuel G. Freedman, "A State of Limbo Rules the Lives of Polish Aliens," *New York Times*, February 21, 1982.

31 Wayne King, "Many Poles Lose Bid for Asylum," *New York Times*, December 17, 1983.

32 See, e.g., Mary Thornton, "Federal Agencies Polarized by Move to Deport Poles," *Washington Post*, June 18, 1987.

33 Robert Pear, "Plan to Give More Poles Asylum Is under Study by the Administration," *New York Times*, March 29, 1985; David Brough, "Study Finds Poles, Iranians Favored: Bias Suggested in U.S. Refugee Policy," *Globe and Mail*, March 10, 1987.

34 Robert J. McCartney, "Thousands from East Bloc Drawn by Westward Hopes; Largest European Migration in 30 Years," *Washington Post*, March 31, 1989.

35 Tony Judt, *Postwar: A History of Europe since 1945* (New York, 2005), 612–13.

36 Theo Sommer, "Mehr Angst als Vaterlandsliebe," *Die Zeit*, August 12, 1988; McCartney, "Thousands from East Bloc Drawn by Westward Hopes."

37 Bethany E. Hicks, "Germany after the Fall: Migration, Gender, and East-West Identities" (PhD diss., Michigan State University, 2010).

38 "Ende der Schönezeit," *Der Spiegel*, December 11, 1989.

39 Nicola Fuchs-Schündeln and Matthias Schündeln, "Who Stays, Who Goes, Who Returns? East–West Migration within Germany since Reunification," *Economics of Transition* 17, no. 4 (2009): 703–38; Hicks, "Germany after the Fall," 186.

40 The leading exporters of citizens were Romania (with a net emigration of 1,245,000), Bulgaria (688,000), and Poland (667,000). Amazingly, the Czech Republic registered a net inflow of 19,000 migrants, and Hungary of 26,000, as emigrants returned from the

West, and immigrants arrived from within the region or from farther afield. Godfried Engbersen et al., "Introduction," in *A Continent Moving West? EU Enlargement and Labour Migration from Central and Eastern Europe*, ed. Richard Black et al. (Amsterdam, 2010), 9–10.

41 Agnieszka Fihel and Agata Górny, "To Settle or to Leave Again? Patterns of Return Migration to Poland during the Transition Period," *Central and Eastern European Migration Review* 2, no. 1 (June 2013): 63.

42 Milan Kundera, *Ignorance*, trans. Linda Asher (New York, 2002), 52, 54, 45.

43 On the Yugoslav wars, see Norman Naimark and Holly Case, *Yugoslavia and Its Historians* (Stanford, 2003).

44 Steven Kinzer, "Germany Chides Europe about Balkan Refugees," *New York Times*, July 29, 1992.

45 http://www.migrationpolicy.org/article/refugee-resettlement-metropolitan-america, accessed May 12, 2014.

46 Cited in Reed Coughlan and Judith Owens-Manley, *Bosnian Refugees in America: New Communities, New Cultures* (New York, 2006), 93.

47 Ibid., 97.

48 Ibid., 146.

49 Burcu Akan Ellis, *Catapulted: Youth Migration and the Making of a Skilled Albanian Diaspora* (New York, 2013).

50 Ibid., 104, 108.

51 Julie Vullnetari, *Albania on the Move: Links between Internal and International Migration* (Amsterdam, 2012), 70.

52 "Albanians Flee to Foreign Embassies," *Toronto Star*, July 3, 1990; "Albanians Reportedly Stream into Embassies in the Capital," *New York Times*, July 7, 1990; "To Albanians, 'Ciao Europa!' Means Haven," ibid., July 14, 1990.

53 Alan Cowell, "Italy Starts to Turn Back Albanian Wave," *New York Times*, August 10, 1991; Alan Cowell, "Italy's Handling of Albanians Is Drawing Criticism," ibid., August 12, 1991.

54 Vullnetari, *Albania on the Move*, 67–76.

55 Béatrice Khadige, "'Le plombier polonais': Un épouvantail pour la France, vu de Varsovie," Agence France-Presse, June 2, 2005.

56 For numbers, see Agnieszka Fihel and Paweł Kaczmarczyk, "Migration: A Threat or a Chance? Recent Migration of Poles and Its Impact on the Polish Labour Market," in *Polish Migration to the UK in the "New" European Union after 2004*, ed. Kathy Burrell (Burlington, VT, 2009), 25–26. On the return program, see Magdalena Lesińska, "The Dilemmas of Policy towards Return Migration: The Case of Poland after the EU Accession," *Central and East European Migration Review* 2, no. 1 (June 2013): 77–90.

57 Veronika Bern, "Vraťte se, vzkazuje Česko krajanům," *NEWTON Industry Specialized Digest*, October 2, 2013, p. 5.

58 Lucy Ash, "Hungarian Government 'Traps' Graduates to Stop Brain Drain," BBC News, http://www.bbc.co.uk/news/world-europe-19213488, accessed January 31, 2014.

59 Kathy Burrell, "Introduction," in *Polish Migration to the UK*, 9; Marta Anacka and Marek Okólski, "Direct Demographic Consequences of Post-Accession Migration for Poland," in *A Continent Moving West?*, 143–45; Bozena Leven and Michal Schwabe, "The Impact of Changing Entry Barriers on Polish Migration," *Journal of Global Economics, Management, and Business Research* 2, no. 1 (2015): 25–34.

60 Kirk Semple, "A Land of Opportunity Lures Poles Home," *New York Times*, September 21, 2008; http://travel.state.gov/content/dam/visas/Statistics/AnnualReports/FY2013AnnualReport/FY13AnnualReport-TableXVIII.pdf, accessed March 24, 2015.

61 Melissa Thompson, "Poles Vault; Polish Leaps up Lingo List to Be Our Second Tongue," *Daily Mirror*, January 31, 2013.

62 Cited in Burrell, "Introduction," 8.

63 Lech Mintowt-Czyz, "There Are Bad Polish Plumbers—But They Stayed at Home: The Teeth-suckers Are in Poznan, Scratching Their Backsides," *Times*, February 1, 2013.

64 World Bank, *Migration and Remittance Factbook 2008* (Washington, DC, 2008), 3.

65 Adrian Lee, "How Poles Conquered Britain," *Express*, February 2, 2013, pp. 24–25.

66 "Tebbit: Immigrants Are Creating Separate Societies," *Daily Telegraph*, September 23, 2013, p. 2.

67 Katrin Benhold and Stephen Castle, "E.U. Calls Roma Expulsions by France a 'Disgrace': Deportations by Paris Violate European Law, Top Justice Official Asserts," *International Herald Tribune*, September 15, 2010, p. 3.

68 "France Sends Roma Gypsies Back to Romania," BBC News, August 10, 2010.

69 Celestine Bohlen, "Talked About, But Seldom Heard From: Letter from Europe," *International Herald Tribune*, October 12, 2013.

70 John Lichfield, "Hollande Urged to Resolve Roma Row," *Independent*, October 1, 2013, p. 29.

71 Peter Allen, "Invasion of the Pickpockets," *Daily Mail*, July 18, 2013.

72 "Bulgarian und Rumänien: Friedrich kündigt Veto gegen Schengen-Erweiterung an," *Spiegel Online*, March 3, 2013.

73 Deutscher Bundestag, 17. Wahlperiod, Haltung der Bundesregierung zum Umgang mit EU-Bürgerinnen und EU-Bürgern aus Rumänien und Bulgarien, April 26, 2013.

74 Hauke Janssem, "Münchhausen-Check: Friedrich und die Einwanderer," *Der Spiegel*, May 28, 2013.

75 For an analysis of postsocialist sex trafficking, see Gail Kligman and Stephanie Limoncelli, "Trafficking Women after Socialism: To, through, and from Eastern Europe," *Social Politics* 12, no. 1 (2005): 118–40.

76 On gay male sex tourism in the Czech Republic, see Matti Bunzl, "The Prague Experience: Gay Male Sex Tourism and the Neocolonial Invention of an Embodied Border," in *Altering States: Ethnographies of Transition in Eastern Europe and the Former Soviet Union*, ed. Daphne Berdahl, Matti Bunzl, and Martha Lampland (Ann Arbor, 2000), 70–95.

77 Jon Henley, "Stolen Bodies," *Guardian*, September 10, 1993, p. 12.

78 Mark Townsend, "In Focus: Kidnap, Beating, Rape: My Story of Sex Slavery in UK," *Guardian*, February 6, 2011.

79 Ibid.; Katherine Butler, "Tricked, Beaten and Sold as a Sex Slave—The Diary of Mia, Aged 14," *Independent*, October 12, 1997.

80 On the history of international activism around sex trafficking, see esp. Stephanie Limoncelli, *The Politics of Trafficking: The First International Movement to Combat the Sexual Exploitation of Women* (Stanford, 2010); Eileen Boris and Heather Berg, "Protecting Virtue, Erasing Labor: Historical Responses to Trafficking," in *Human Trafficking Reconsidered: Rethinking the Problem, Envisioning New Solutions*, ed. Kimberly Kay Hoang and Rhacel Salazar Parrenas (New York, 2014), 19–29.

81 Emma Goldman, *The Traffic in Women and Other Essays on Feminism* (New York, 1971), 96, cited in Boris and Berg, "Protecting Virtue, Erasing Labor," 19.

82 Tim Rayment, "Gangs Enslave Disabled Romanians as Street Beggars," *Sunday Times*, July 21, 2013.

83 Anca Parvulescu, *The Traffic in Women's Work: East European Migration and the Making of Europe* (Chicago, 2014), 40.

84 Liz Alderman, "Young and Educated in Europe, but Desperate for Jobs," *New York Times*, November 15, 2013; "Poland Braces for Fresh Exodus of Young Workers," *Financial Times*, January 23, 2013, p. 2; Michael Stothard, "Island Faces Economic Hurt from 'Lost Generation,'" ibid., March 30, 2013, p. 7.

85 Paul Collier, "How Migration Hurts Poor Countries," *New York Times*, December 1, 2010, p. 3.

86 Yoani Sánchez, "Leaving Home, Coming Home," *New York Times*, November 28, 1913.

87 "Fatal Journeys: Tracking Lives Lost during Migration," International Organization for Migration (Geneva, 2014), 92; Jim Yardley, "Hundreds of Migrants Are Feared Dead as Ship Capsizes off Libyan Coast," *New York Times*, April 19, 2015; Jim Yardley, "Rising Toll on Migrants Leaves Europe in Crisis; 900 May Be Dead at Sea," ibid., April 20, 2015.

88 Jerzy Sawka, "Przystanek Świat: Wyjechać, zostać, wrócić?," *Gazeta Wyborcza*, March 9, 2008.

Bibliography

ARCHIVAL SOURCES AND ABBREVIATIONS

ARCHIWUM AKT NOWYCH, WARSAW (AAN)
Konsulat Generalny RP w Londynie
Konsulat Generalny RP w Nowym Yorku
Konsulat RP w Marsylii
Komitet Centralny (KC), Polska Zjednoczna Partia Robotnicza
    (PZPR), Wydział Administracyny
Ministerstwo Spraw Zagranicznych (MSZ)
Ministerstwo Opieki Społecznej (MOS)
Panstowy Urząd Emigracyny

ARCHIWUM PAŃSTOWE W KRAKOWIE (APKR)
k.u.k. Polizei-Direktion in Krakau, 1852–1918
k.u.k. Landesgericht in Strafsachen in Krakau, 1855–1918
Sąd Okręgowy Cywilny w Krakowie, 1919–50
k.u.k. Bezirkshauptmannschaft in Biała, 1869–1918
k.u.k. Bezirkshauptmannschaft in Chrzanów, 1869–1918
k.u.k. Bezirkshauptmannschaft in Auschwitz, 1909–18
k.u.k. Bezirkshauptmannschaft in Saybusch, 1867–1918

Starostwo Grodzie Krakowskie, 1919–39
Starostwo Grodzie w Białej, 1919–39

HAUS-, HOF- UND STAATSARCHIV, VIENNA, AUSTRIA
Politisches Archiv XXXIII: USA
Berichte, Weisungen, Varia, 1838–1918 USA
Administrative Registratur
Fach 7: Fremde Missionen
Fach 8: Konsolate
Fach 15: Aus- und Einwanderung

ÖSTERREICHISCHES STAATSARCHIV, VIENNA
AT-OeStA/AVA Inneres
AT-OeStA/AVA Justiz

NÁRODNÍ ARCHIV, PRAGUE
Ministerstvo zemědelství IV, Spisy 1918–34
Nejvyšší správní soud, 1918–40
Ministerstvo sociální péče, 1918–51
Československý úřad zahraniční, 1918–39, 1945–
Politické buro ÚVKSČ, 1954–62
KSČ—Ústřední výbor 1945–89. Politické buro ÚVKSČ 1954–62
Ministerstvo práce a sociální péče, Praha (1945–50)
Uřad předsednictva vlády—bězná spisovná, 1945–59
Ministerstvo práce a sociální péče—repatriace
Ministerstvo vnitra—stára registratura
Ministerstvo zahraničních věcí—výstřižkový archiv, Praha, III.
    Část

ŽIDOVSKÉ ARCHIV, PRAGUE
Sbírky k dějinám šoa, Dokumenty perzekuce

ARCHIVES DES AFFAIRES ÉTRANGÈRES, PARIS (MAE)
Z-Europe, Tchécoslovaquie
Z-Europe, Pologne

Series C, Étrangers en France
SDN, Émigration et immigration
Europe, 1944–70, Pologne
Europe, 1944–70, Tchécoslovaquie
Europe, 1944–70, Yougoslavie
Europe, 1944–70, Hongrie
Prisonniers de Guerre, Déportés et Réfugiés

ARCHIVES NATIONALES, PARIS

F7, Ministère de l'intérieur, police générale
F10, Agriculture
F60, Secrétariat général du Gouvernement et services du Premier
    ministre
AJ43, Organisation internationale pour les réfugiés (OIR)

POLITISCHES ARCHIV DES AUSWÄRTIGEN AMT, BERLIN (MFAA)

U.S. ARCHIVES

Archive of Czechs and Slovaks Abroad, University of Chicago
Center for Jewish History, New York
Immigrants Protective League, University of Illinois, Chicago
Chicago History Museum Archive
U.S. Holocaust Memorial, Museum, and Archive (USHMMA)
RG-11.001M.36, Records of the Executive Committee of the World
    Jewish Congress, Paris
RG-11.001M94, Records of the Hebrew Immigrant Assistance
    Society, Paris

SELECTED SECONDARY SOURCES

Ackermann, Volker. Der "echte" Flüchtling: Deutsche Vertriebene und
    Flüchtlinge aus der DDR, 1945–61. Osnabrück: Universitätsverlag
    Rasch, 1995.
Ahonen, Pertti. Death at the Berlin Wall. New York: Oxford University
    Press, 2011.
Alroey, Gur. An Unpromising Land: Jewish Migration to Palestine in

the Early Twentieth Century. Stanford: Stanford University Press, 2014.

Bauer, Yehuda. *Jews for Sale? Nazi-Jewish Negotiations, 1933–1945*. New Haven: Yale University Press, 1994.

Benda, Jan. *Útěky a vyhánění z pohraničí českých zemí, 1938–1939*. Prague: Karolinum, 2013.

Bon Tempo, Carl. *Americans at the Gate: The United States and Refugees during the Cold War*. Princeton: Princeton University Press, 2008.

Breitman, Richard, and Alan M. Kraut. *American Refugee Policy and European Jewry, 1933–1945*. Bloomington: Indiana University Press, 1987.

———. *FDR and the Jews*. Cambridge, MA: Harvard University Press, 2013.

Brinkmann, Tobias, ed. *Points of Passage: Jewish Transmigrants from Eastern Europe in Scandinavia, Germany, and Britain, 1880–1914*. New York: Berghahn, 2013.

———. "Why Paul Nathan Attacked Albert Ballin: The Transatlantic Mass Migration and the Privatization of Prussia's Eastern Border Inspection, 1886–1914." *Central European History* 43 (2010): 47–83.

Bristow, Edward J. *Prostitution and Prejudice: The Jewish Fight against White Slavery*. Oxford: Oxford University Press, 1982.

Brown, Wendy. *Walled States, Waning Sovereignty*. Cambridge, MA: MIT Press, 2010.

Brunnbauer, Ulf, ed. *Transnational Societies, Transterritorial Politics: Migrations in the (Post) Yugoslav Region, 19th–21st Century*. Munich: Oldenbourg, 2009.

Burrell, Kathy, ed. *Polish Migration to the UK in the "New" European Union after 2004*. Burlington, VT: Ashgate, 2009.

Čapková, Kateřina, and Michal Frankl. *Nejisté útočiště: Československo a uprchlíci před nacismem, 1933–1938*. Prague: Paseka, 2008.

Caron, Vicki. *Uneasy Asylum: France and the Jewish Refugee Crisis, 1933–1942*. Stanford: Stanford University Press, 1999.

Carruthers, Susan L. *Cold War Captives: Imprisonment, Escape, and Brainwashing*. Berkeley: University of California Press, 2009.

Choate, Mark. *Emigrant Nation: The Making of Italy Abroad.* Cambridge, MA: Harvard University Press, 2008.

Cohen, Gerard Daniel. *In War's Wake: Europe's Displaced Persons in the Postwar Order.* Oxford: Oxford University Press, 2012.

Conrad, Sebastian. *Globalization and the Nation in Imperial Germany.* Translated by Sorcha O'Hagan. Cambridge: Cambridge University Press, 2010.

Dowty, Alan. *Closed Borders: The Contemporary Assault on Freedom of Movement.* New Haven: Yale University Press, 1987.

Dwork, Deborah, and Robert Jan van Pelt. *Flight from the Reich: Refugee Jews, 1933–1946.* New York: W. W. Norton, 2012.

Fahrmeir, Andreas, Olivier Faron, and Patrick Weil, eds. *Migration Control in the North Atlantic World: The Evolution of State Practices in Europe and the United States from the French Revolution to the Interwar period.* New York: Berghahn Books, 2003.

Foner, Eric. *The Story of American Freedom.* New York: W. W. Norton, 1998.

Frommer, Benjamin. "Expulsion or Integration: Unmixing Interethnic Marriage in Postwar Czechoslovakia." *East European Politics and Societies* 14, no. 2 (Spring 2000): 381–410.

Gammerl, Benno. *Staatsbürger, Untertanen und Andere: Der Umgang mit ethnischer Heterogenität im Britischen Weltreich und im Habsburgerreich, 1867–1918.* Göttingen: Vandenhoeck & Ruprecht, 2010.

Gatrell, Peter. *Free World? The Campaign to Save the World's Refugees, 1956–63.* Cambridge: Cambridge University Press, 2011.

Genizi, Haim. *America's Fair Share: The Admission and Resettlement of Displaced Persons, 1945–1952.* Detroit: Wayne State University Press, 1993.

Green, Nancy L. "The Politics of Exit: Reversing the Immigration Paradigm." *Journal of Modern History* 77 (June 2005): 263–89.

Green, Nancy L., and François Weil. *Citizenship and Those Who Leave: The Politics of Emigration and Expatriation.* Urbana: University of Illinois Press, 2007.

Grossmann, Atina. *Jews, Germans, and Allies: Close Encounters in Occupied Germany.* Princeton: Princeton University Press, 2007.

Holian, Anna. *Between National Socialism and Soviet Communism: Displaced Persons in Postwar Germany.* Ann Arbor: University of Michigan Press, 2011.

Hübscher, Roland. *L'immigration dans les campagnes françaises, XIXe–XXe siècle.* Paris: Odile Jacob, 2005.

Iglicka, Krystyna. *Poland's Post-War Dynamic of Migration.* Aldershot: Ashgate Press, 2001.

Jacobson, Matthew Frye. *Whiteness of a Different Color: European Immigrants and the Alchemy of Race.* Cambridge, MA: Harvard University Press, 1998.

Jennings, Eric T. "Last Exit from Vichy France: The Martinique Escape Route and the Ambiguities of Emigration." *Journal of Modern History* 74 (June 2002): 289–324.

———. "Writing Madagascar Back into the Madagascar Plan." *Holocaust and Genocide Studies* 21, no. 2 (Fall 2007): 187–217.

Kaplan, Marion A. *Dominican Haven: The Jewish Refugee Settlement in Sosúa, 1940–1945.* New York: Museum of Jewish Heritage, 2008.

Kowalski, Grzegorz. *Przestępstwa emigracyjne w Galicji, 1897–1918.* Cracow: Jagiellonian University Press, 2003.

Kuzmany, Börries. "Center and Periphery at the Austrian-Russian Border: The Galician Border Town of Brody in the Long Nineteenth Century." *Austrian History Yearbook* 42 (2011): 67–88.

Lake, Marilyn, and Henry Reynolds. *Drawing the Global Colour Line: White Men's Countries and the International Challenge of Racial Equality.* Cambridge: Cambridge University Press, 2008.

Lesser, Jeffrey. *Welcoming the Undesirables: Brazil and the Jewish Question.* Berkeley: University of California Press, 1995.

Lewis, Mary Dewhurst. *The Boundaries of the Republic: Migrant Rights and the Limits of Universalism in France, 1918–1940.* Stanford: Stanford University Press, 2007.

Lohr, Eric. *Russian Citizenship: From Empire to Soviet Union.* Cambridge, MA: Harvard University Press, 2012.

London, Louise. *Whitehall and the Jews, 1933–1948: British Immigration Policy, Jewish Refugees, and the Holocaust.* Cambridge: Cambridge University Press, 2003.

Major, Patrick. *The Rise and Fall of the Berlin Wall: A Concrete History.* Oxford: Oxford University Press, 2009.

Marrus, Michael. *The Unwanted: Refugees from the First World War through the Cold War.* Philadelphia: Temple University Press, 2002.

McKeown, Adam M. *Melancholy Order: Asian Migration and the Globalization of Borders.* New York: Columbia University Press, 2011.

Mendelsohn, Ezra. *Zionism in Poland: The Formative Years, 1915–1926.* New Haven: Yale University Press, 1981.

Miletic, Aleksander R. *Journey under Surveillance: The Overseas Emigration Policy of the Kingdom of Serbs, Croats, and Slovenes in Global Context, 1918–1928.* Berlin: Lit Verlag, 2012.

Moss, Kenneth B. "Thinking with Restriction: Immigration Restriction and Polish Jewish Accounts of the Post-liberal State, Empire, Race, and Political Reason, 1926–39." *East European Jewish Affairs* 44, nos. 2–3 (2014): 205–24.

Murdzek, Benjamin P. *Emigration in Polish Social-Political Thought, 1870–1914.* New York: Columbia University Press, 1977.

Naimark, Norman. *Fires of Hatred: Ethnic Cleansing in Twentieth-Century Europe.* Cambridge, MA: Harvard University Press, 2001.

Nicosia, Francis R. *Zionism and Anti-Semitism in Nazi Germany.* New York: Cambridge University Press, 2008.

Phelps, Nicole. *U.S.-Habsburg Relations from 1815 to the Paris Peace Conference.* Cambridge: Cambridge University Press, 2013.

Pollack, Martin. *Kaiser von Amerika: Die grosse Flucht aus Galizien.* Vienna: Paul Zsolny Verlag, 2010.

Puskás, Julianna. *Ties That Bind, Ties That Divide: 100 Years of Hungarian Experience in the United States.* Translated by Zora Ludwig. New York: Holmes & Meier, 2000.

Reczyńska, Anna. *For Bread and a Better Future: Emigration from Poland to Canada, 1918–1939.* Toronto: Multicultural History Society of Ontario, 1996.

Reeder, Linda. *Widows in White: Migration and the Transformation of Rural Italian Women, Sicily, 1880–1920.* Toronto: University of Toronto Press, 2003.

Rheinisch, Jessica, and Elizabeth White, eds. *The Disentanglement of Populations: Migration, Expulsion and Displacement in Postwar Europe, 1944–49.* New York: Palgrave Macmillan, 2011

Roediger, David R. *Working toward Whiteness: How America's Immigrants Became White: The Strange Journey from Ellis Island to the Suburbs.* New York: Basic Books, 2005.

Rosental, Paul-André. "Protéger et expulser les étrangers en Europe du XIXe siècle à nos jours." *Annales. Histoire, Sciences Sociales* 66 (April–June 2011): 335–73.

Rychlik, Jan. *Cestování do ciziny v habsburské monarchii a v Československu.* Prague: Ústav pro soudobé dějiny, 2007.

Salvatici, Silvia. "From Displaced Persons to Labourers: Allied Employment Policies in Postwar West Germany." In *The Disentanglement of Populations: Migration, Expulsion, and Displacement in Postwar Europe, 1944–49,* edited by Jessica Rheinisch and Elizabeth White, 210–28. New York: Palgrave Macmillan, 2011.

Service, Hugo. *Germans to Poles: Communism, Nationalism, and Ethnic Cleansing after the Second World War.* Cambridge: Cambridge University Press, 2013.

Shanes, Joshua. *Diaspora Nationalism and Jewish Identity in Habsburg Galicia.* Cambridge: Cambridge University Press, 2012.

Sheffer, Edith. *Burned Bridge: How East and West Germans Made the Iron Curtain.* New York: Oxford, 2011.

Smith, Neil. *American Empire: Roosevelt's Geographer and the Prelude to Globalization.* Berkeley: University of California Press, 2003.

Stauter-Halsted, Keely. "'A Generation of Monsters': Jews, Prostitution, and Racial Purity in the 1892 Lviv White Slavery Trial." *Austrian History Yearbook* 38 (2007): 25–35.

Steidl, Annemarie, et al., eds. *European Mobility: Internal, International, and Transatlantic Moves in the 19th and Early 20th Centuries.* Göttingen: V&R Unipress, 2009.

Stola, Dariusz. *Kraj bez wyjścia? Migracje z Polski 1949–1989.* Warsaw: Instytut Pamięci Narodowej, 2010.

Vaculík, Jaroslav. *Nástin českých a slovenských přeshraničních migrací v meziválečném období.* Brno: Masaryk University, 2010.

———. *Poválecná repatriace československých tzv. přemístěných osob.* Brno: Masaryk University, 2004.

Weitz, Eric D. "From the Vienna to the Paris System: International Politics and the Entangled Histories of Human Rights, Forced Deportations, and Civilizing Missions." *American Historical Review* 113 (December 2008): 1313–43.

Wells, Allen. *Tropical Zion: General Trujillo, FDR, and the Jews of Sosúa.* Durham, NC: Duke University Press, 2009.

Wingfield, Nancy M. "Destination: Alexandria, Buenos Aires, Constantinople: 'White Slavers' in Late Imperial Austria." *Journal of the History of Sexuality* 20 (2011): 291–311.

Wyman, Mark. *Round-Trip to America: The Immigrants Return to Europe, 1880–1930.* Ithaca: Cornell University Press, 1993.

Zimmerman, Andrew. *Alabama in Africa: Booker T. Washington, the German Empire, and the Globalization of the New South.* Princeton: Princeton University Press, 2010.

Index

Page numbers in *italics* refer to illustrations.